# between men and women

HANS FAHRMEYER

Universe

4,50

This book is dedicated to King Redman.

First published in the United States of America in 1998 by
UNIVERSE PUBLISHING
A Division of Rizzoli International Publications, Inc.
300 Park Avenue South
New York, NY 10010



Distributed to the U.S. trade by St. Martin's Press, New York
Distributed in Canada by McClelland and Stewart



98 99 00 / 10 9 8 7 6 5 4 3 2 1

Library of Congress Catalog Card Number: 98-60983

Printed in Italy

Design by Amelia Costigan

# foreword

## by David Leddick

The twentieth century has been marked by fundamental change in almost every facet of human life. No change, perhaps, has been more remarkable than that which has taken place in the social and sexual relationships between men and women. Rules and traditions that have governed sexual relations for centuries have been bent, broken, or turned upside down. Capturing these new gender roles in art and imagery is a complex and infinite task—one that Hans Fahrmeyer has undertaken with courage and insight, preserving these new, naked truths in naked images.

In the past, the basic model for men and women was simple: men protected women and women comforted men—a notion dating back to early hunter-gatherer cultures. Much of secular Western art and iconography bore this out. The few portrayals of nude men and women together in pre-Renaissance art followed a conventional motif of well-muscled men pictured with submissive, if full-bodied, women, not seldom in violent scenes invoking events from the classical age (think *The Rape of the Sabine Women*). The Renaissance in Europe brought somewhat more enlightened artistic visions of the naked male and female form—ones that rarely provided real insight into the intricacies of sexual rapports, however.

The modern era succeeded in muddying the waters a bit, if only in its removing of barriers and taboos in the portrayal of the naked body. Yet, while fine art in the modern age has managed successfully to redefine gender boundaries, the bulk of imagery in popular visual media today is no more enlightened than its classical and medieval predecessors. Pornography, for example, is still mired in the image of the dominant, controlling (if not downright tyrannical) male. And until recently, modern pop icons have simply perpetuated traditional gender roles—from Sylvester Stallone to Marilyn Monroe.

As we approach the new millennium, however, refreshing new trends are emerging. A new generation of film stars, for example, is beginning to mark a departure from traditional beefcake/bombshell icons: think the slightly androgynous Leonardo DiCaprio and Johnny Depp, or the aggressive, sassy Linda Fiorentino and Madonna. Women are beginning to shout back; men are beginning to listen.

In real life, too, women are affirming their psychological and physical independence from men, recognizing that traditional dominant-submissive roles can be abandoned and even reversed. With this new awareness has come new, more exciting ways to portray the sexes in art and photography—and in popular visual media. The male body is now, for better or worse, as effective a marketing tool as the sexy female form. It is now more or less openly acknowledged that women react strongly to the male form in the mainstream media, and that men do, too. . . .

Many heterosexual men have had the courage to step outside of their traditional point of view to appreciate the male form. Women, too, are increasingly unashamed of their own impulsive attraction to both the male and female body. All of this is part of a new give-and-take between men and women, one that is unclouded by old conventions and is almost childlike: "You show me yours and I'll show you mine." The puritanical elements in this country will still resist the tides of change, but forward-looking people will continue to widen frontiers.

This new equality—with all its complexities and ambiguities—is beautifully embraced by Hans Fahrmeyer, whose photography celebrates this new freedom. In Fahrmeyer's images, bodies weave together, interlace, fold and unfold, lean against each other in a pure dance of mutual desire and attraction. His models' bodies are lithe, tensile, and supple, but never exaggerated or garish; smooth but not carved in marble. All his subjects exude strength and confidence, sometimes playful, sometimes verging on fury. The vast range of human emotion is celebrated with shadow, light, and texture. These pictures are about real flesh and real people; they express new attitudes about the way the sexes relate. Hans Fahrmeyer's photographs are images for the next millennium.

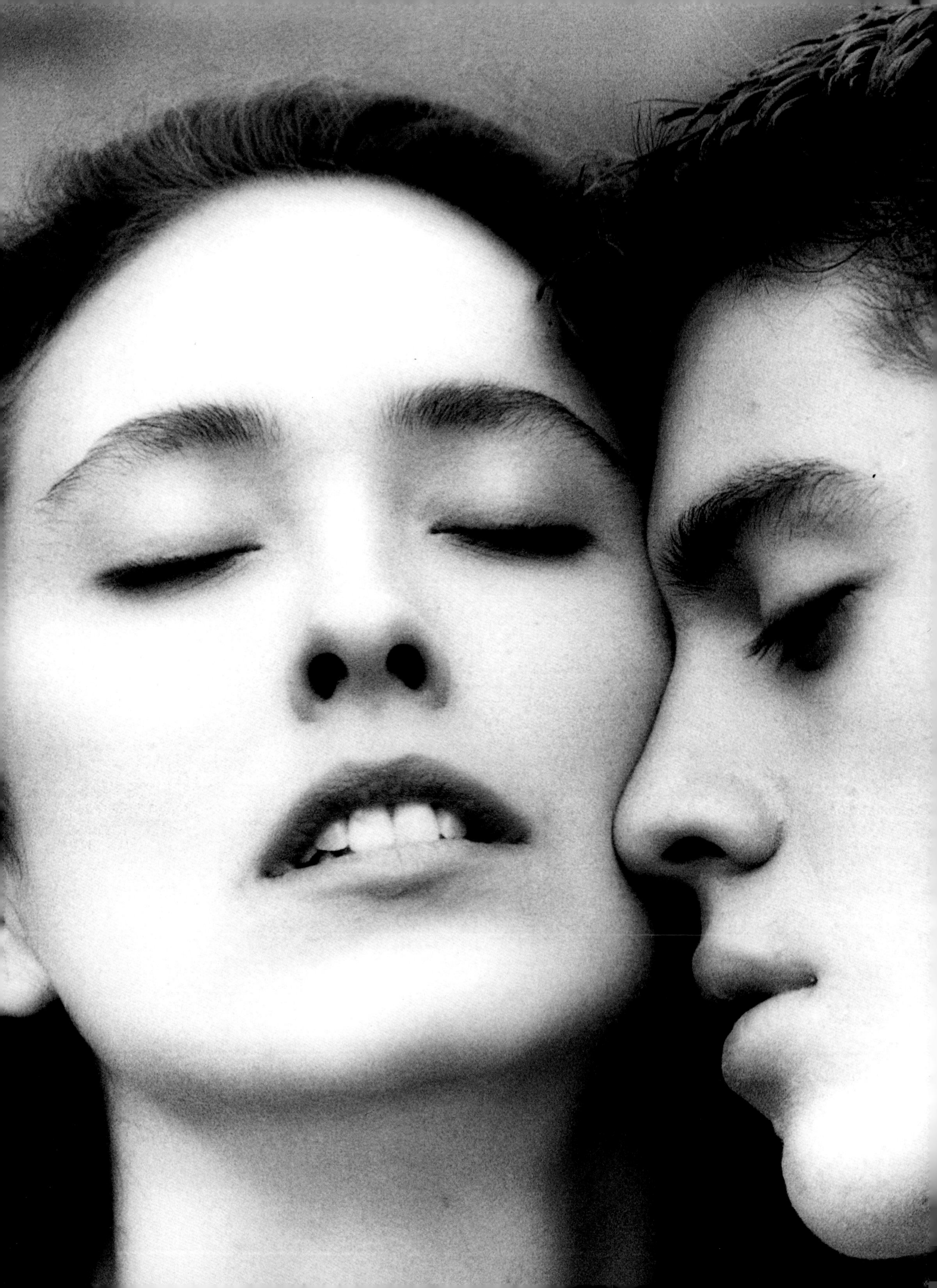

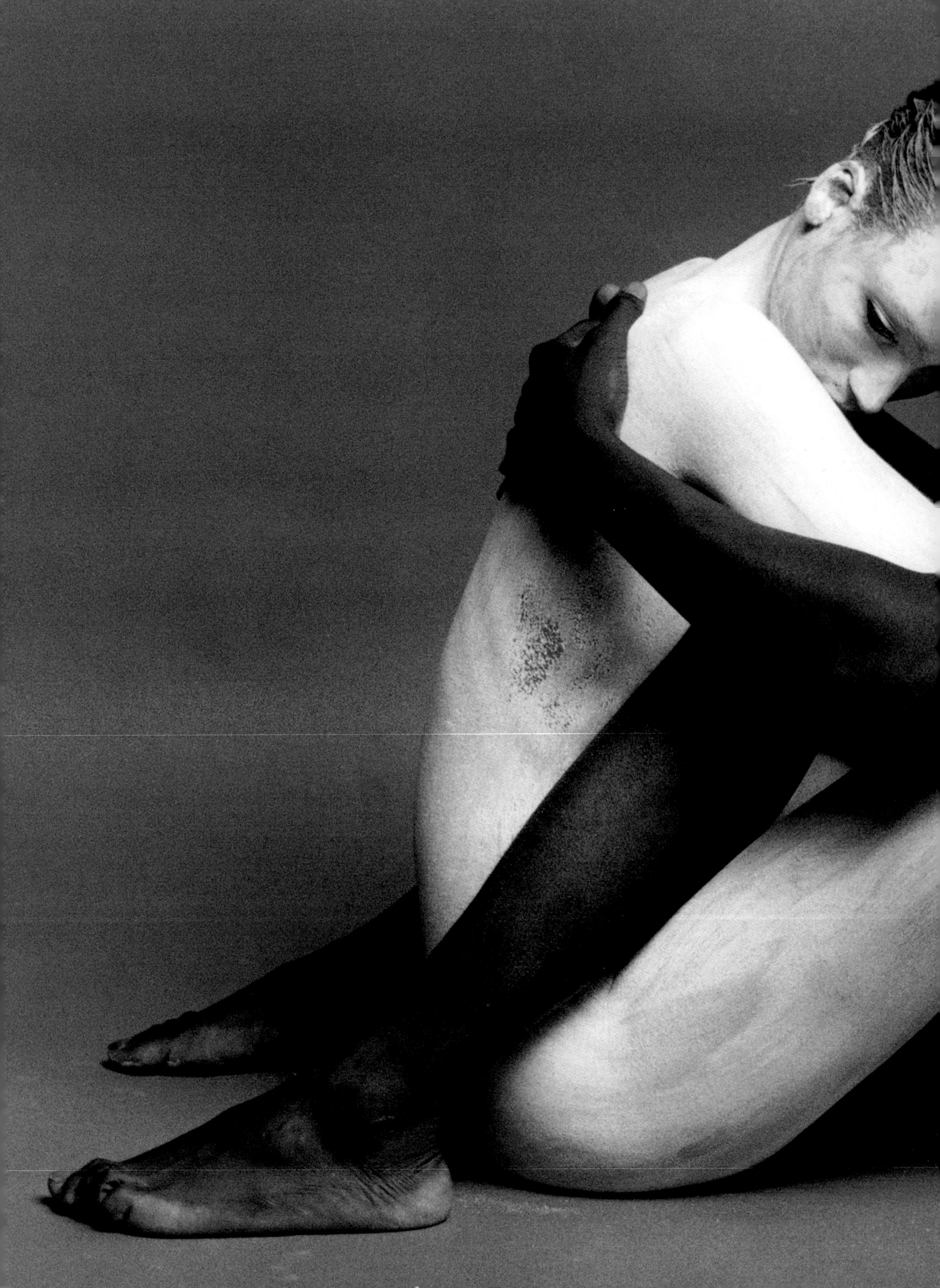

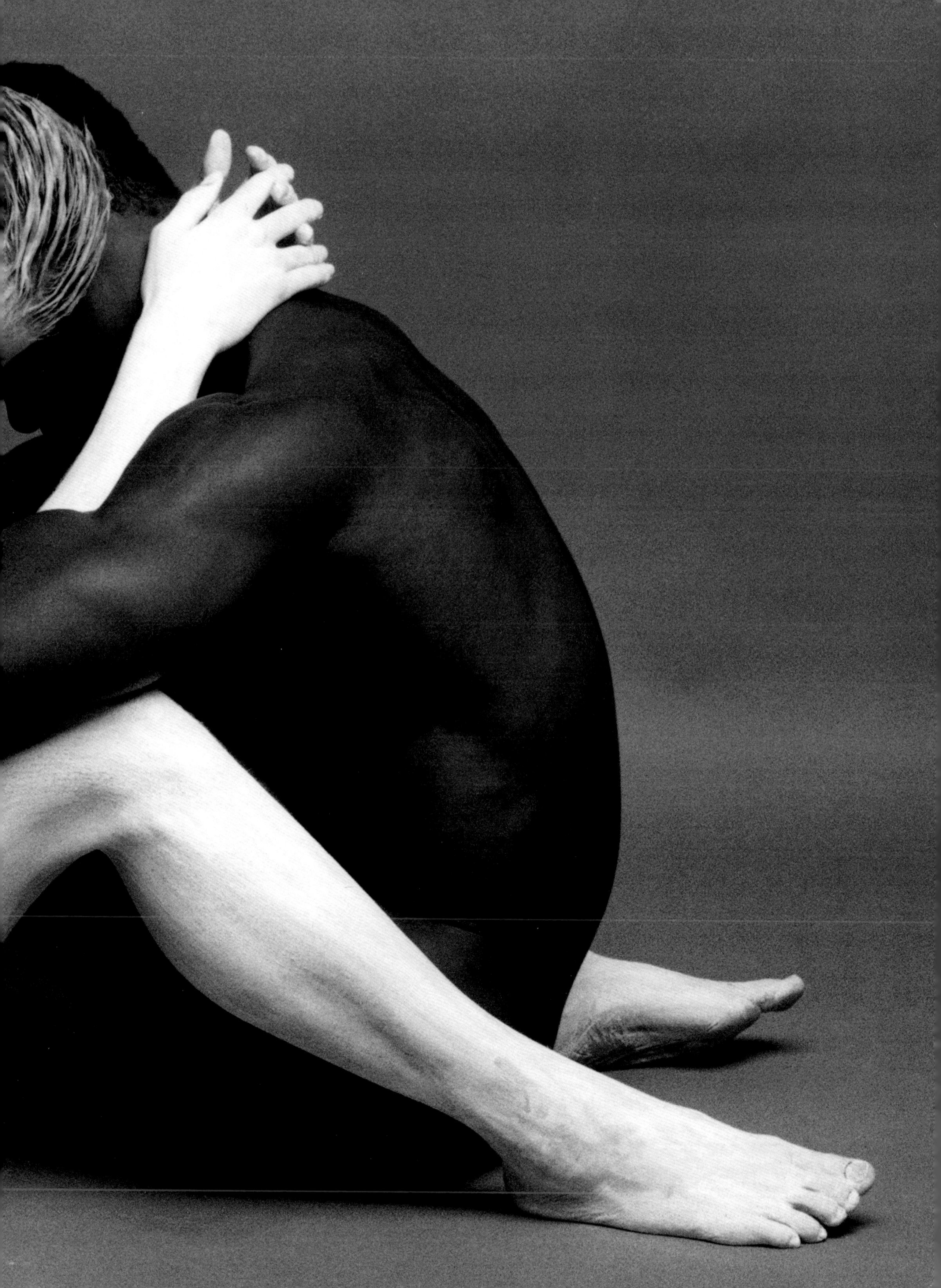

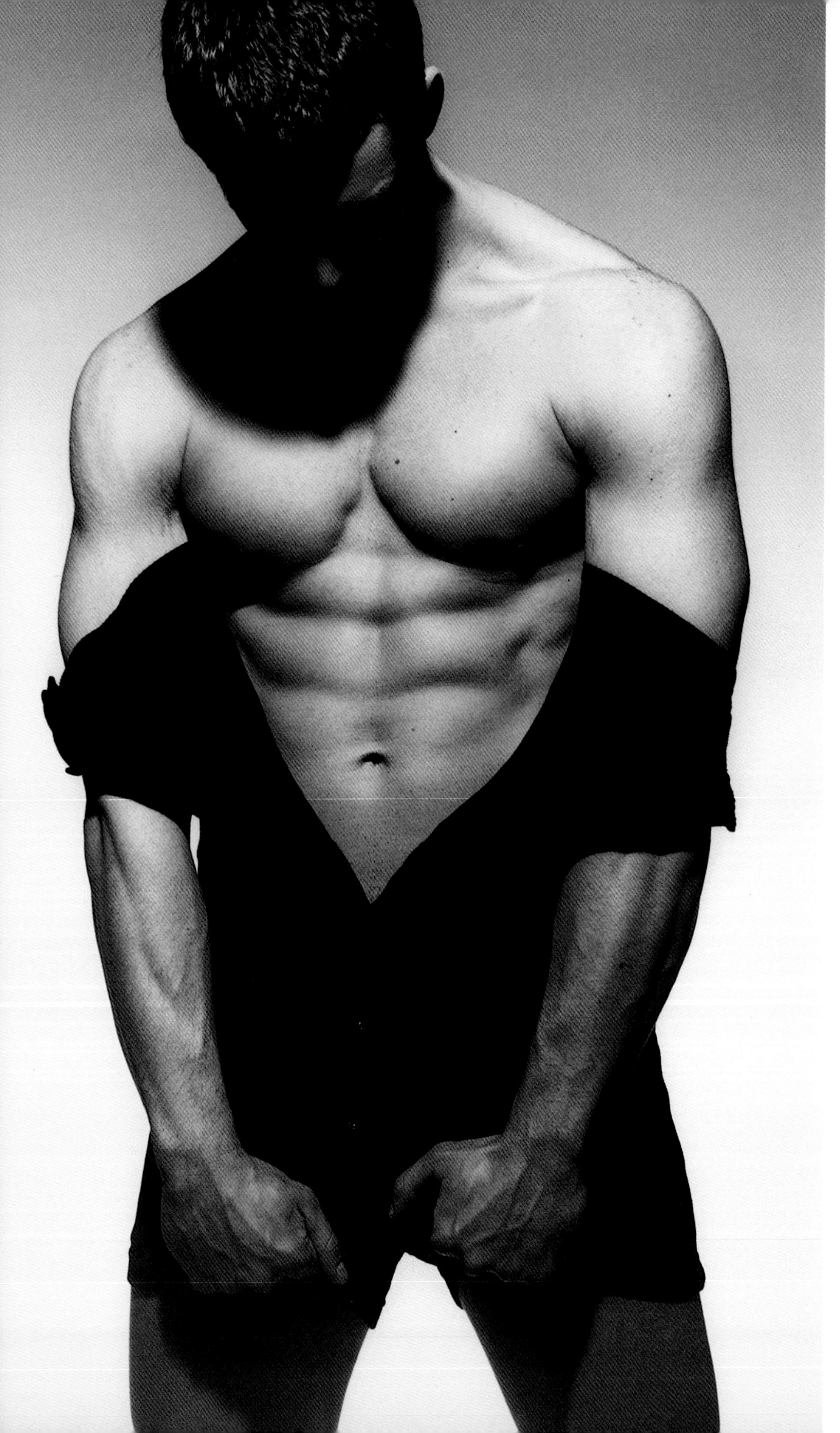

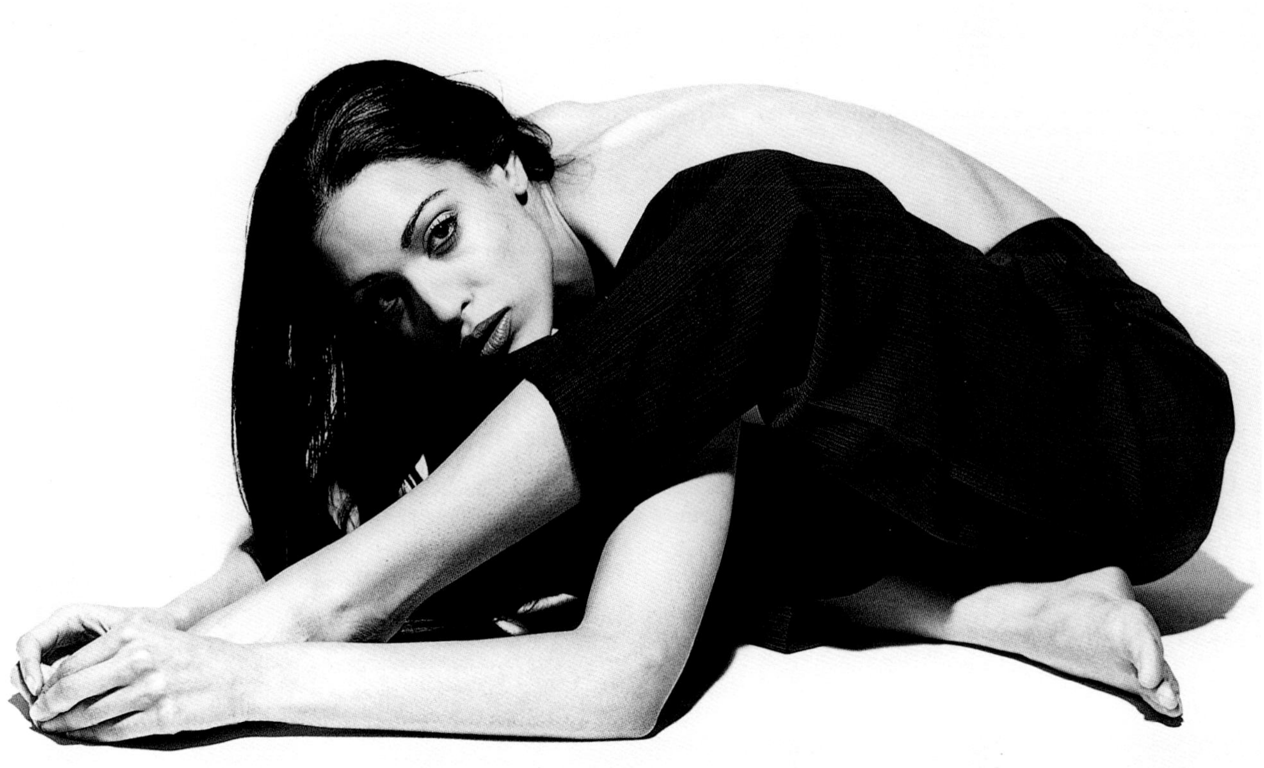

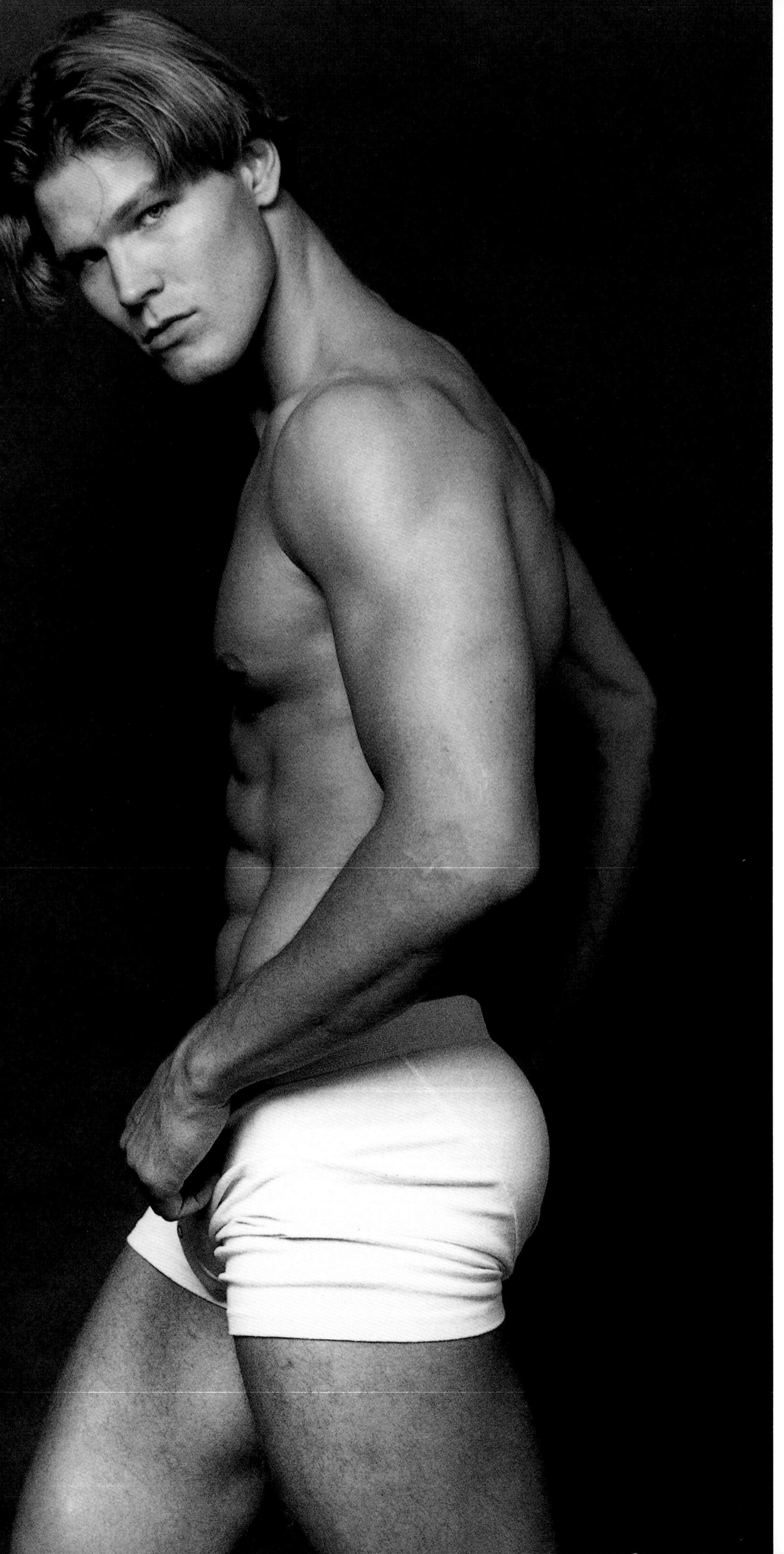

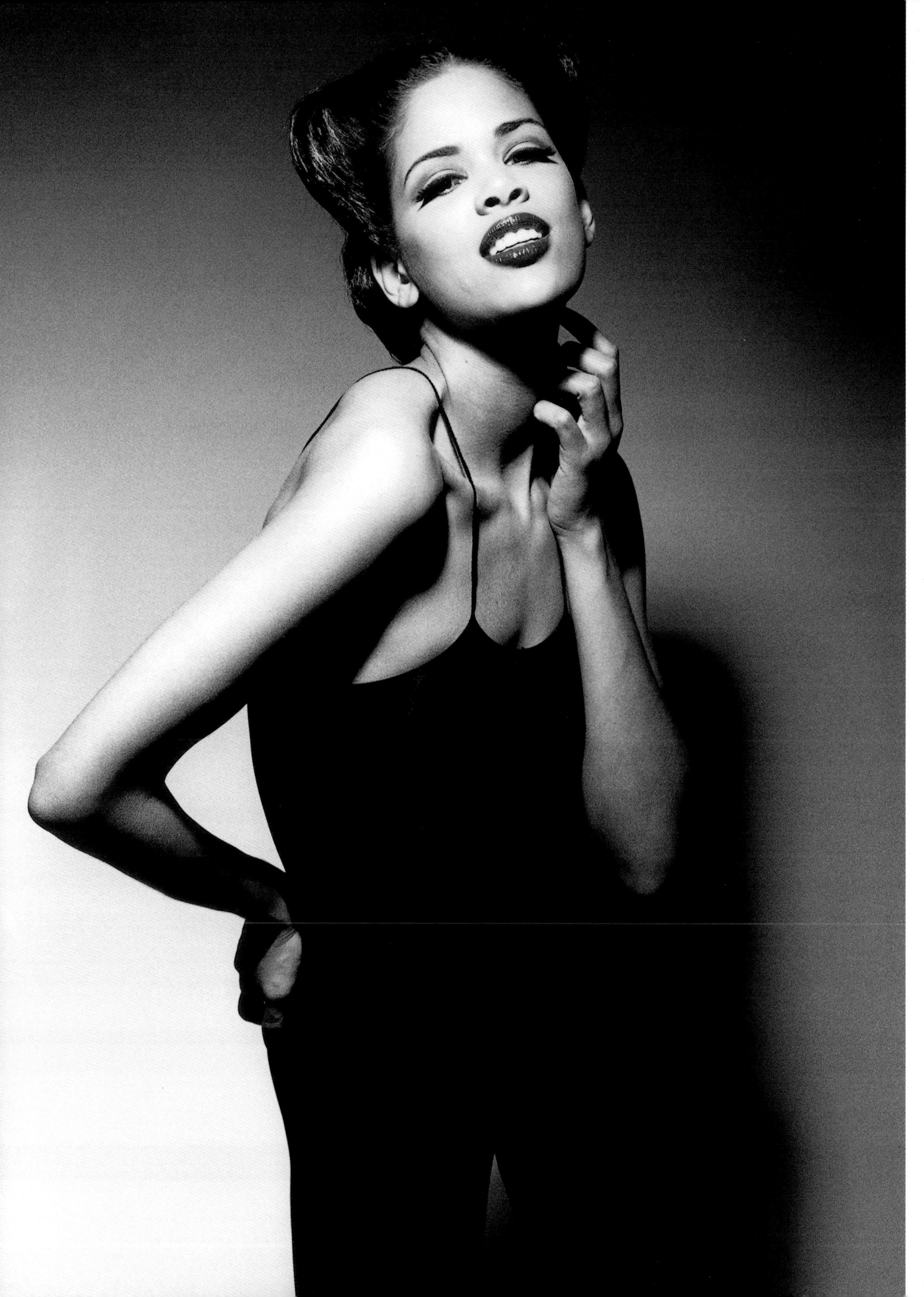

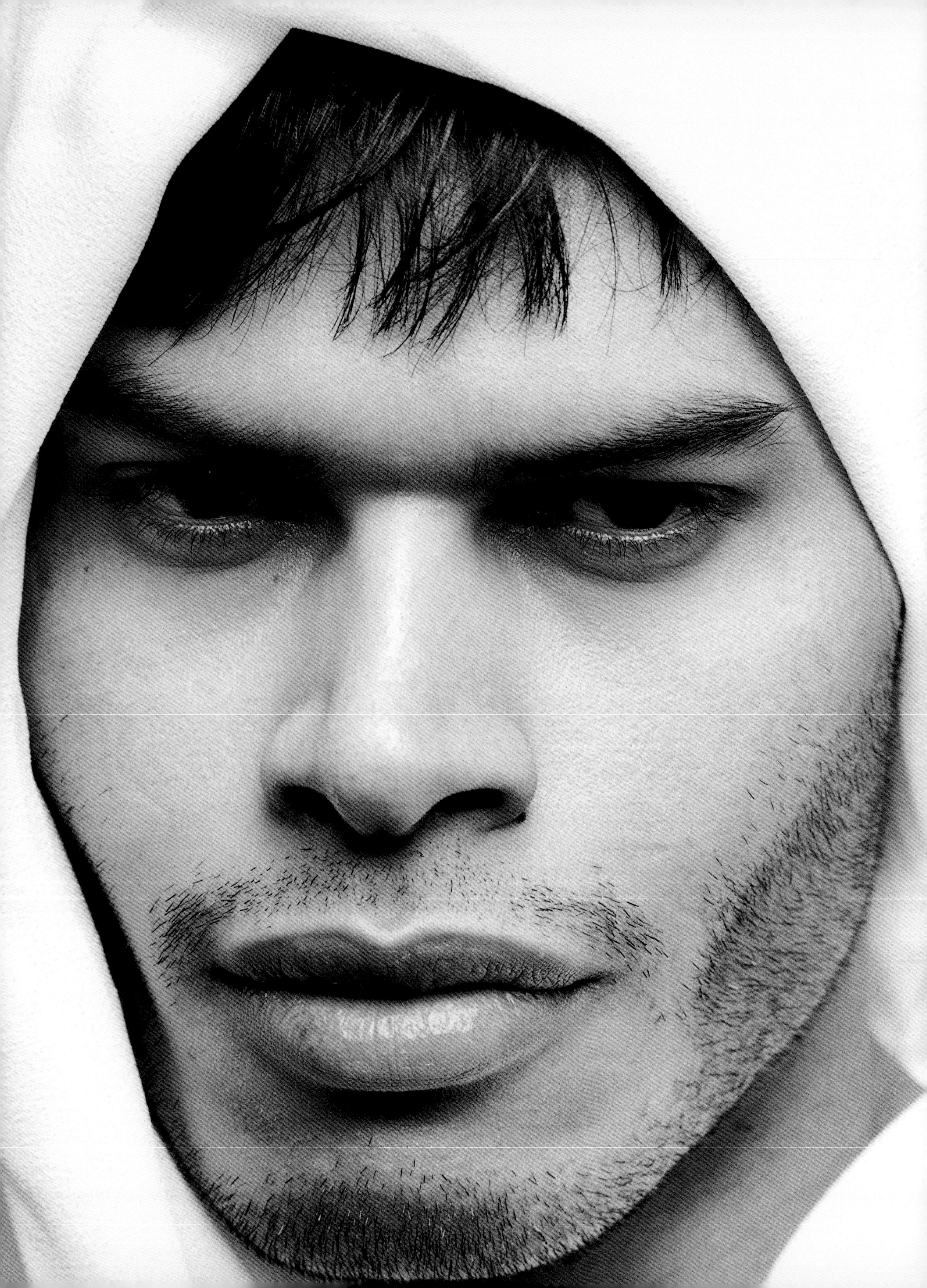

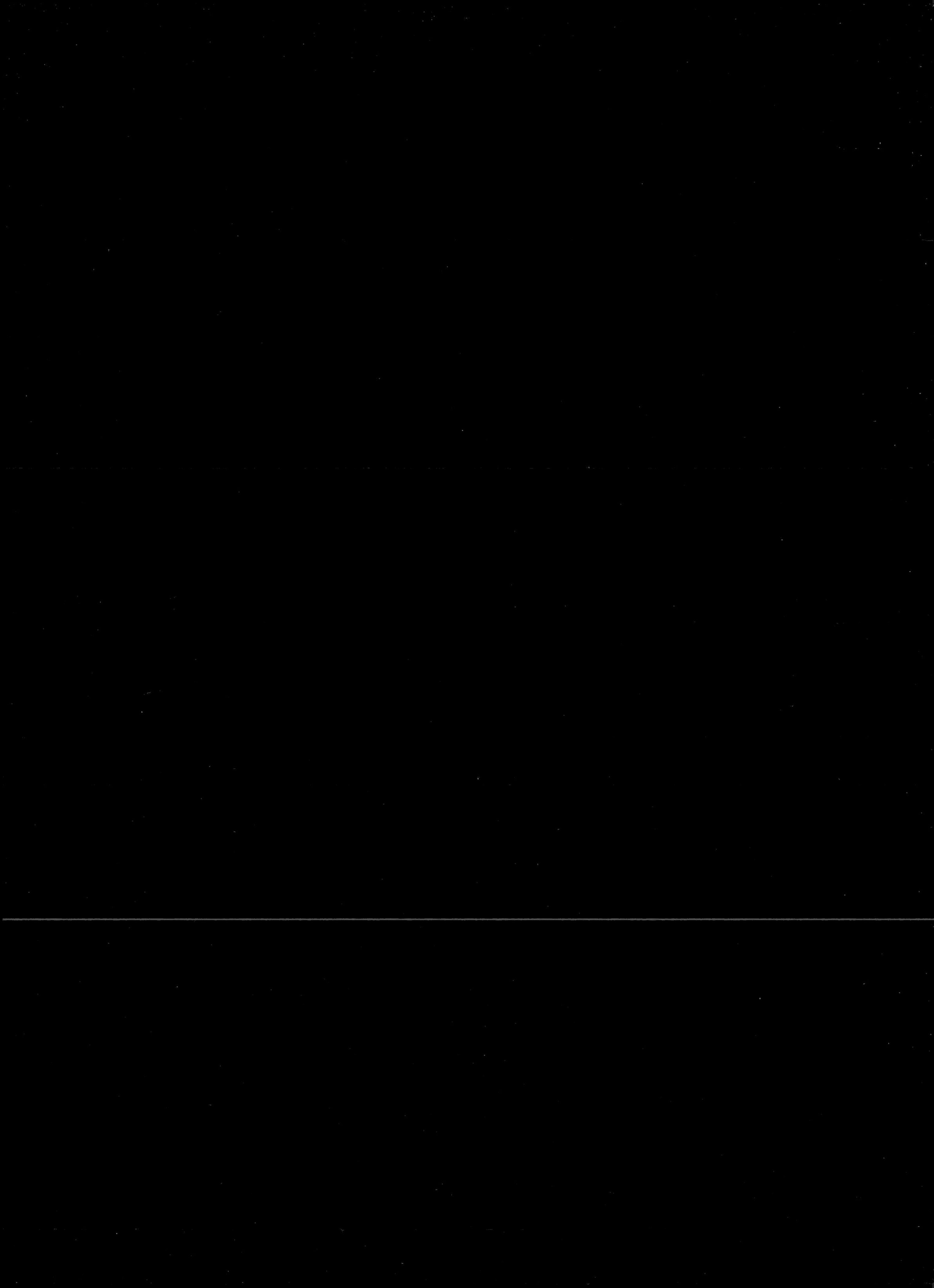

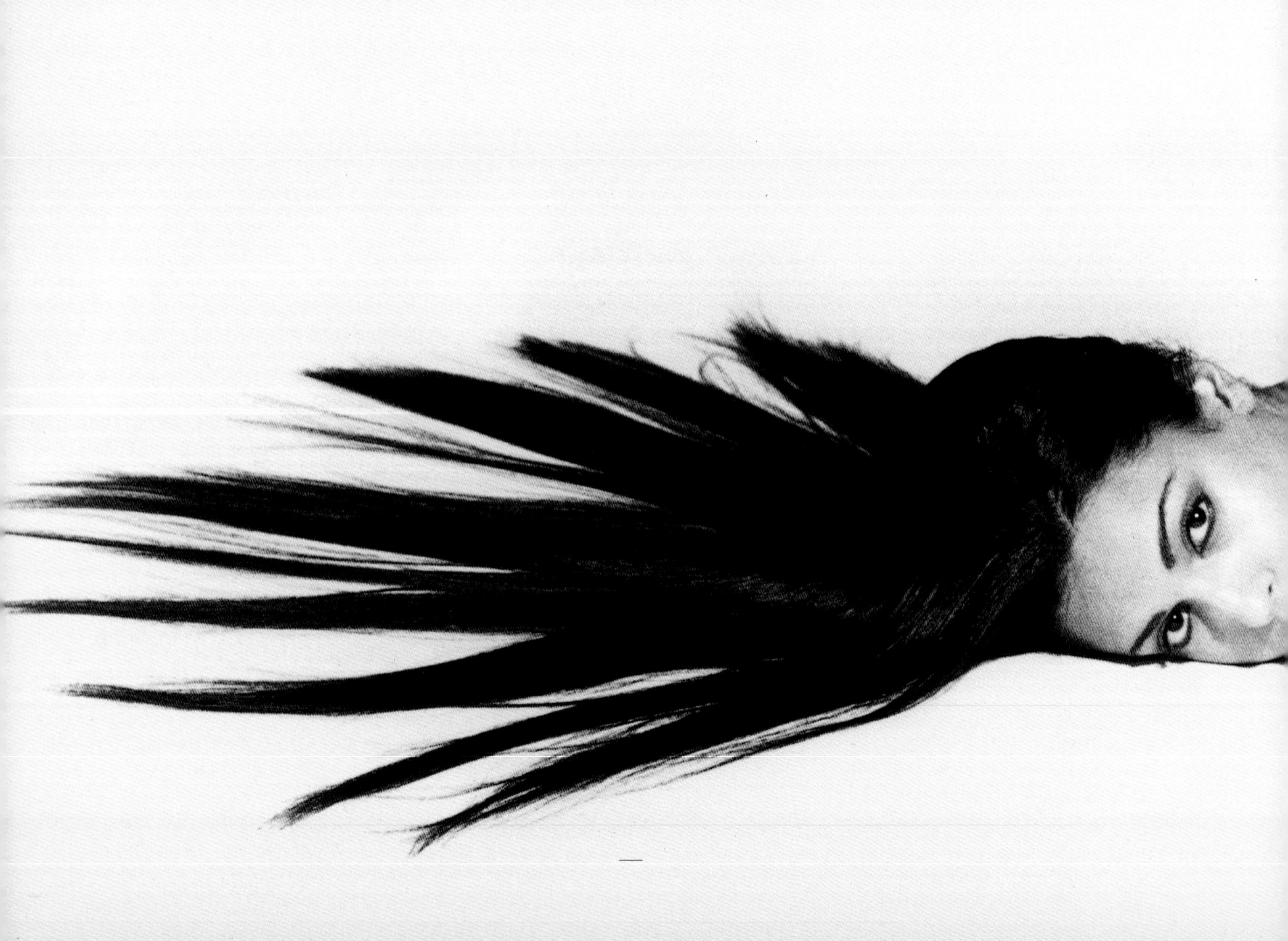

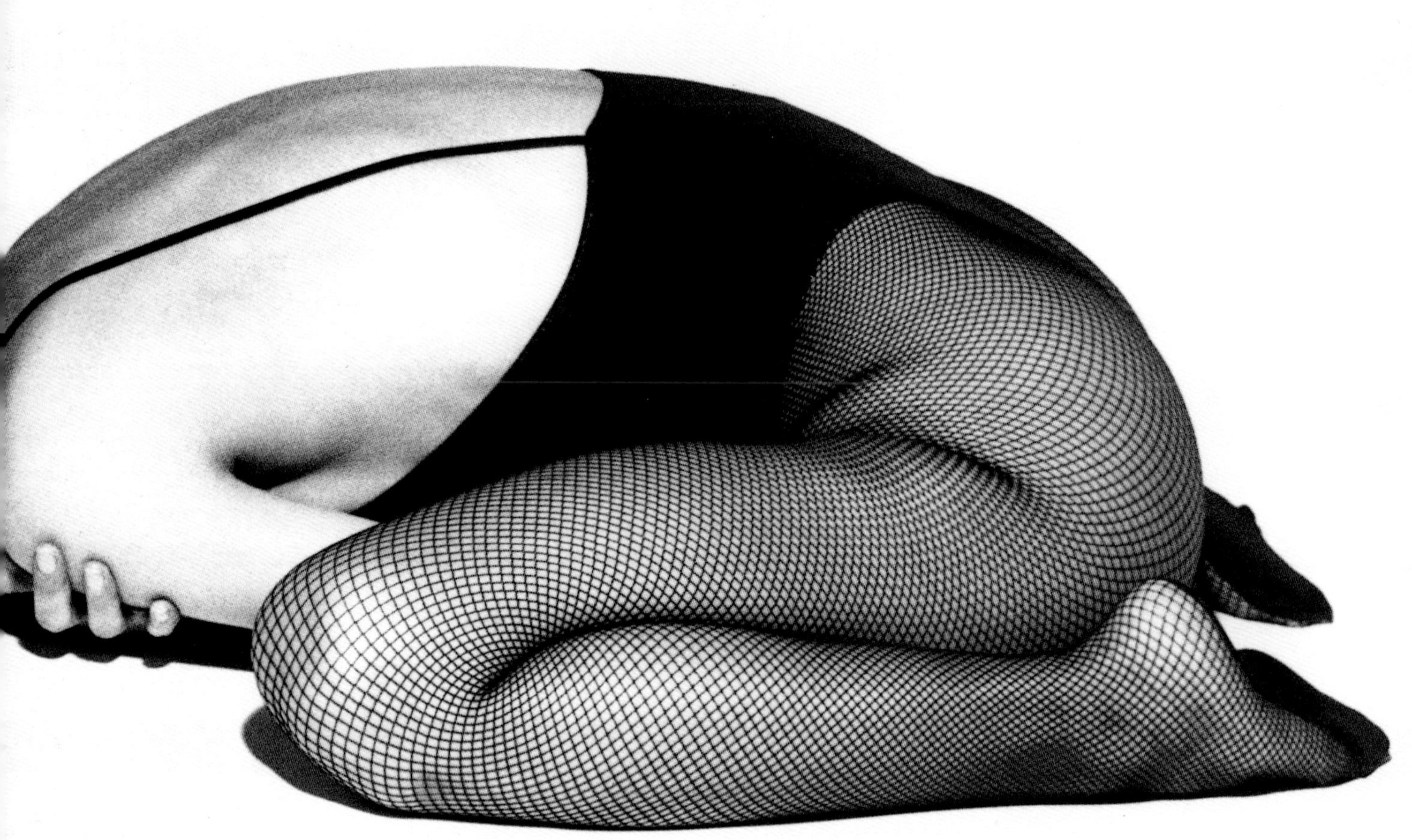

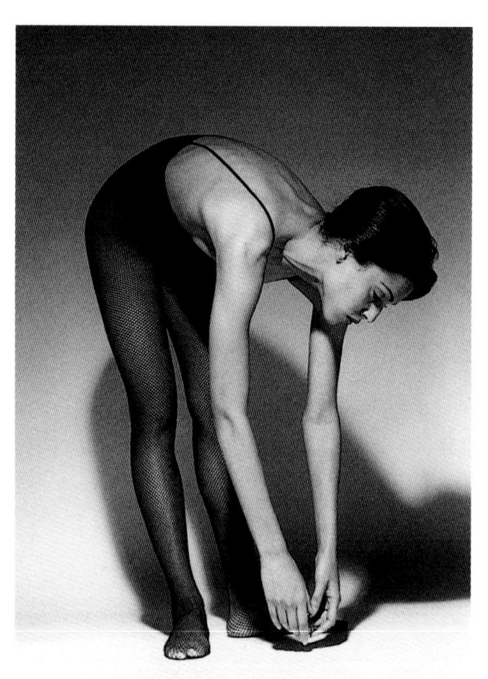

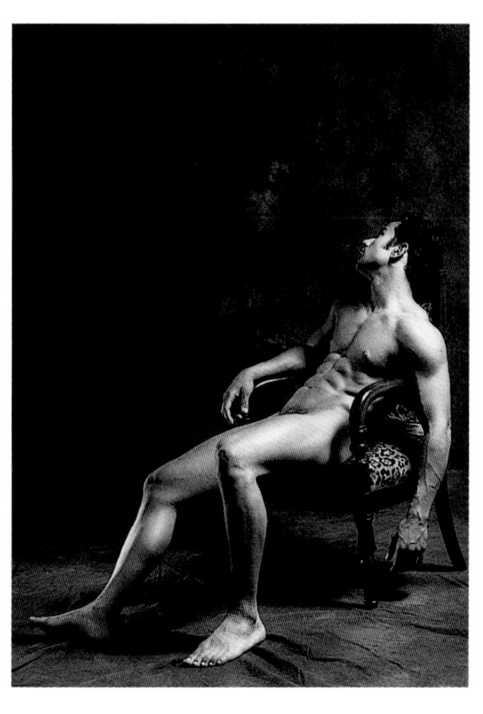

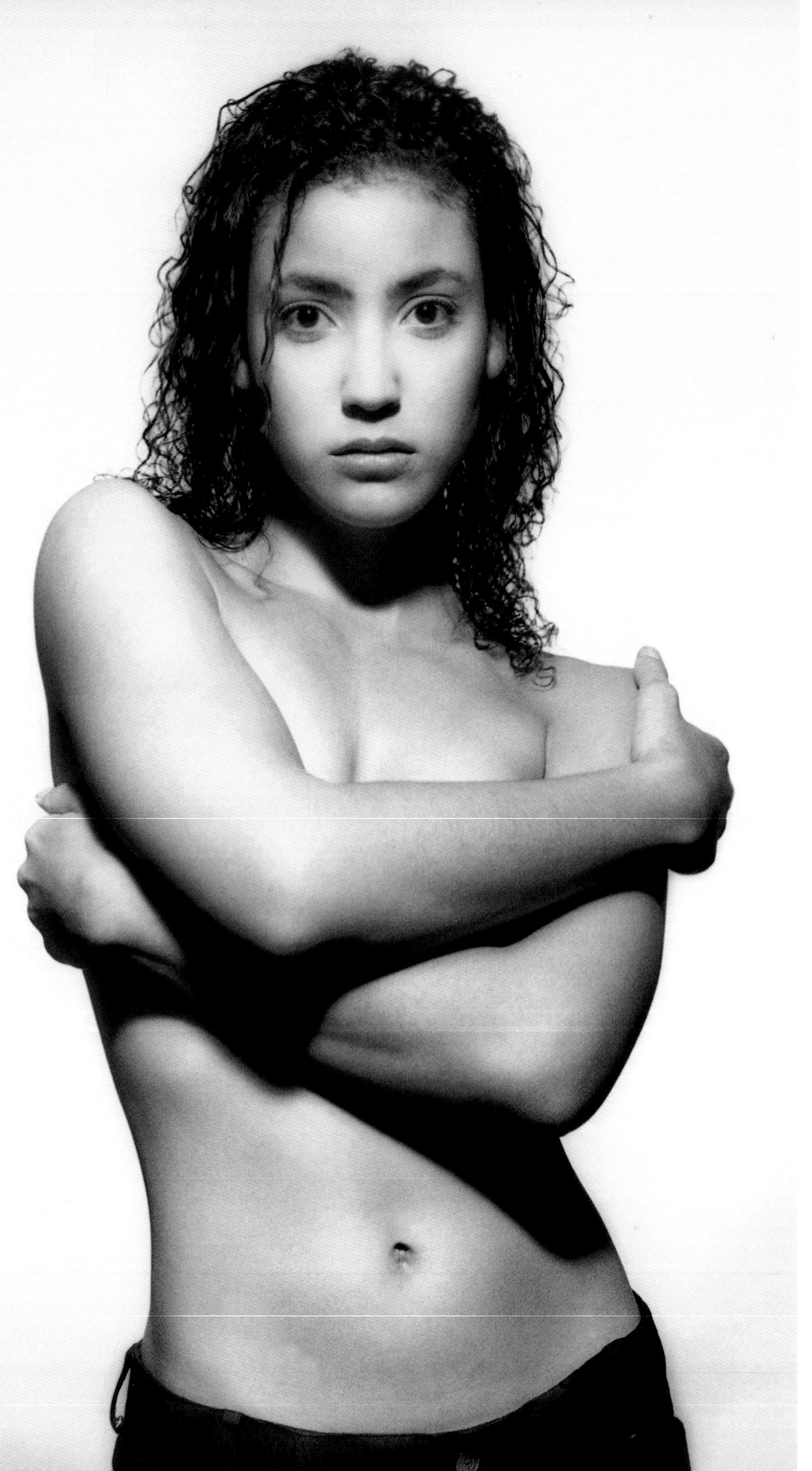

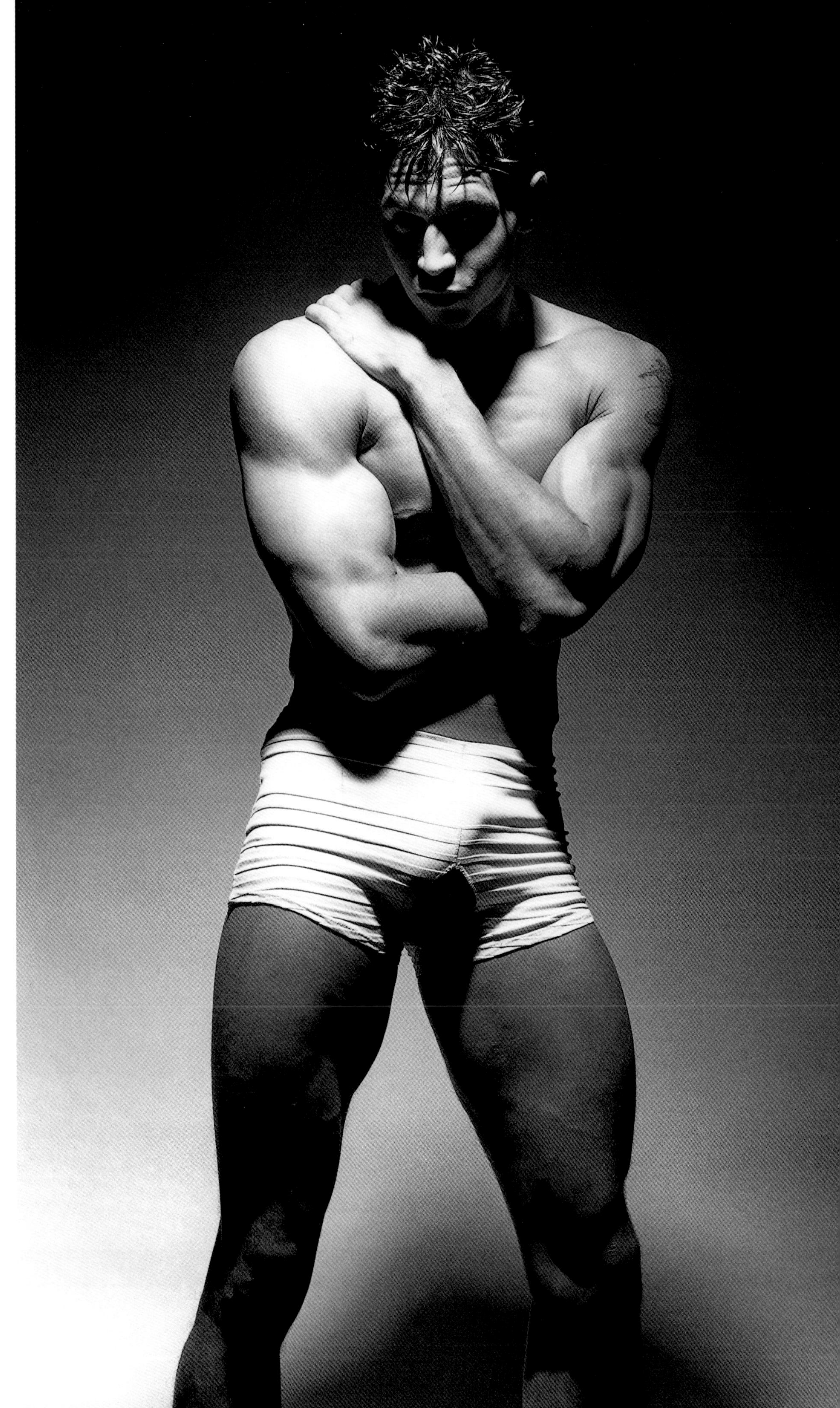

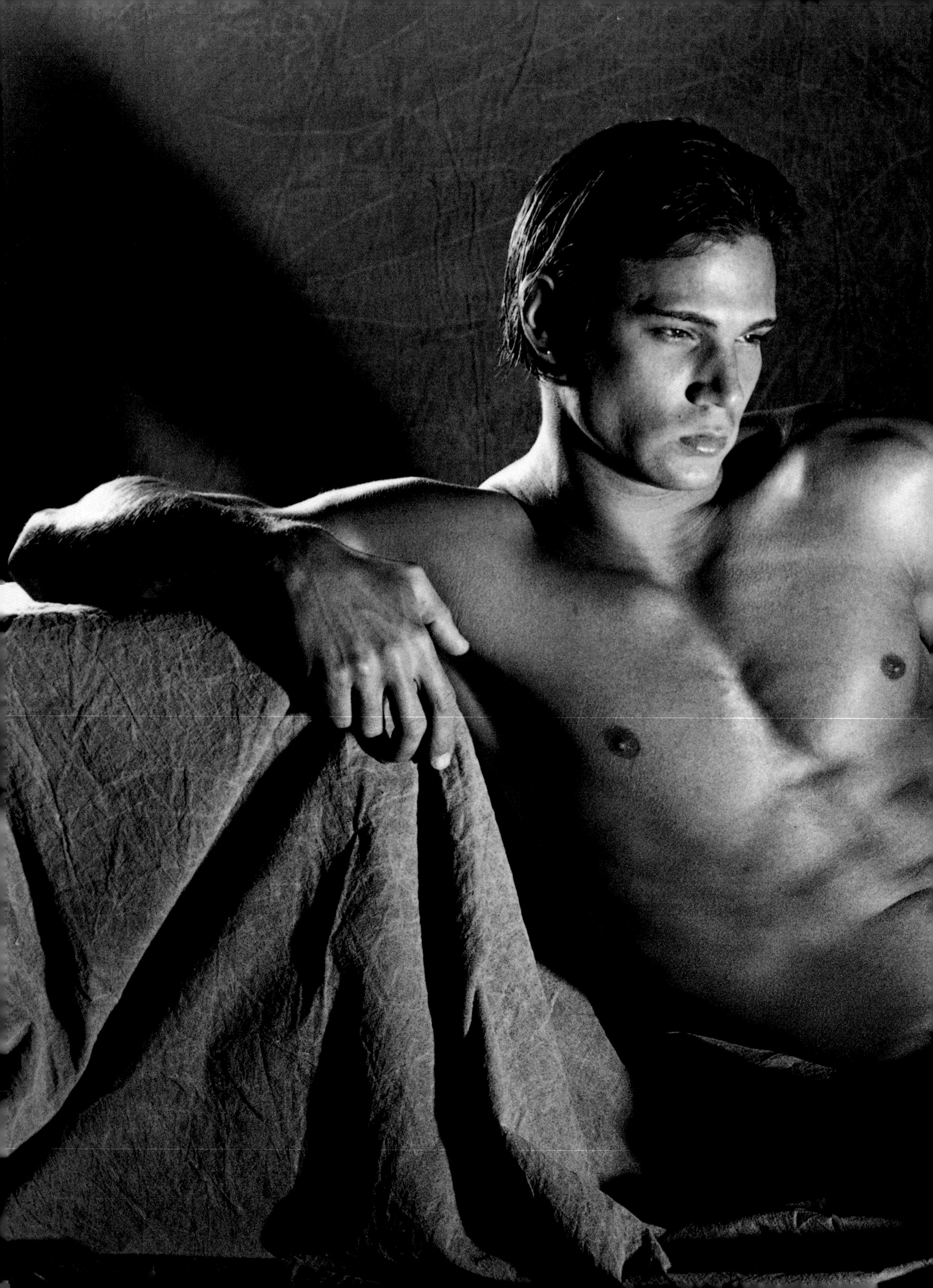

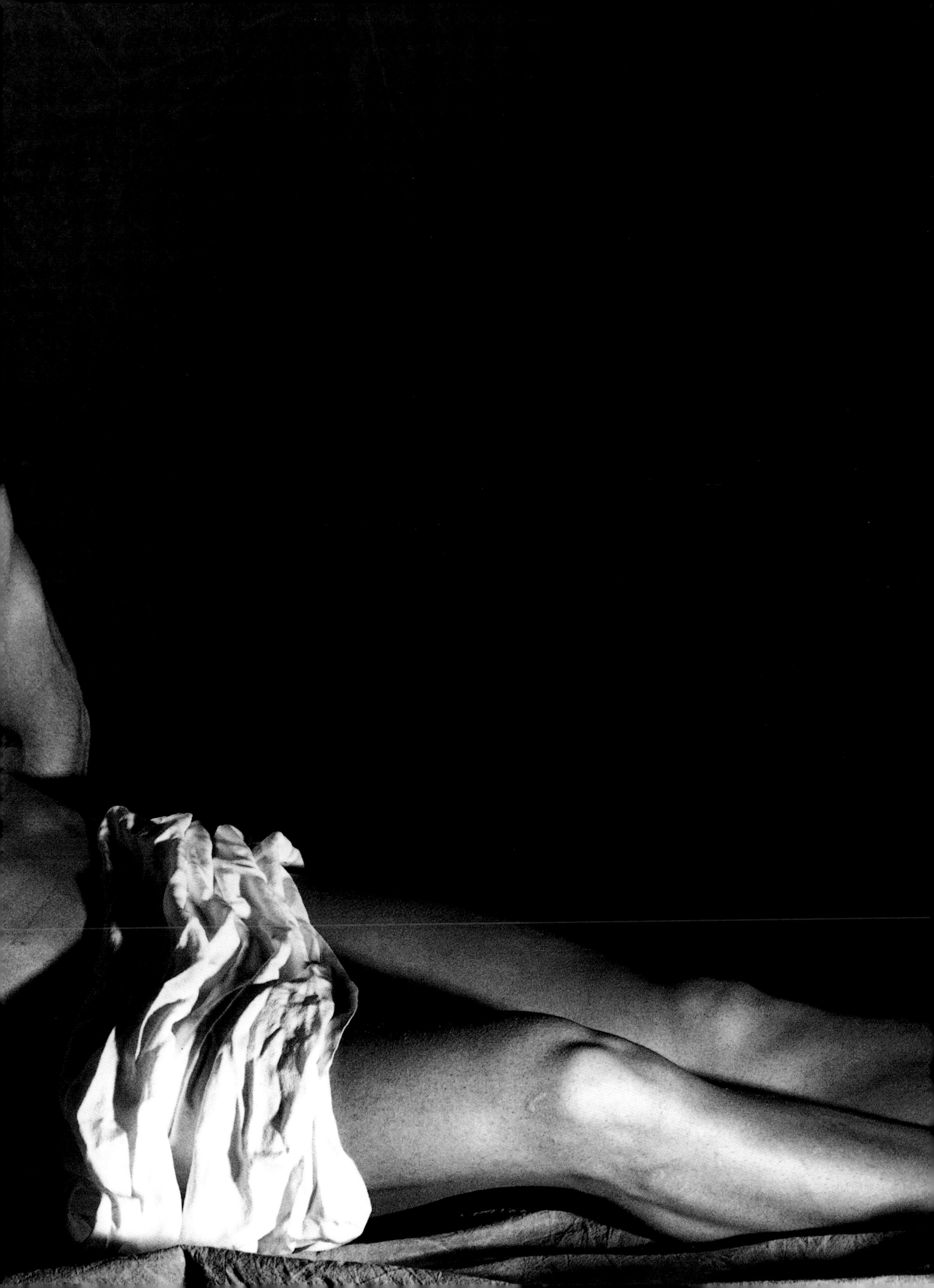

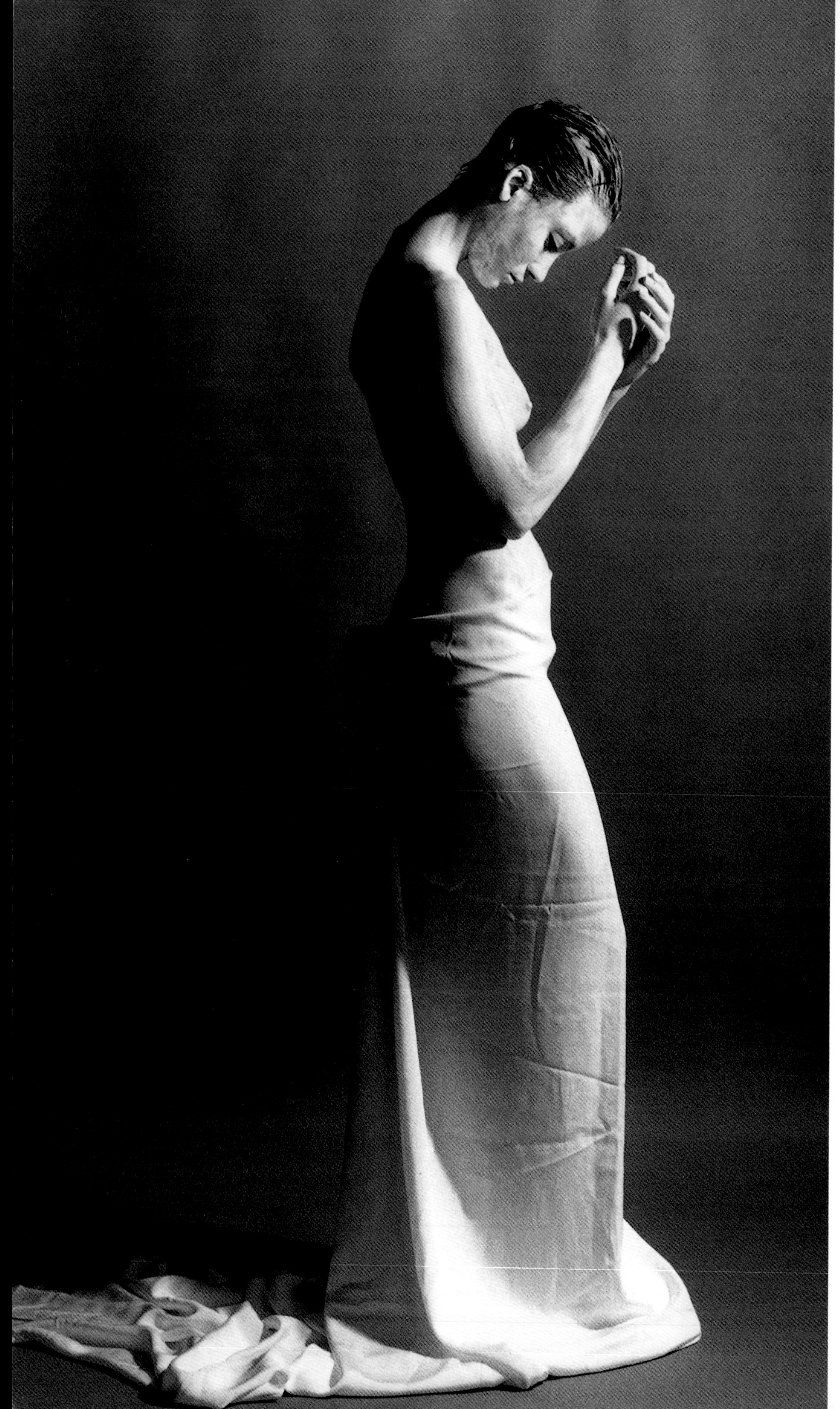

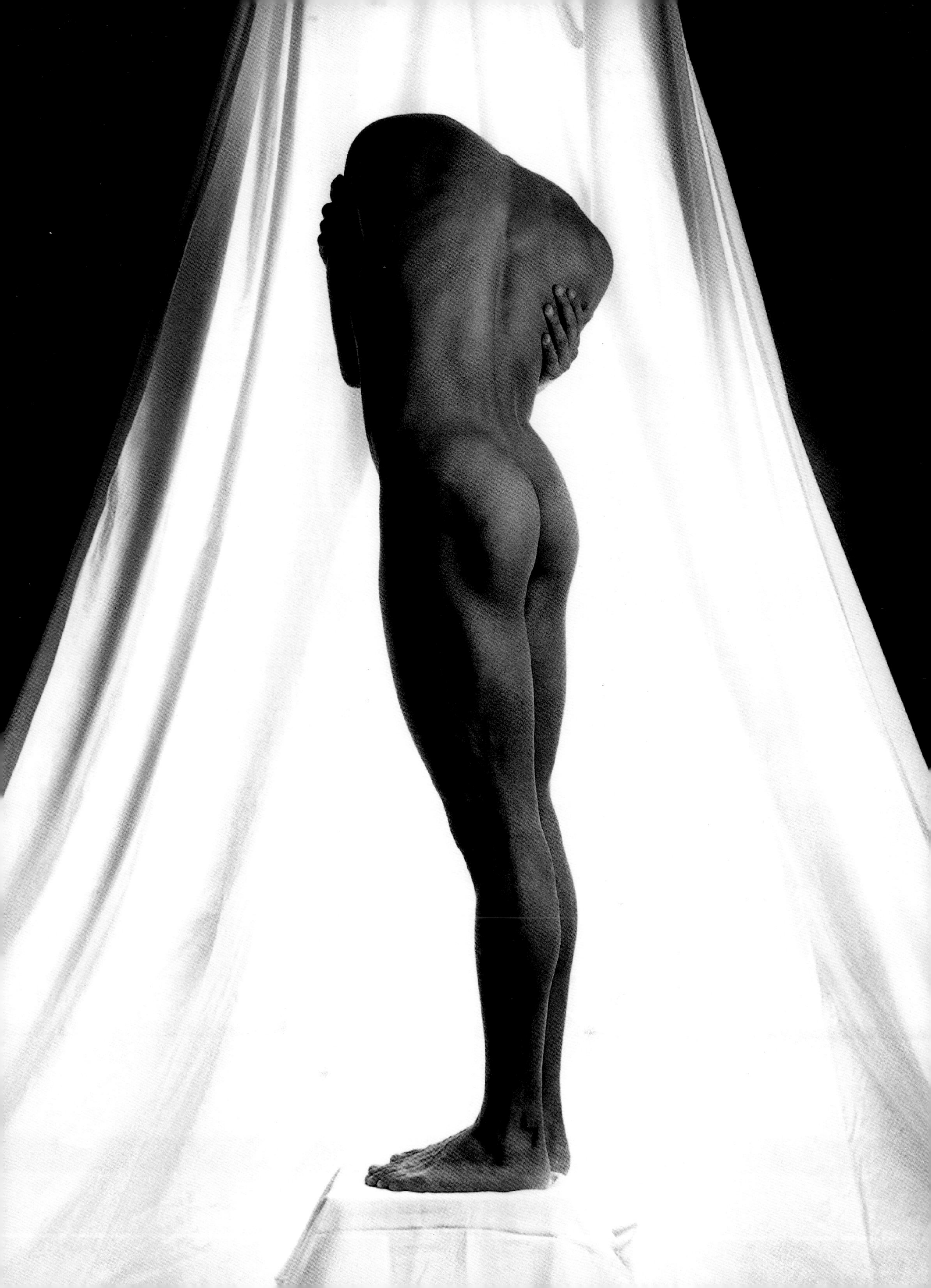

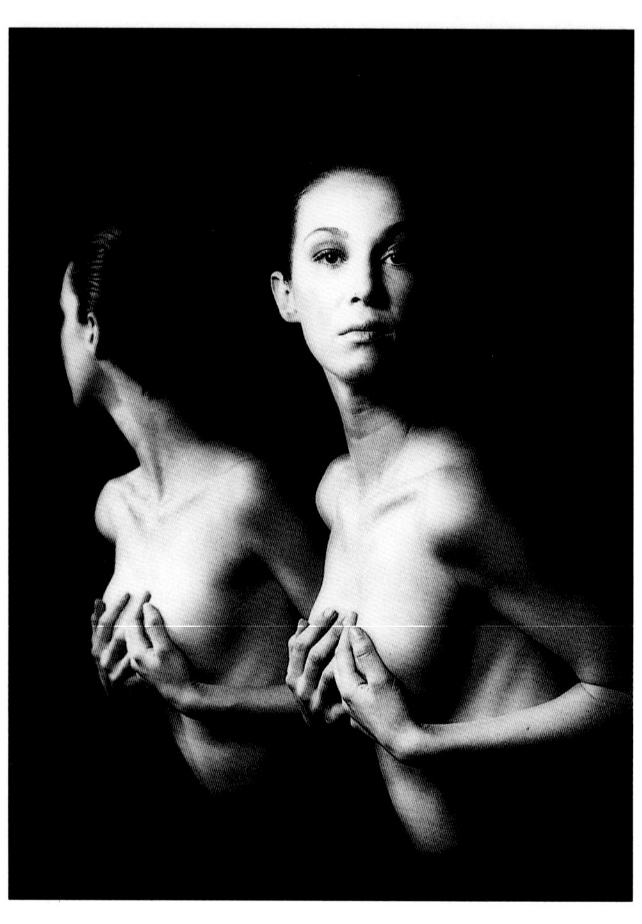

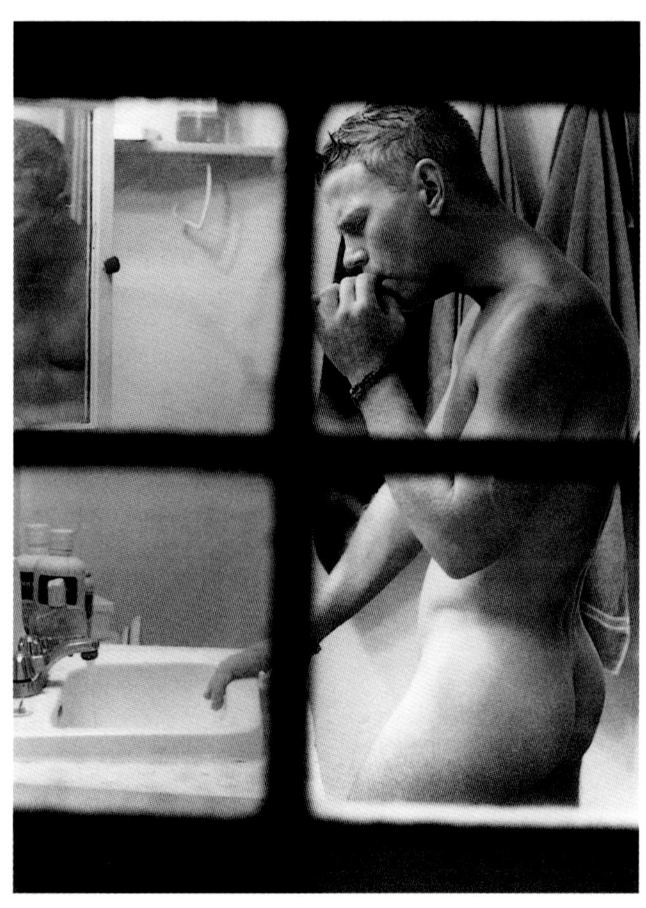

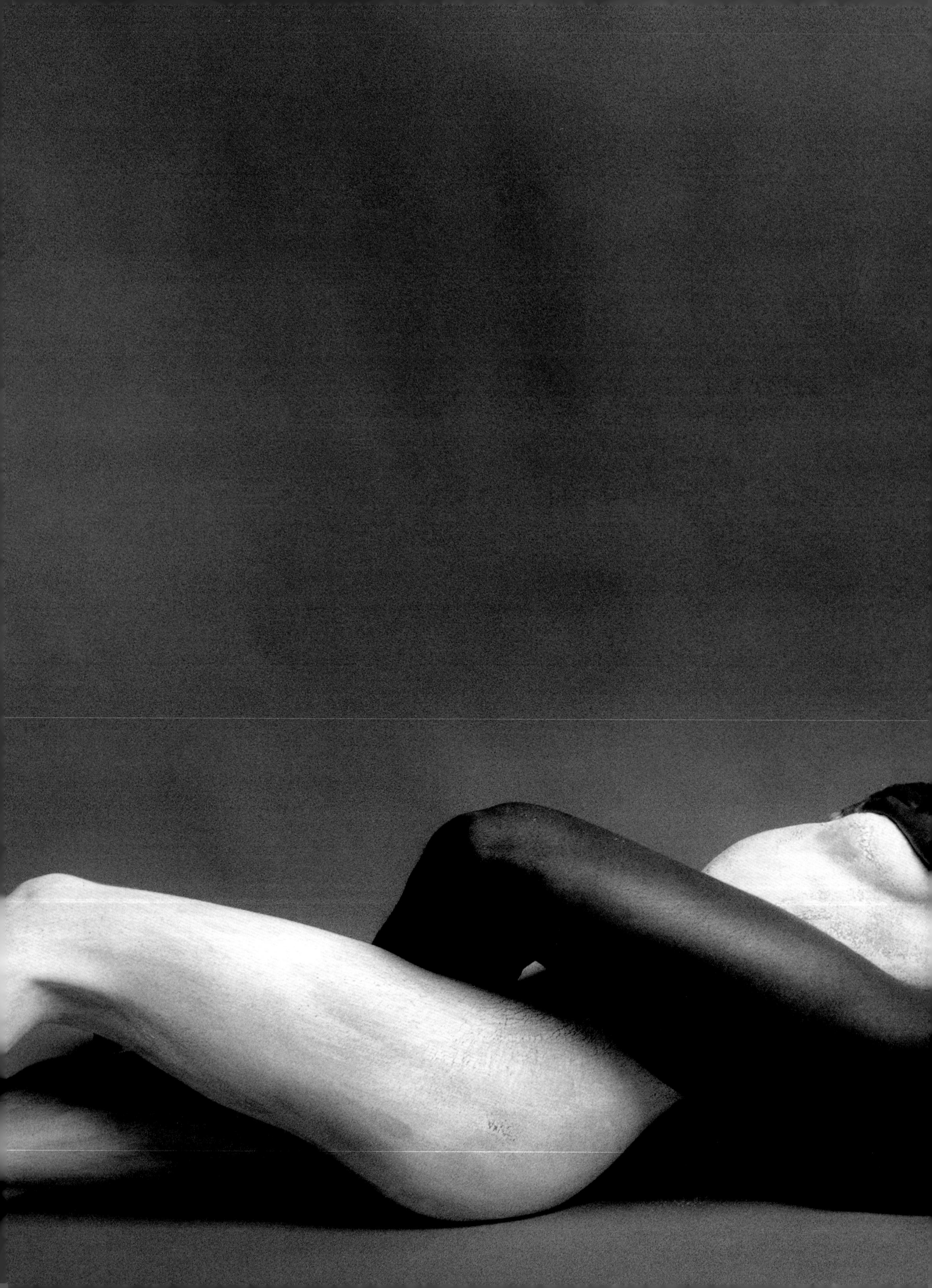

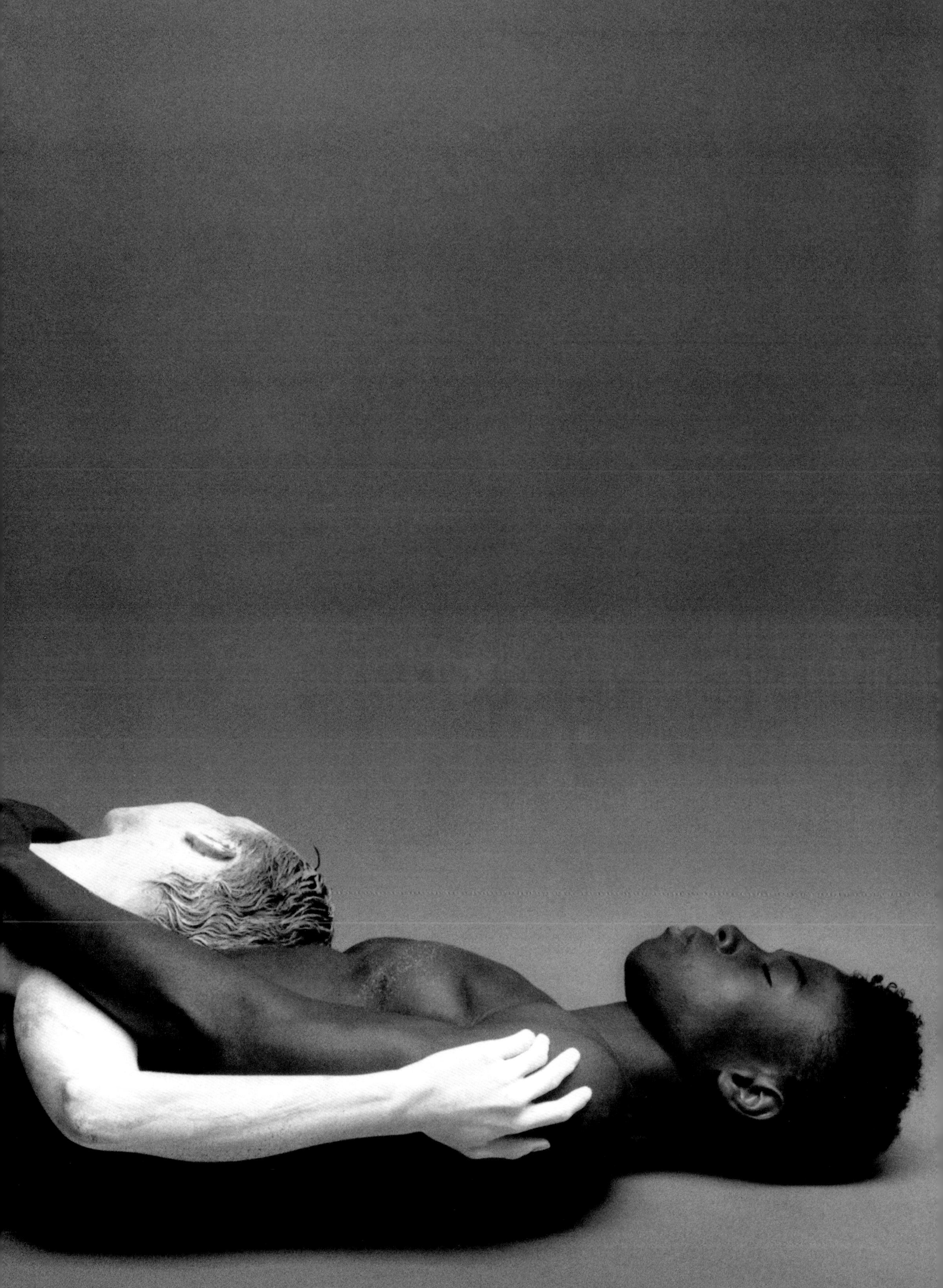

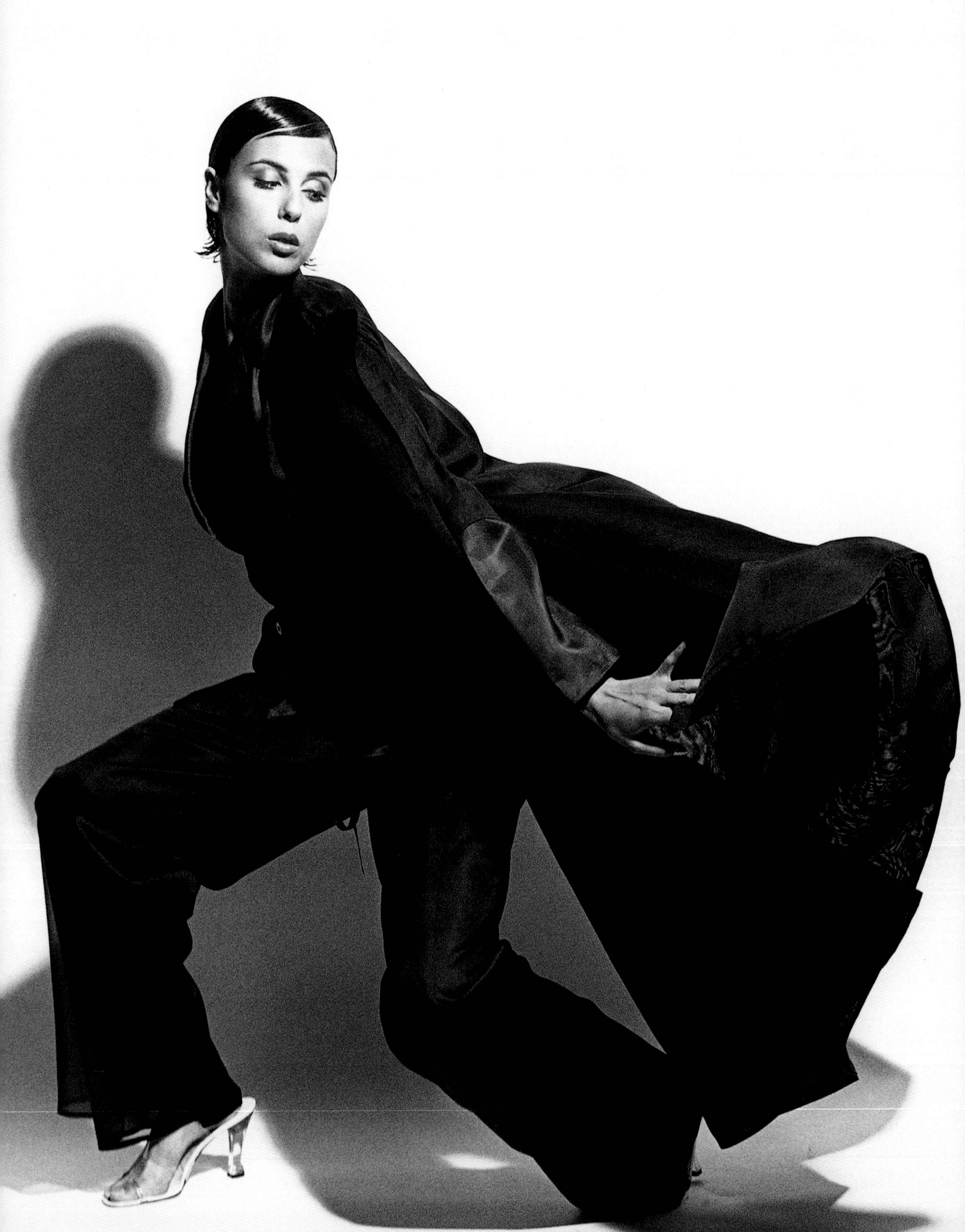

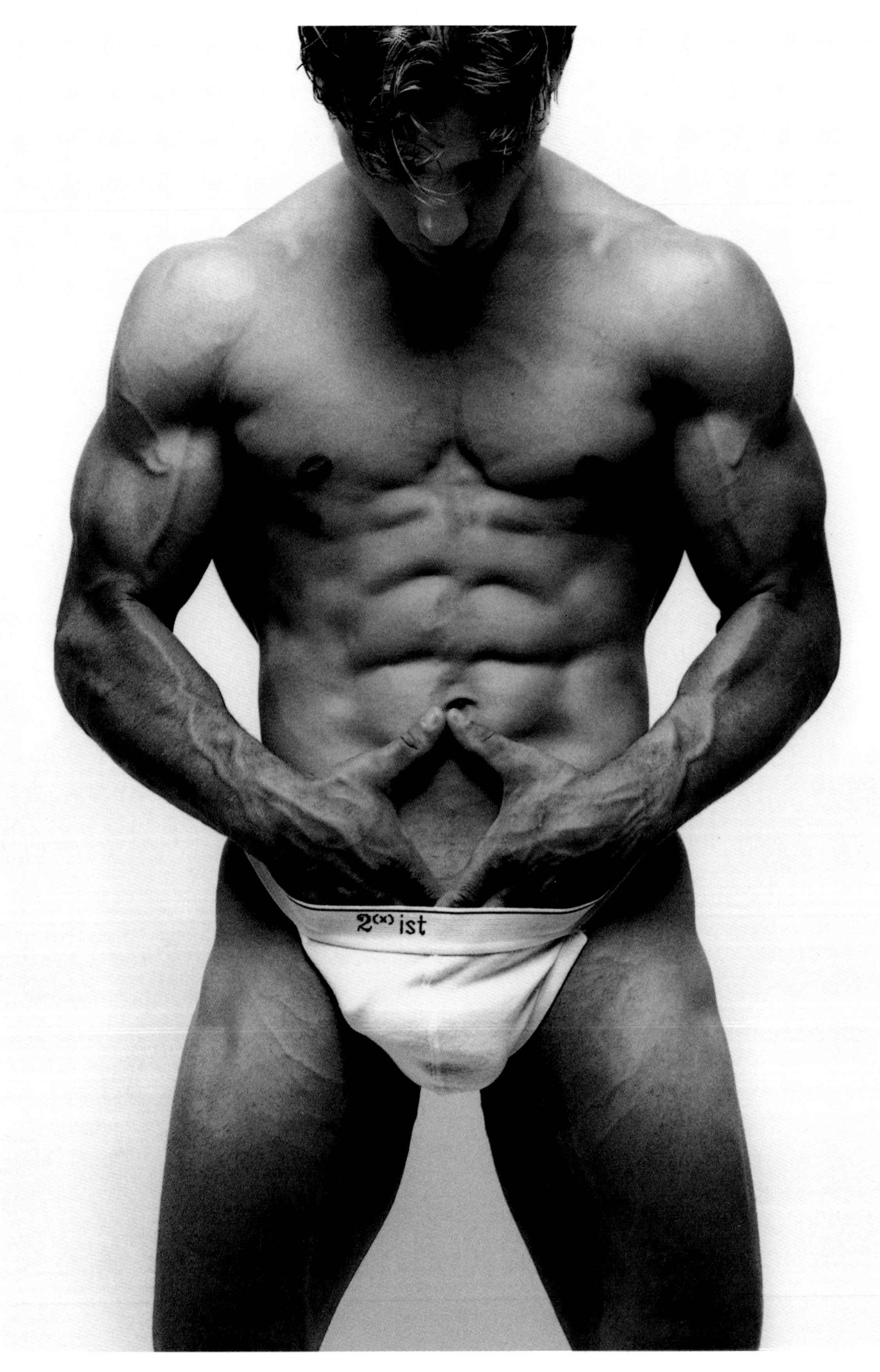
2(x)ist

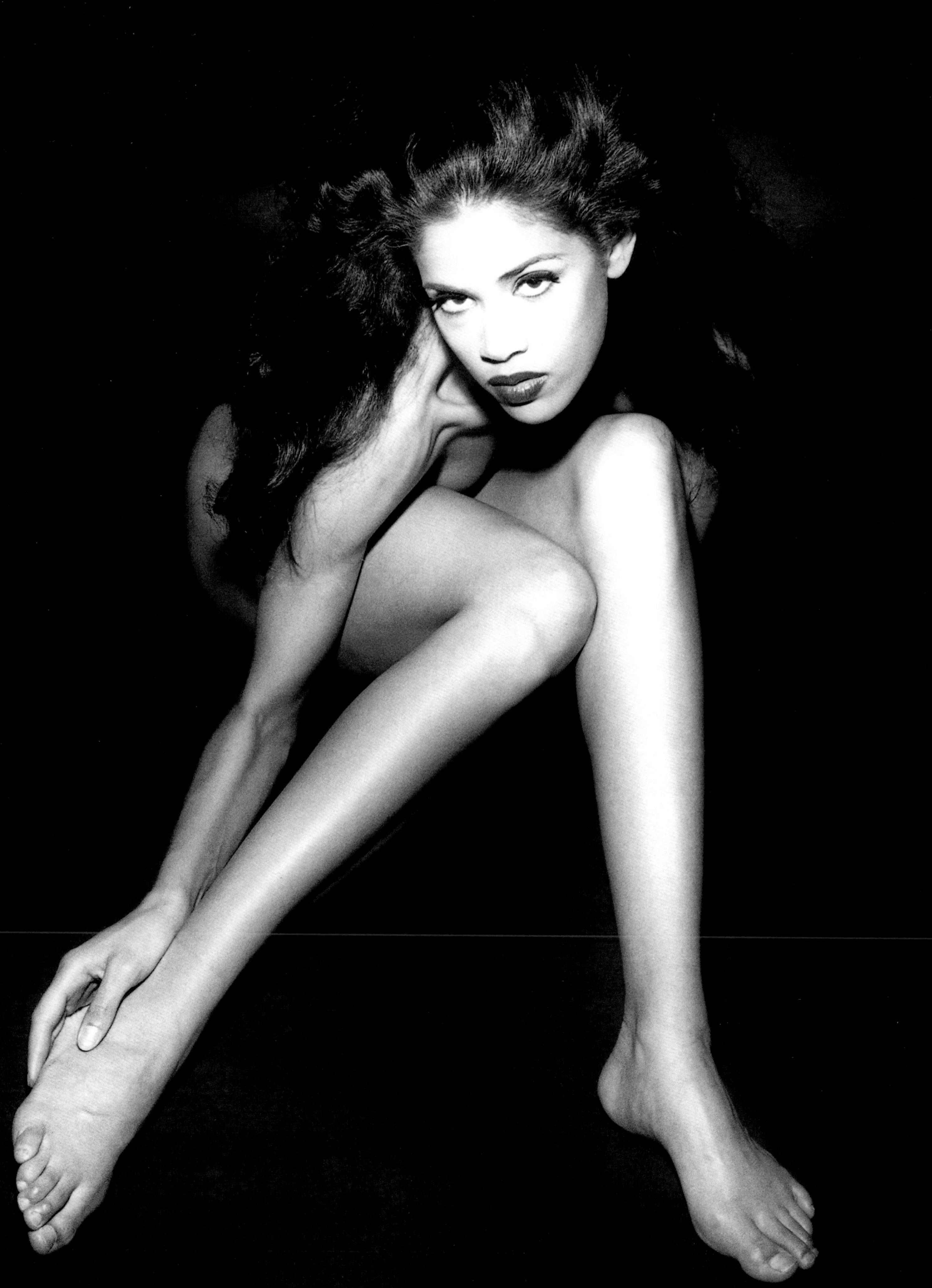

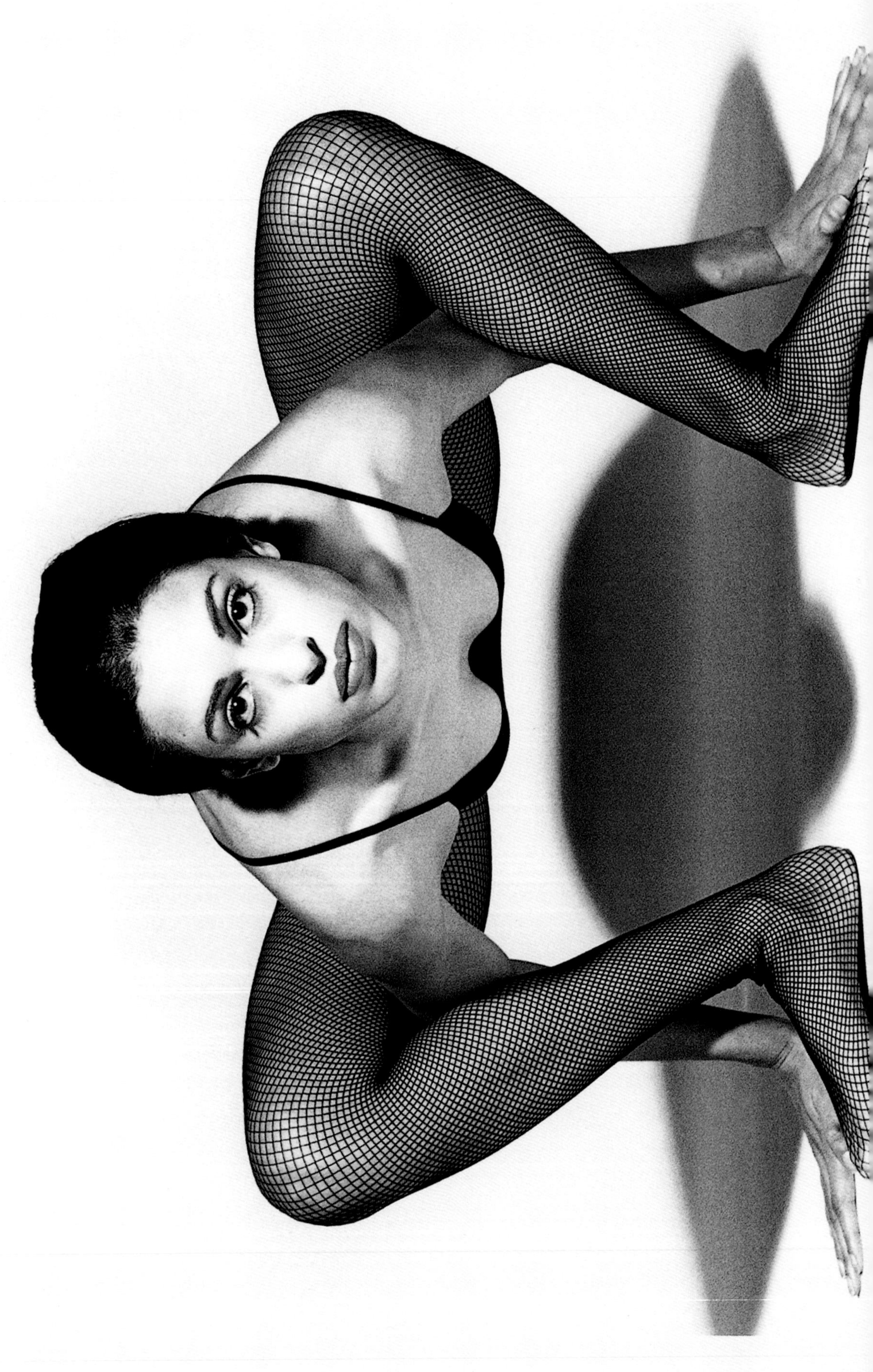

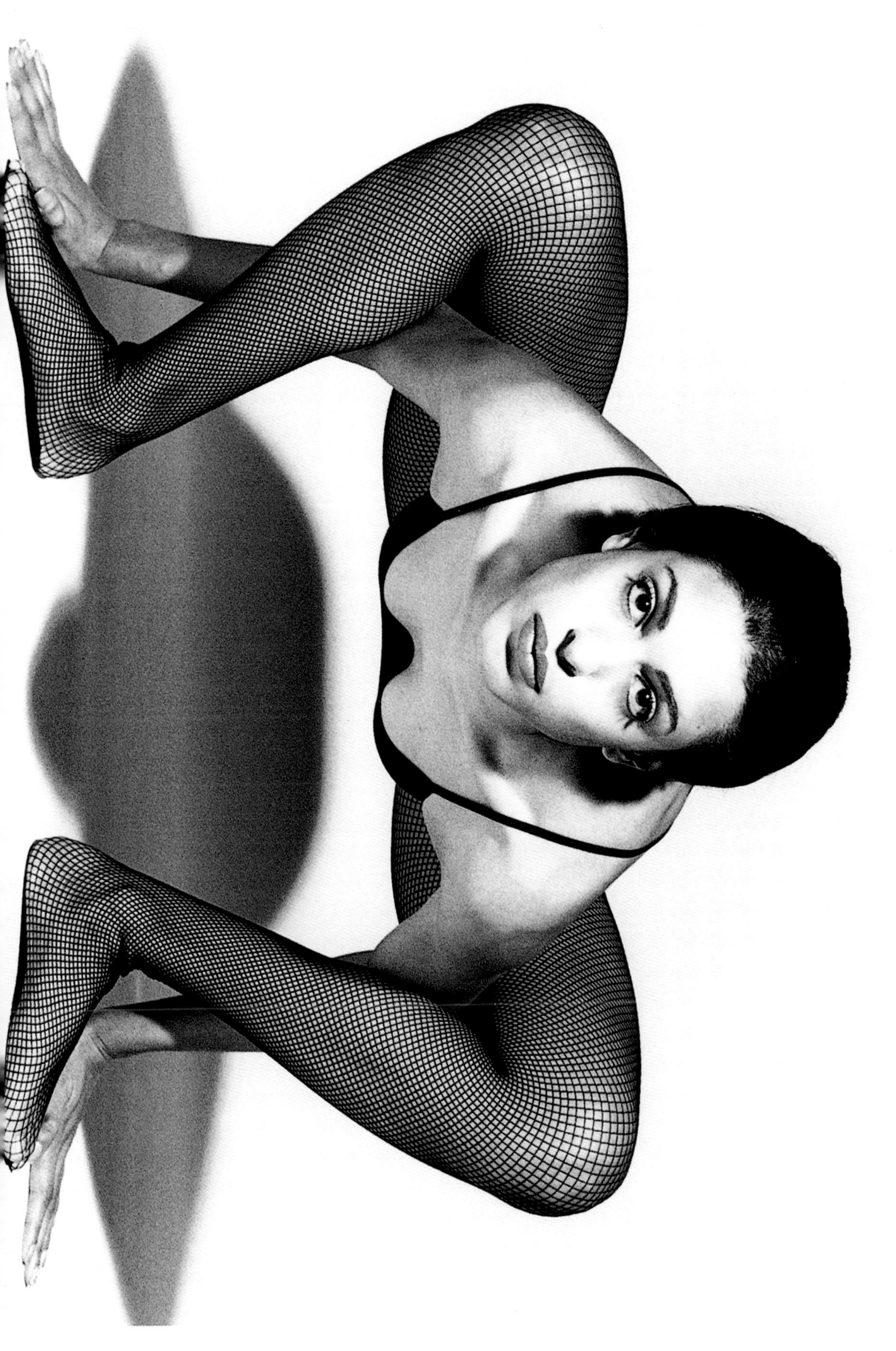

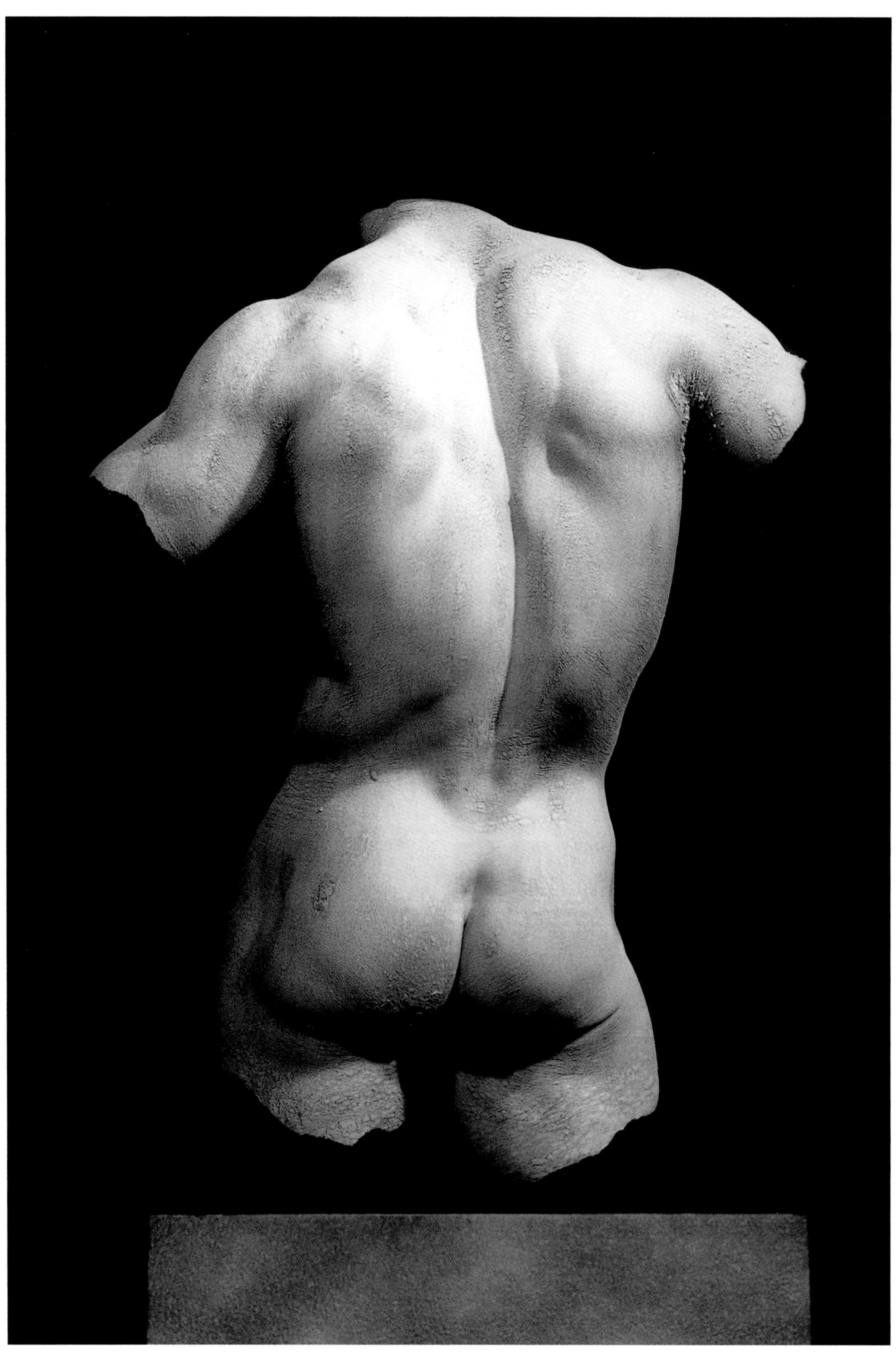

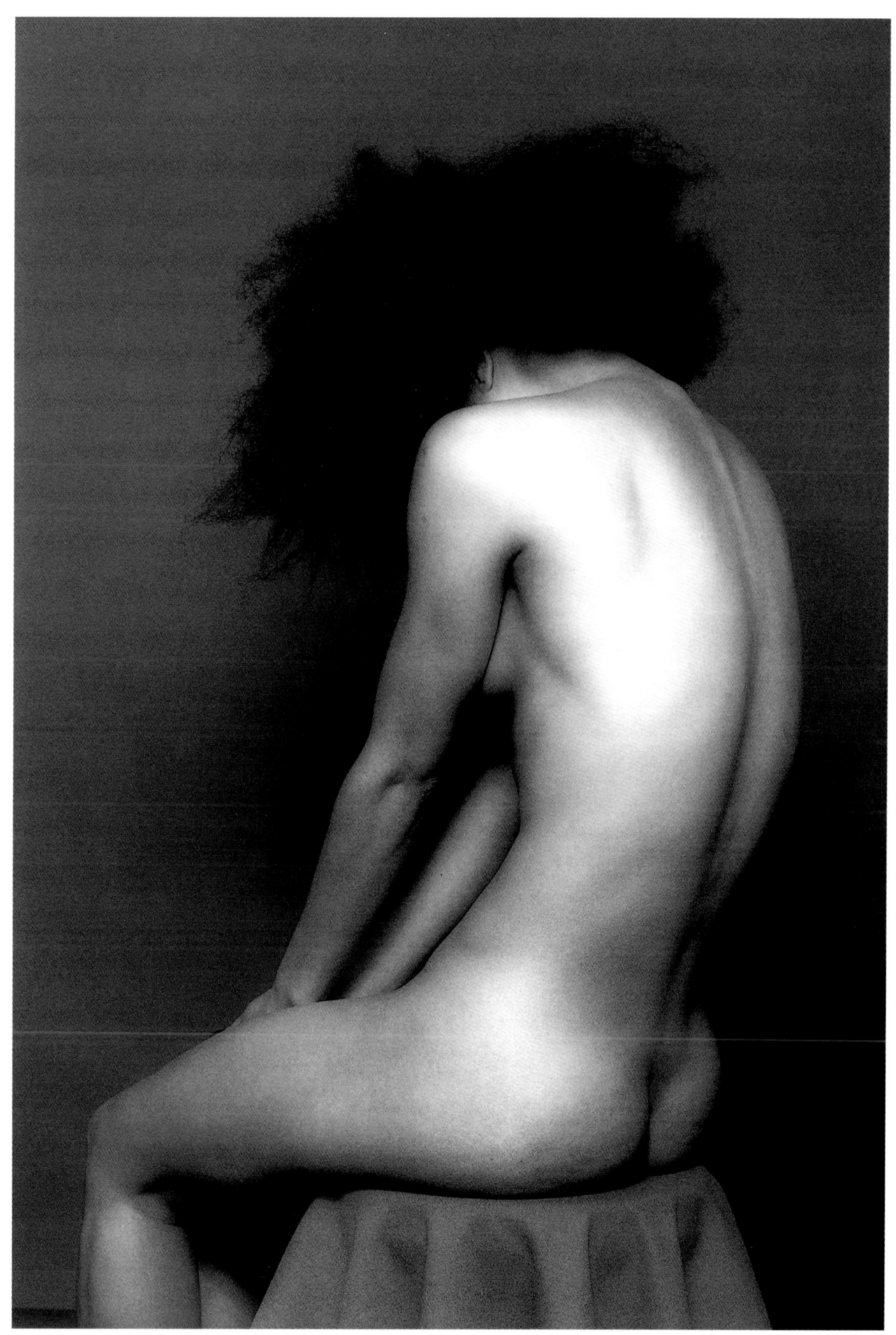

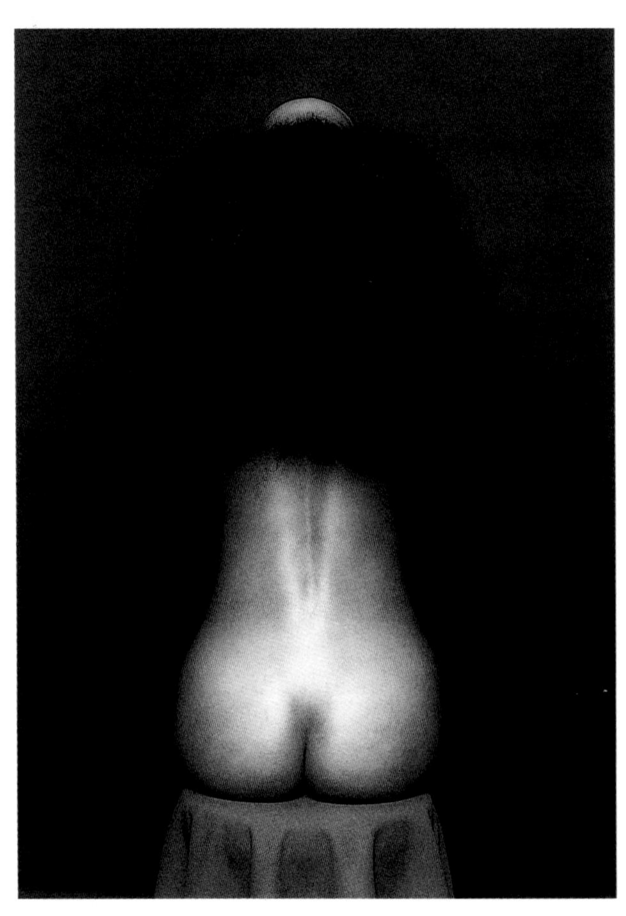

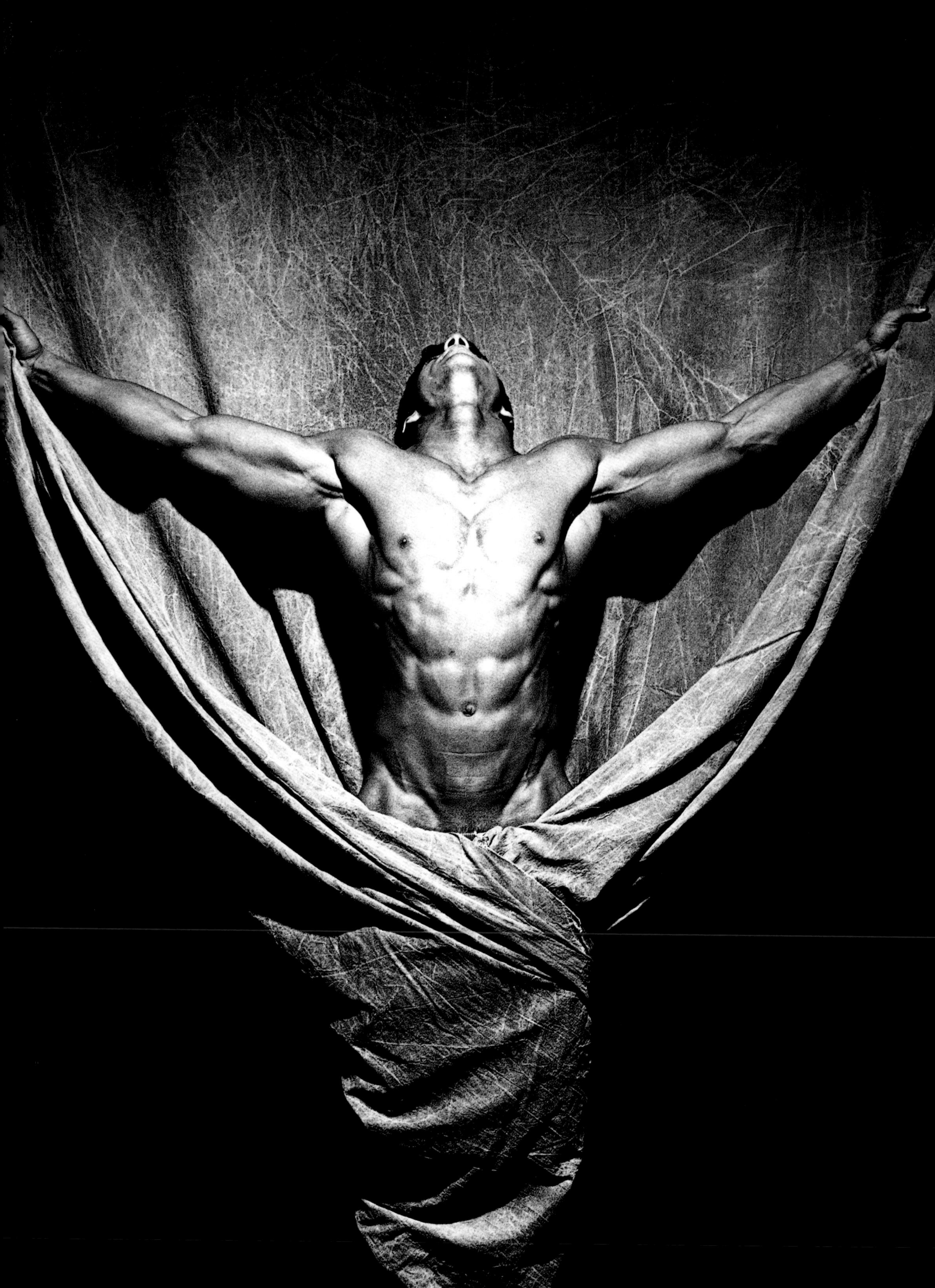

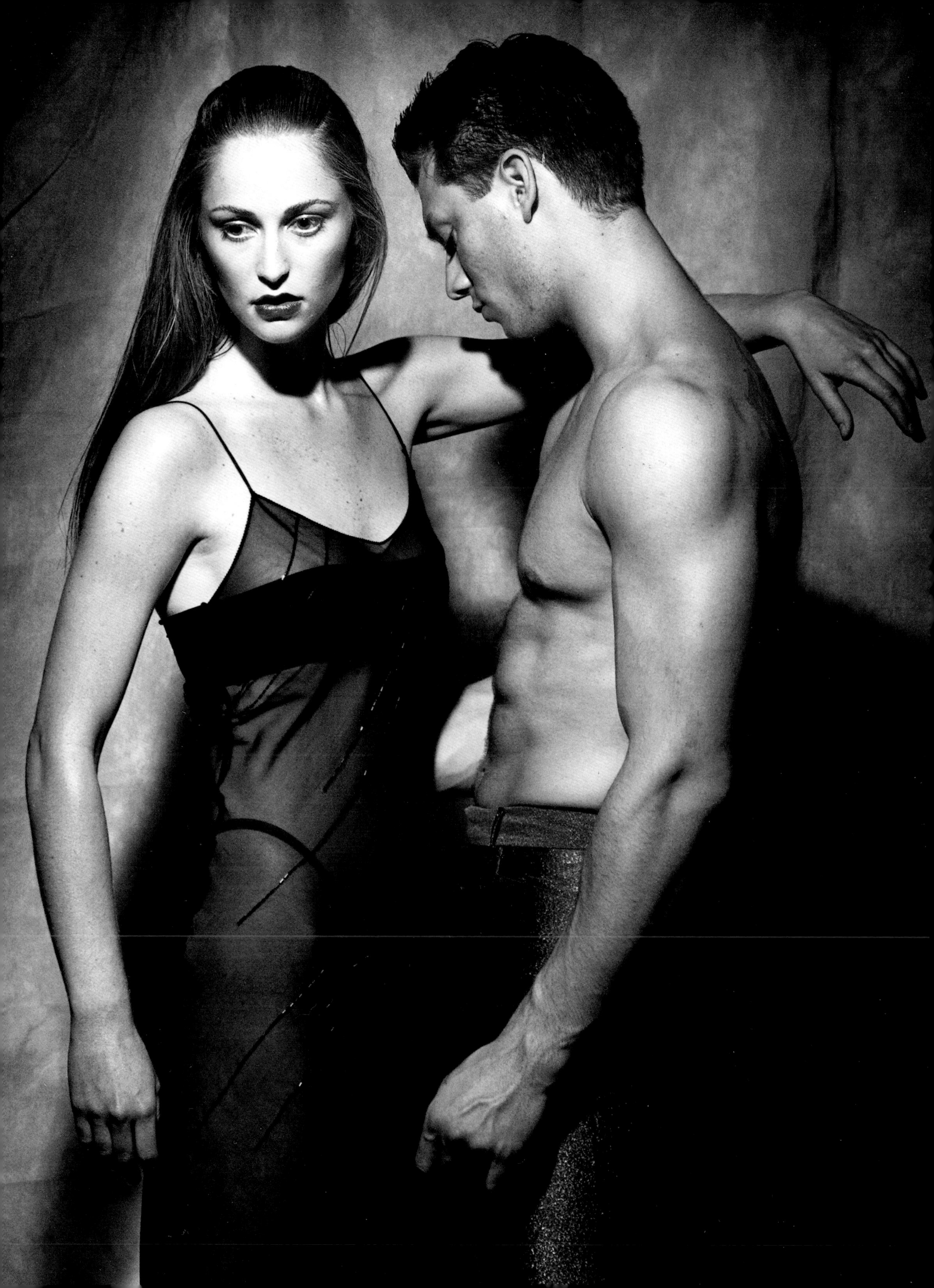

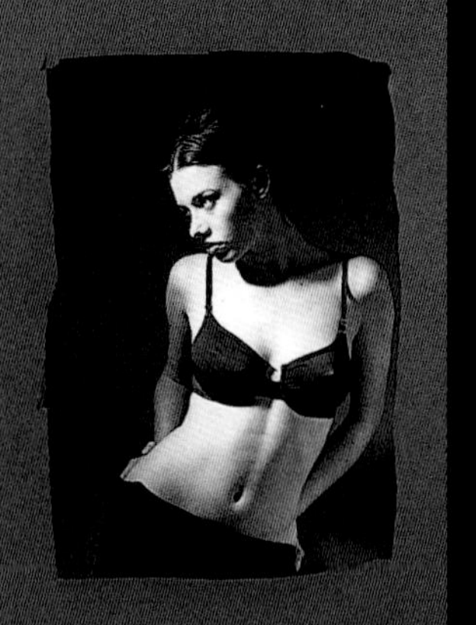
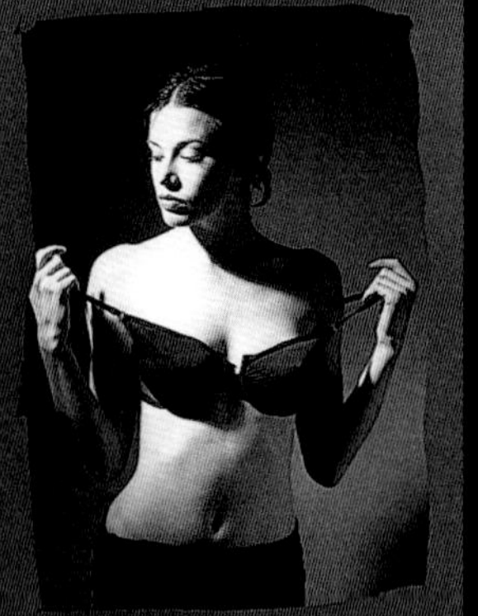
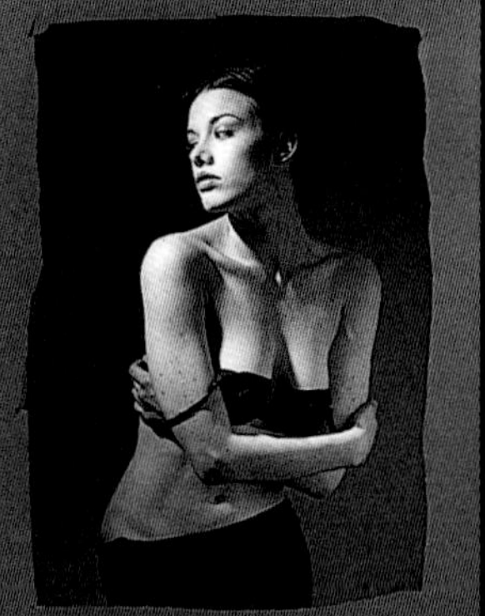
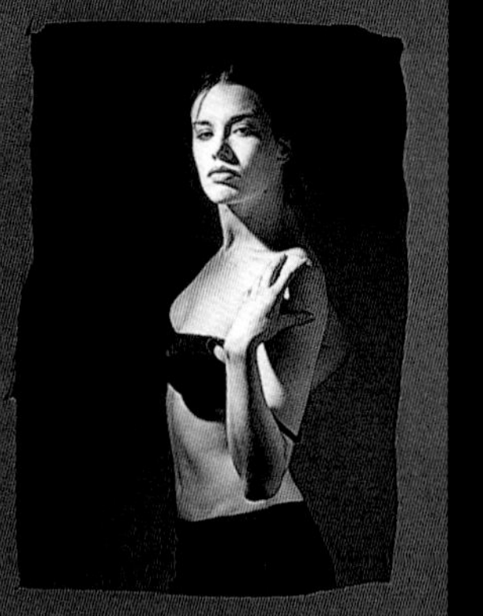

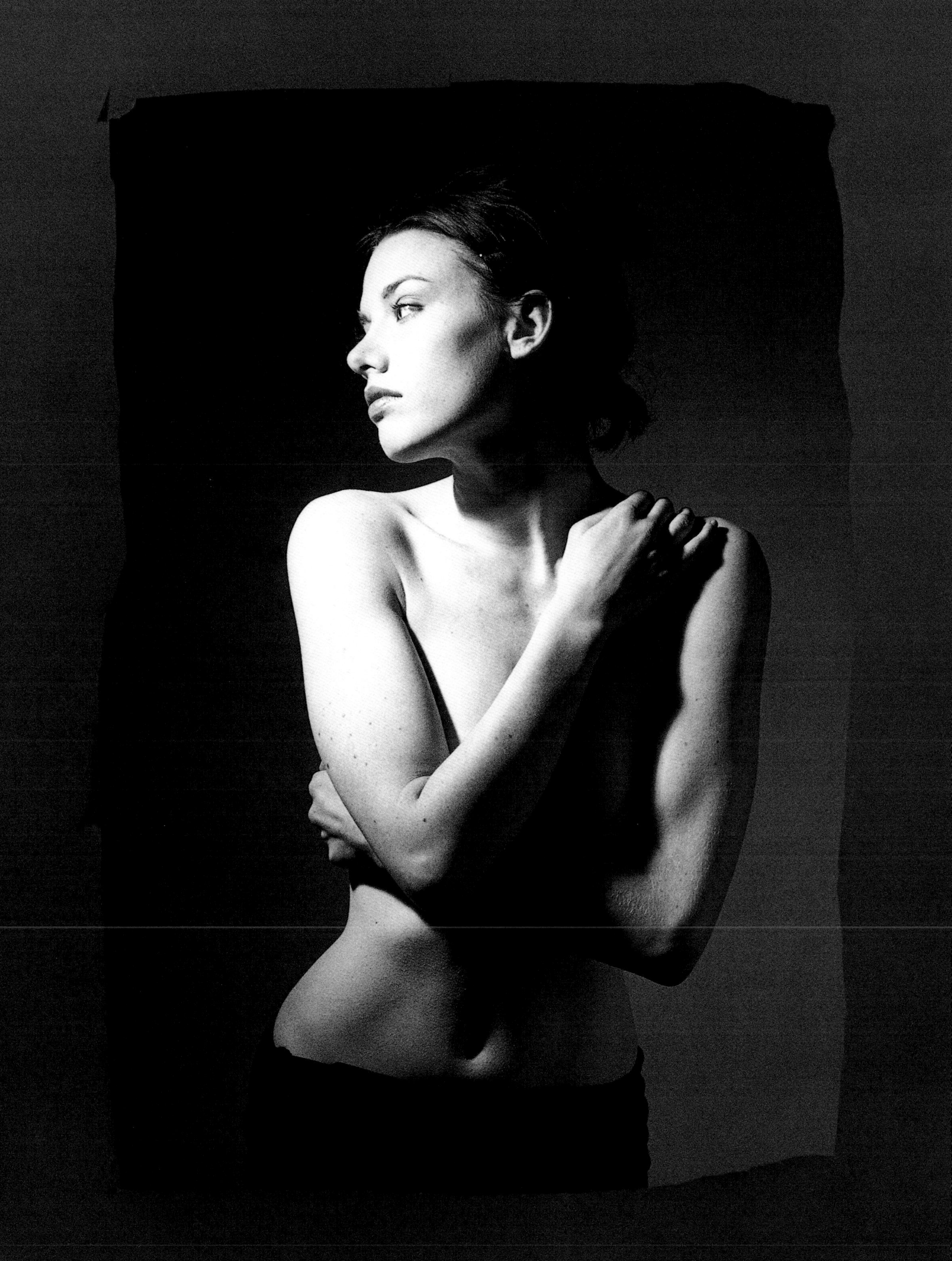

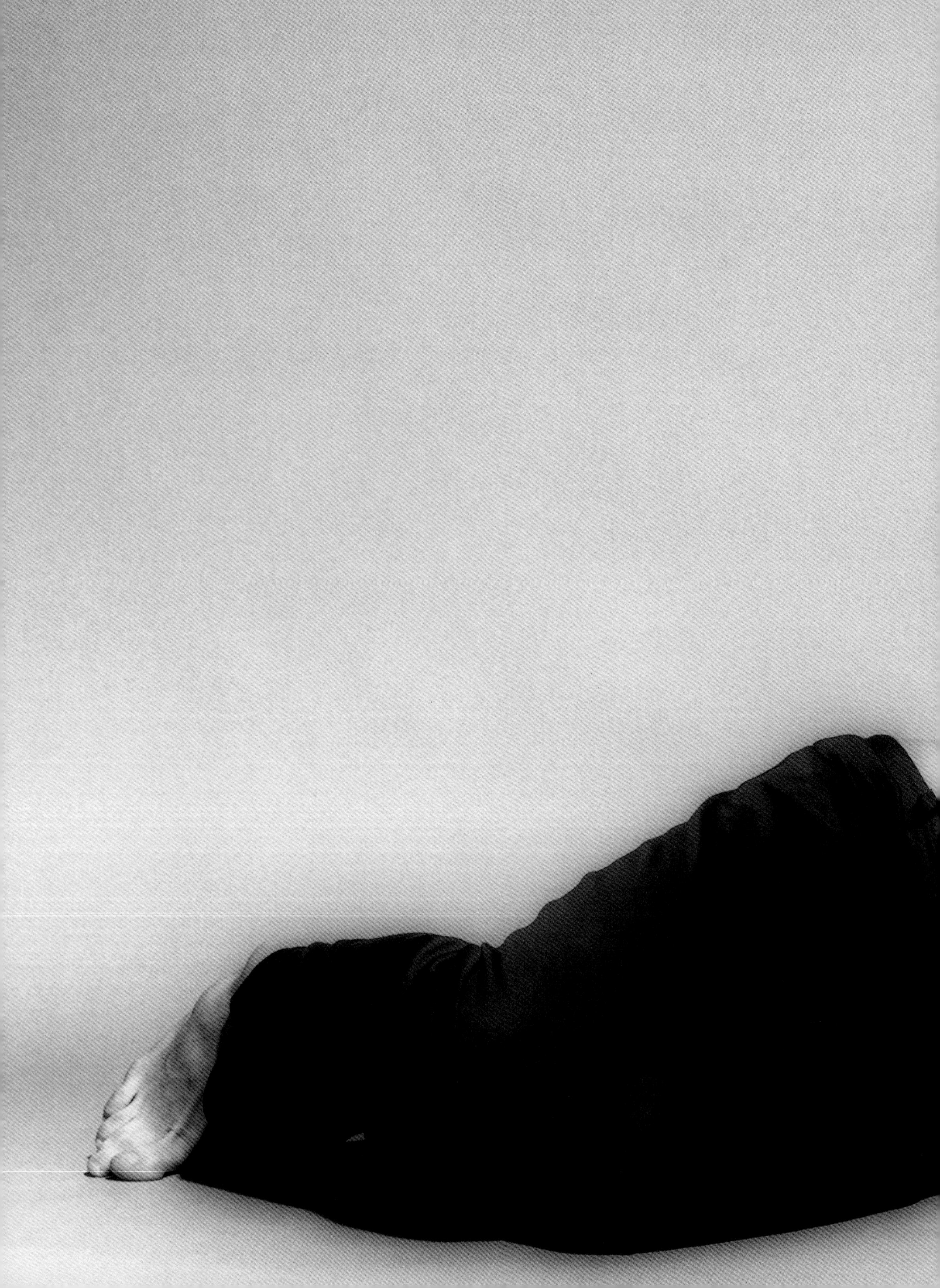

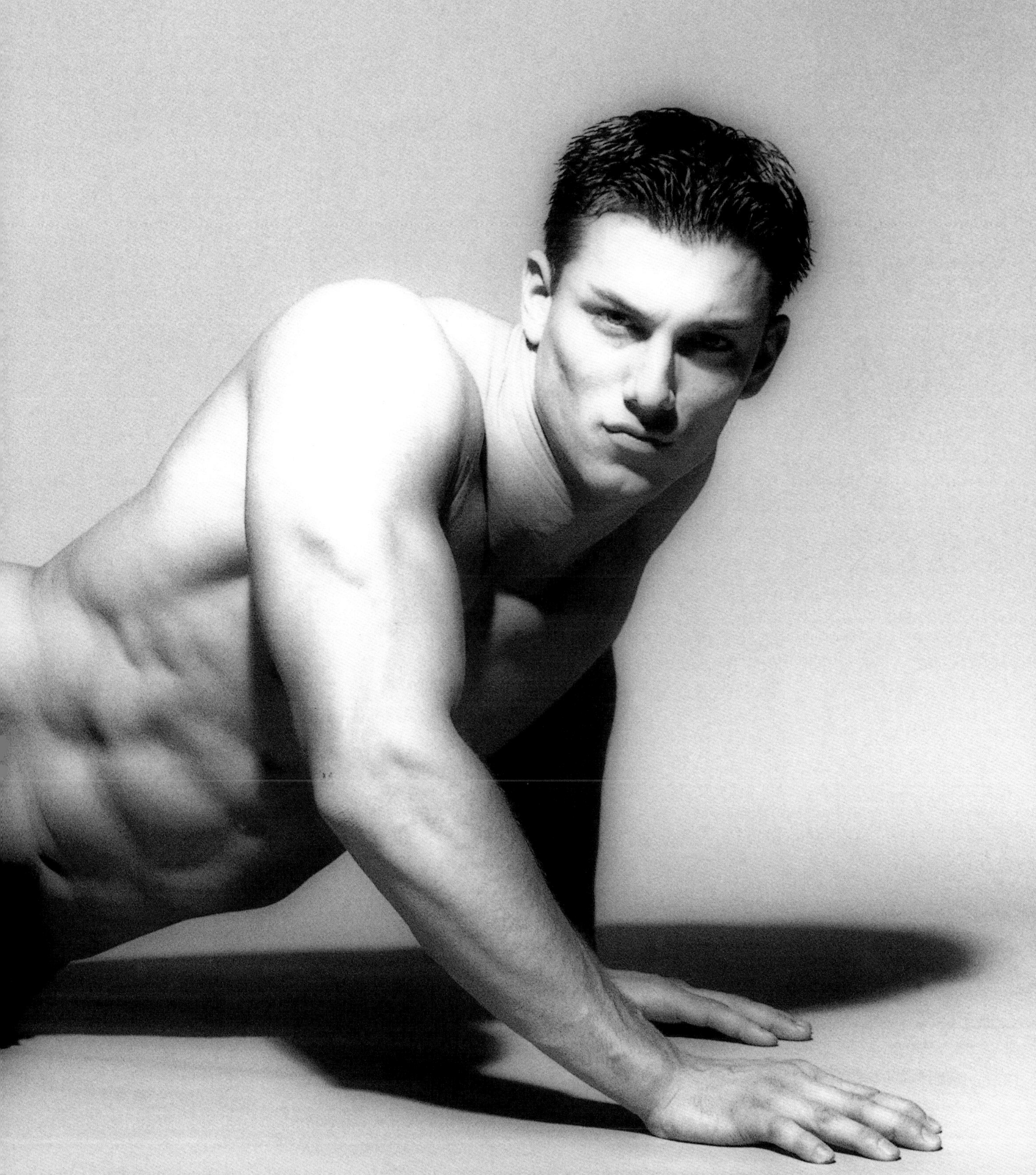

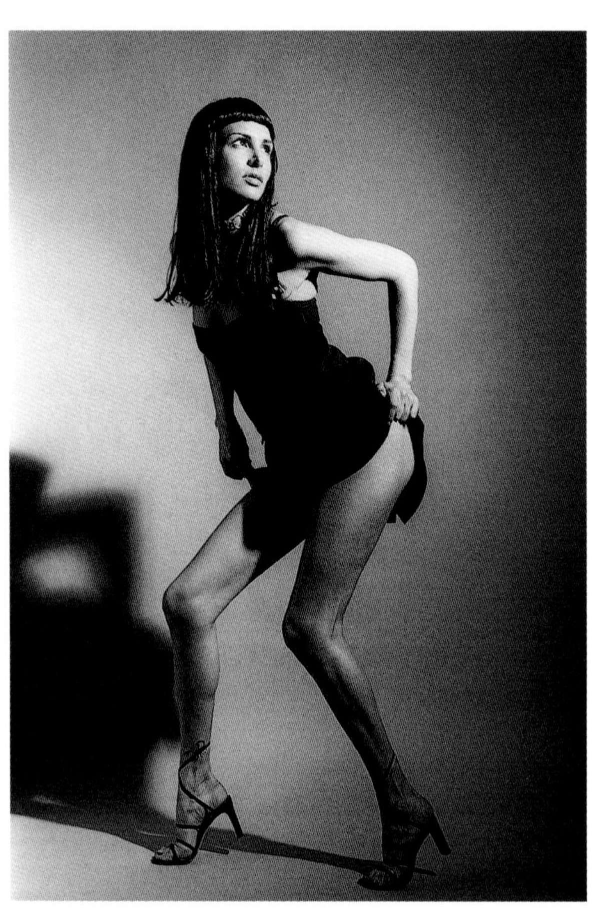

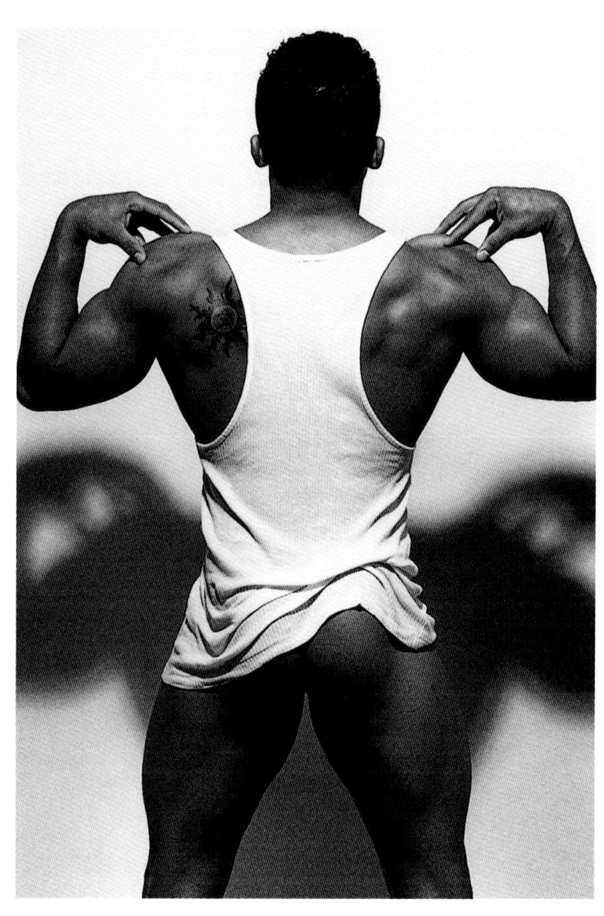

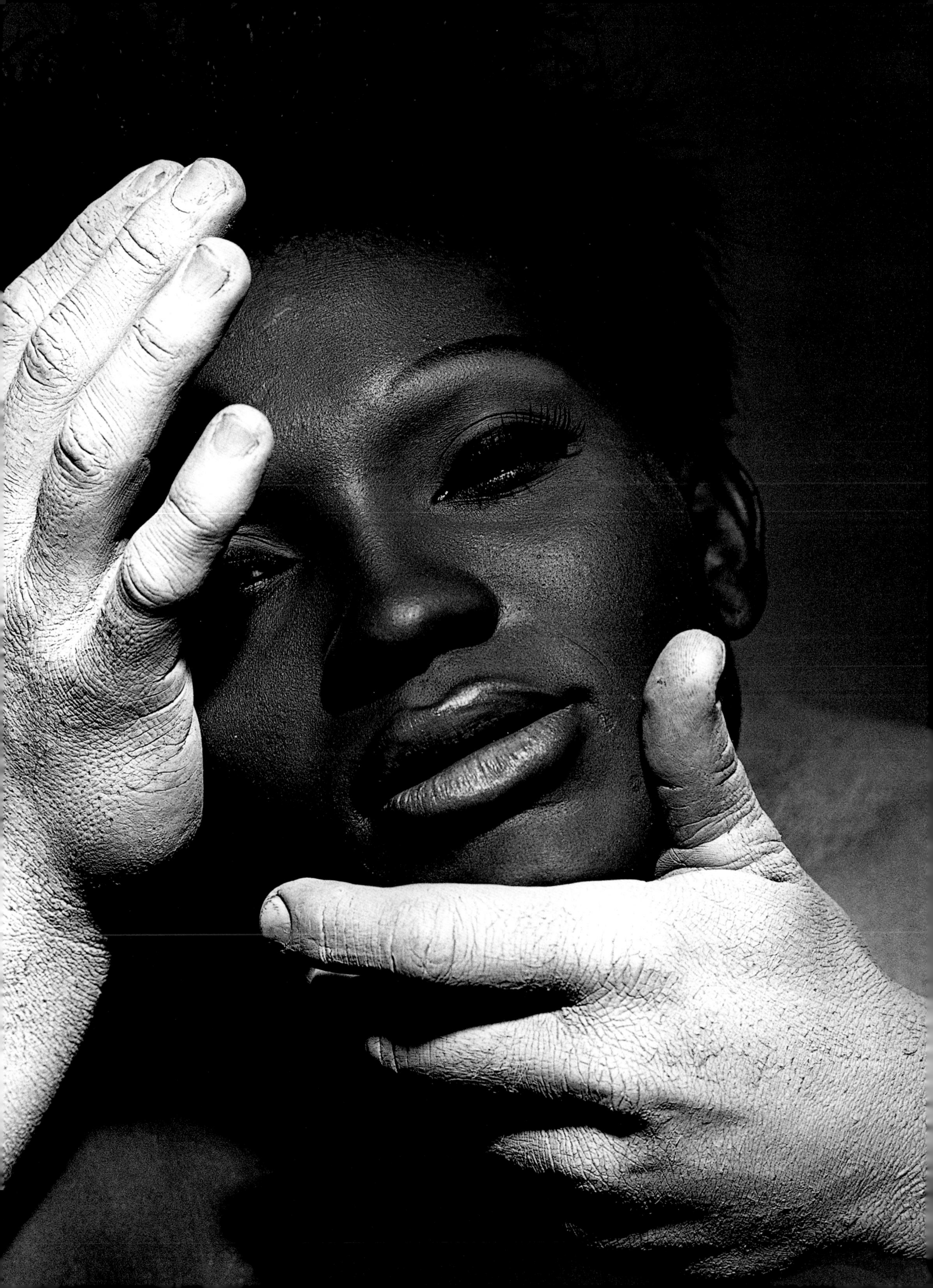

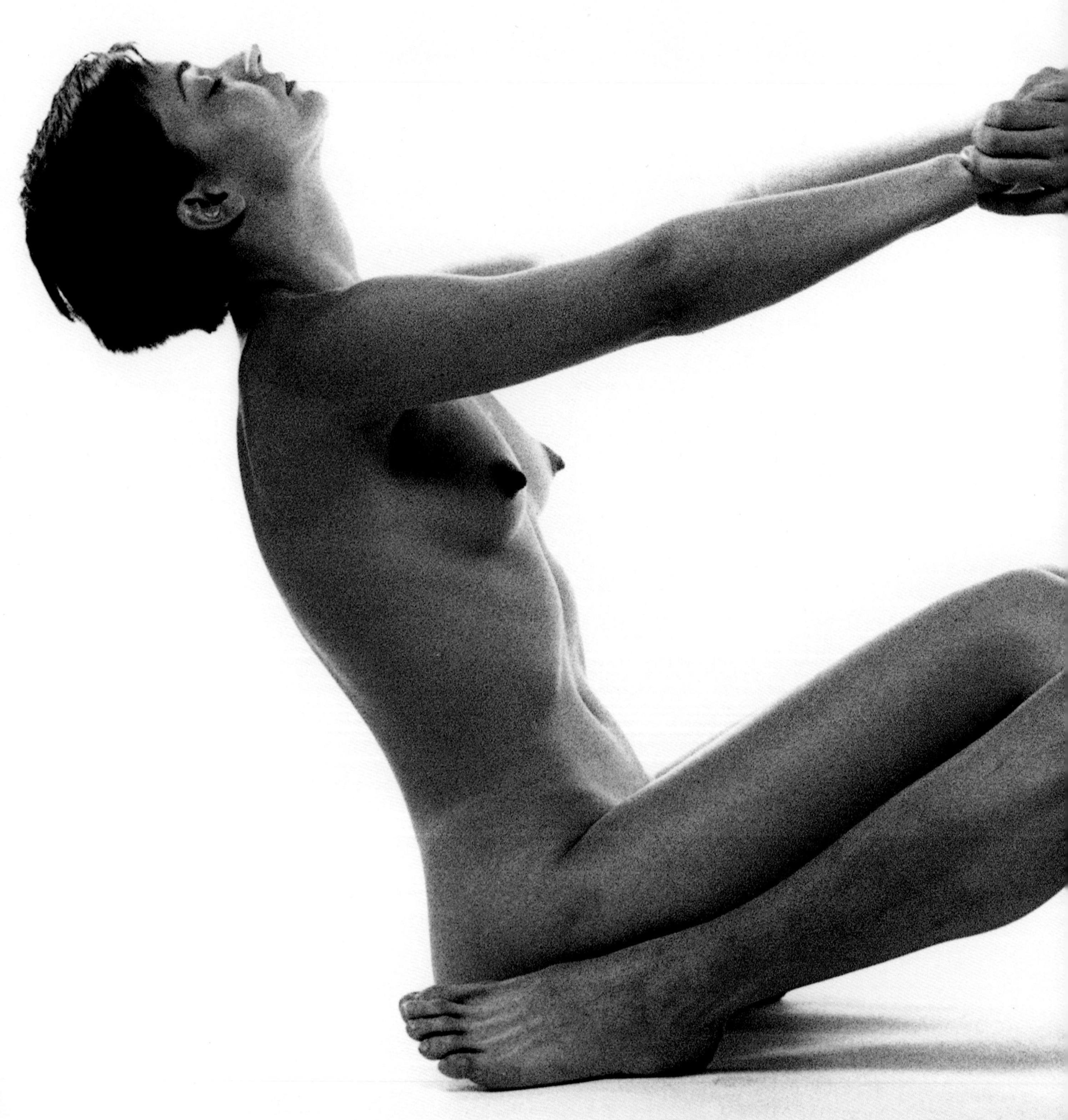

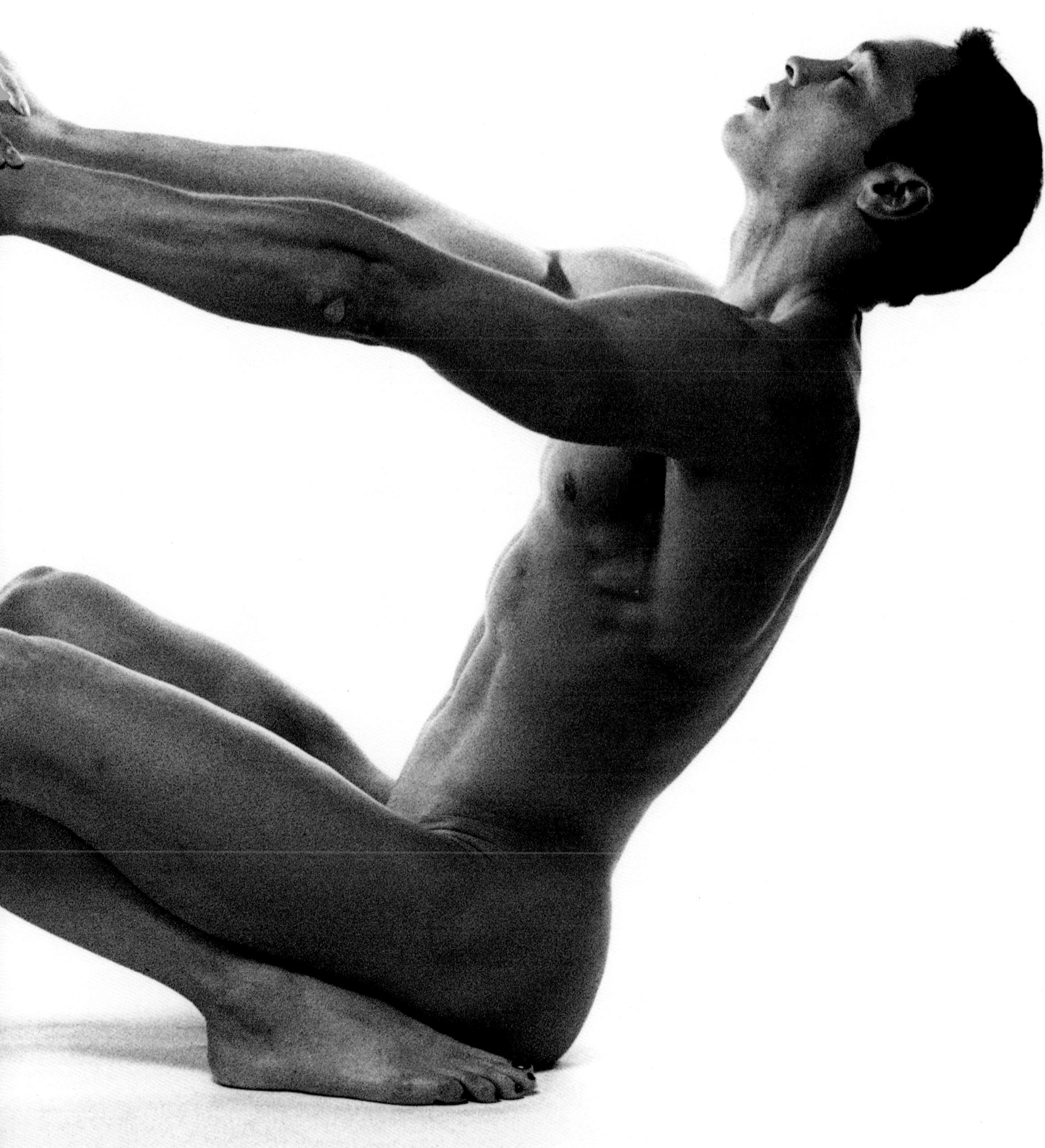

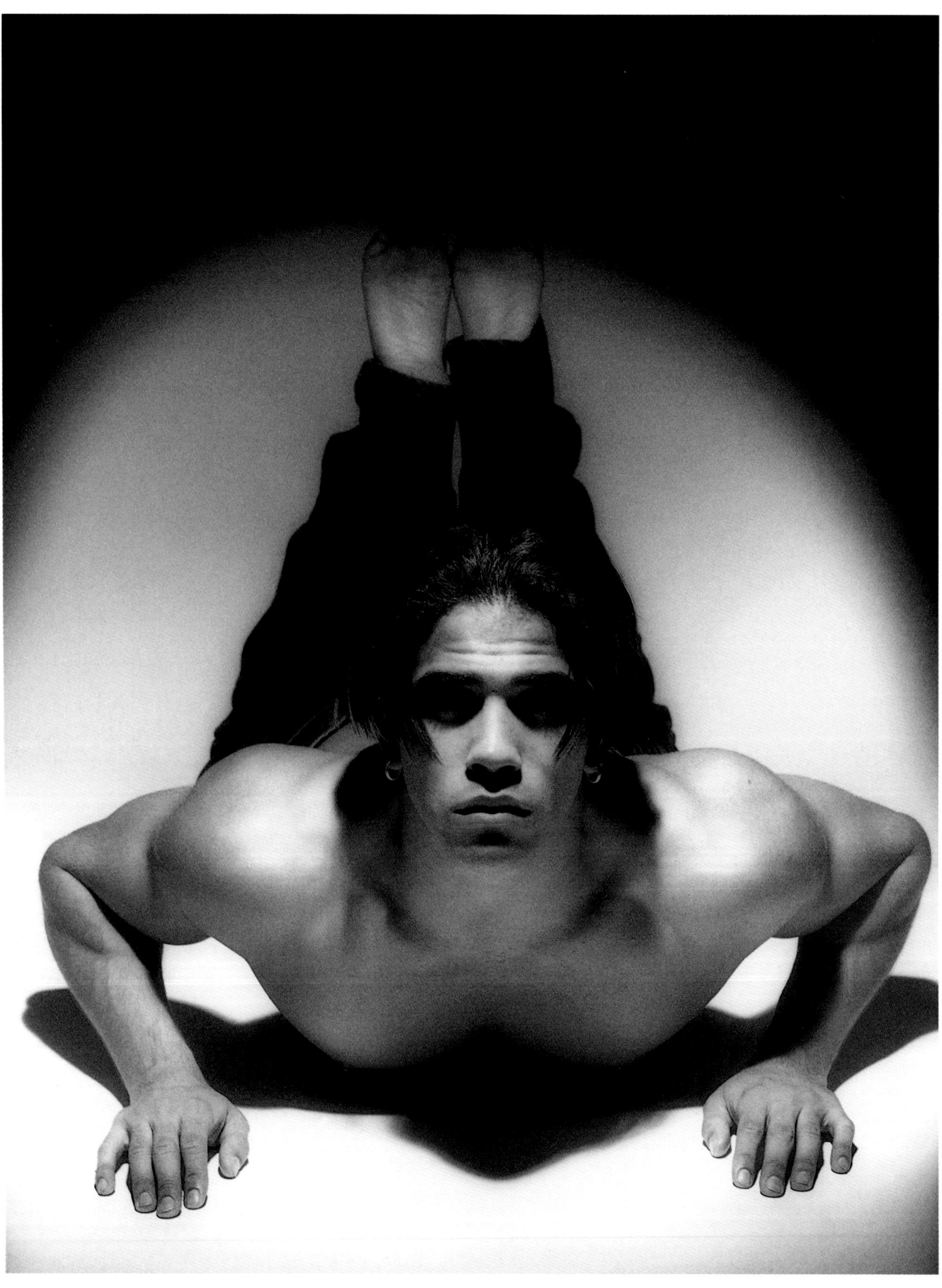

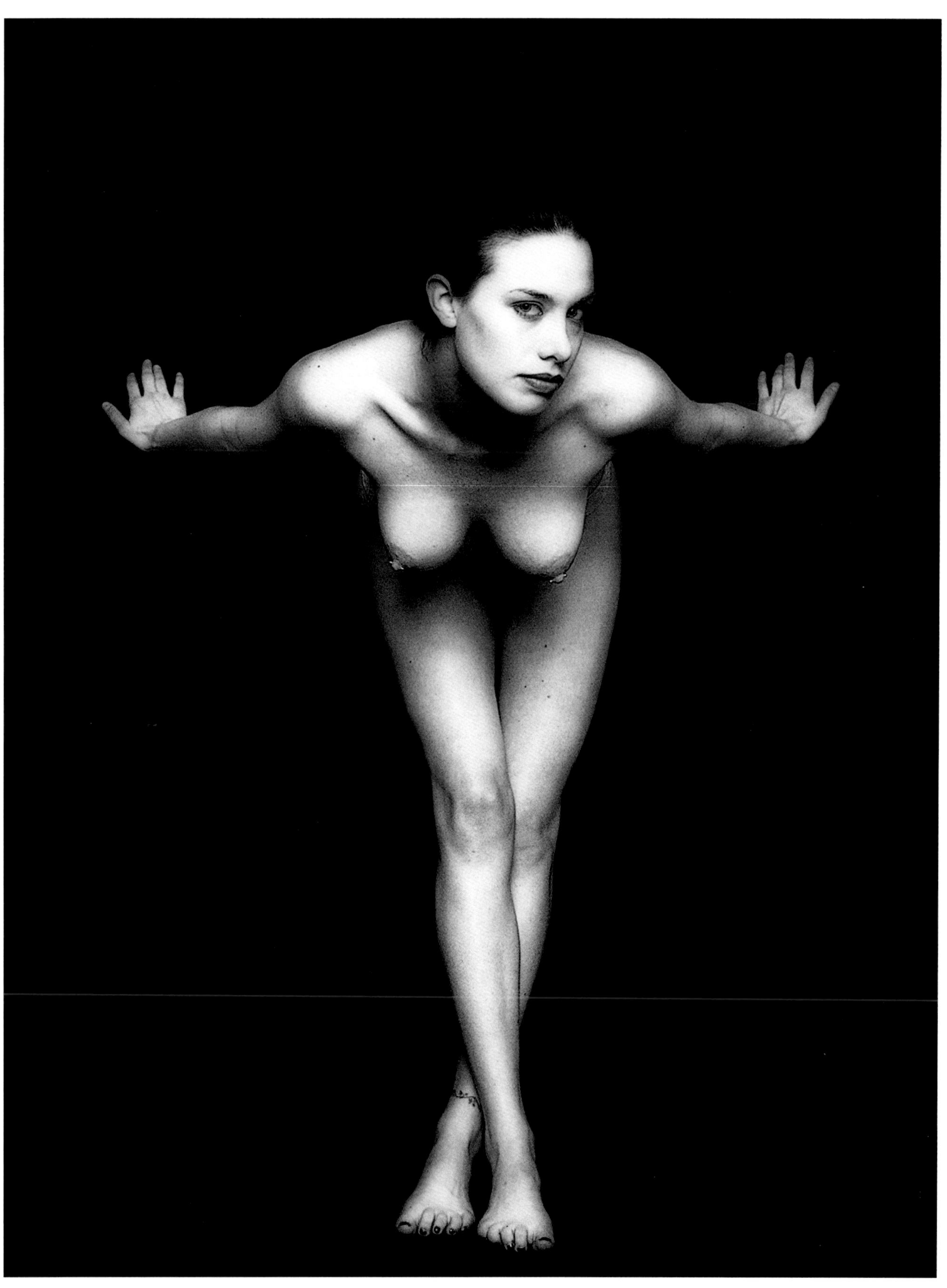

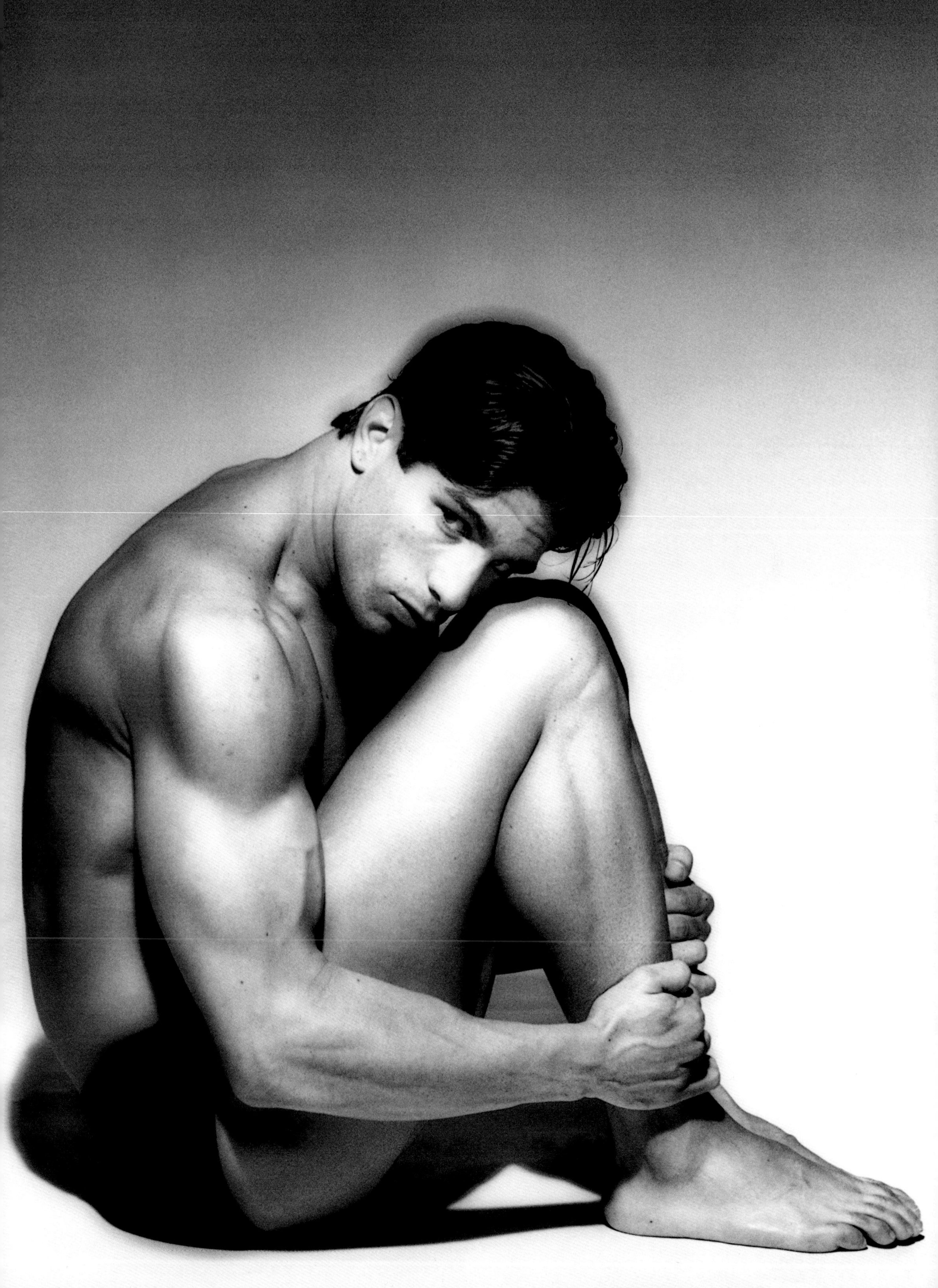

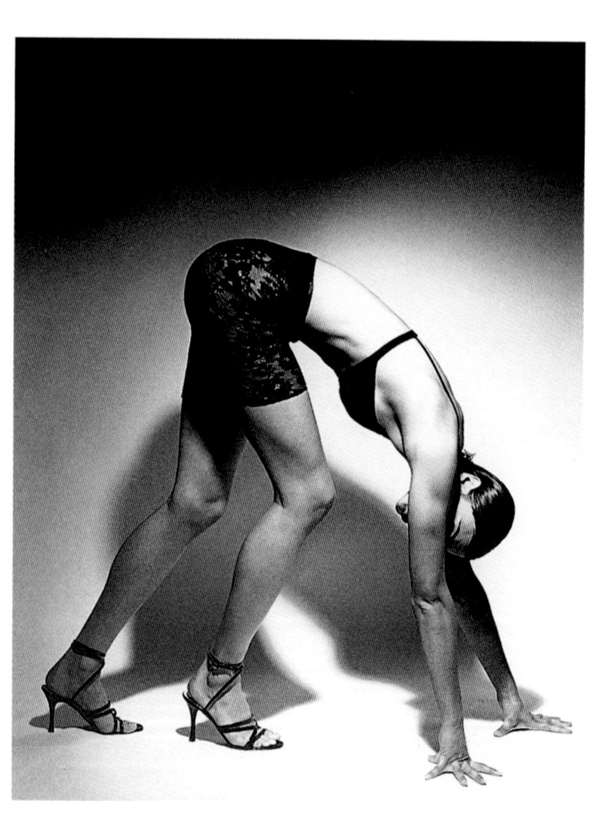

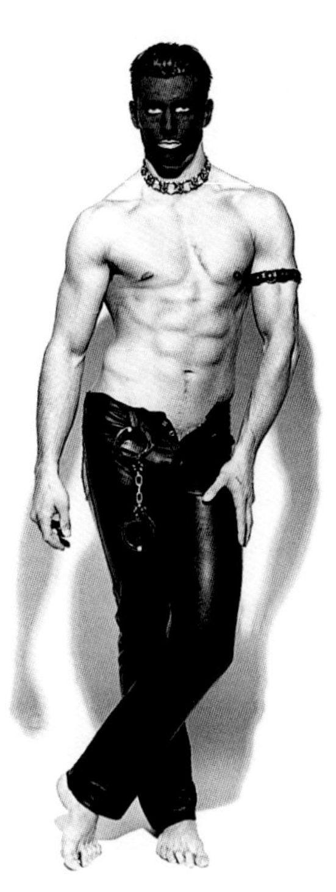

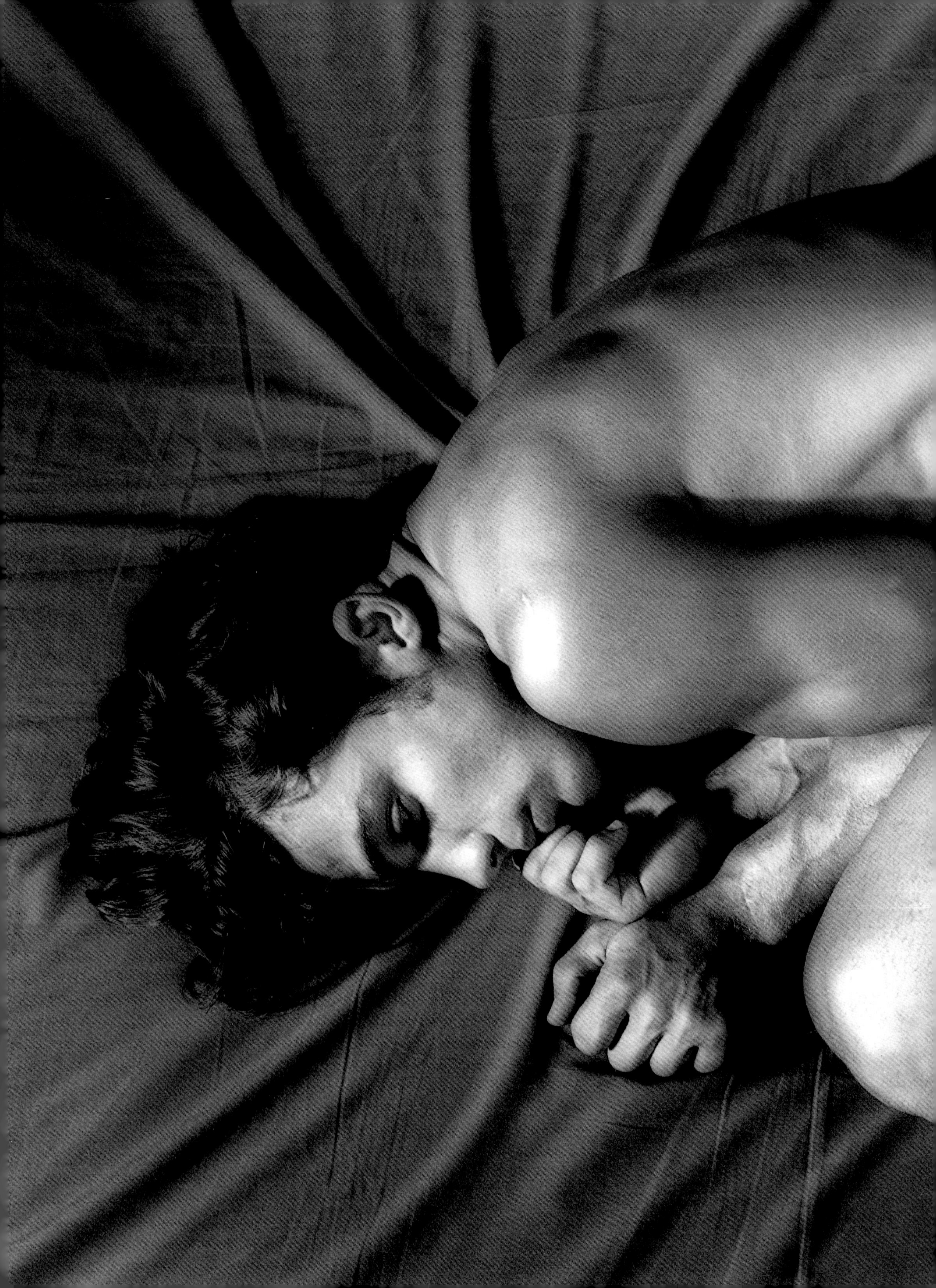

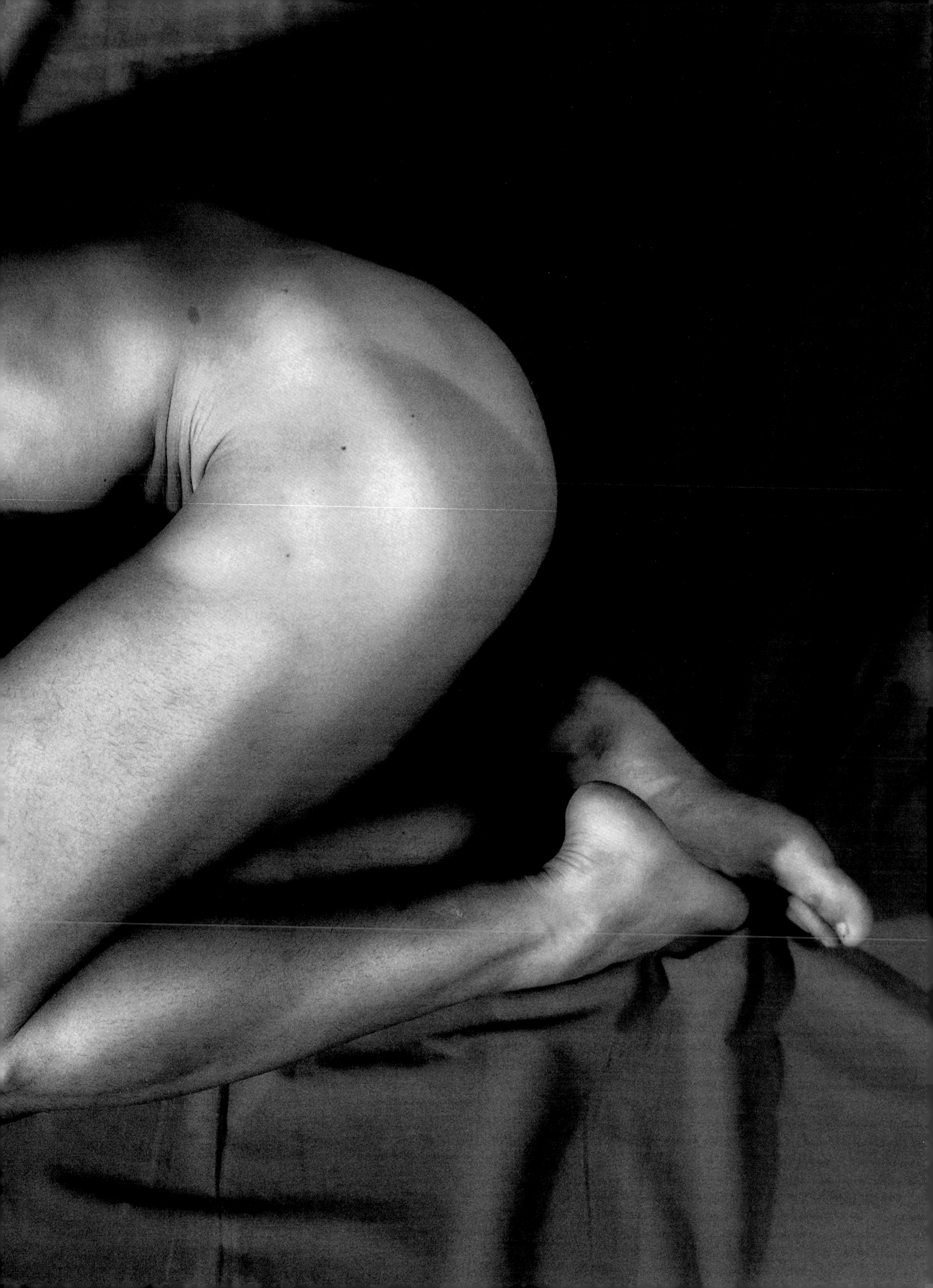

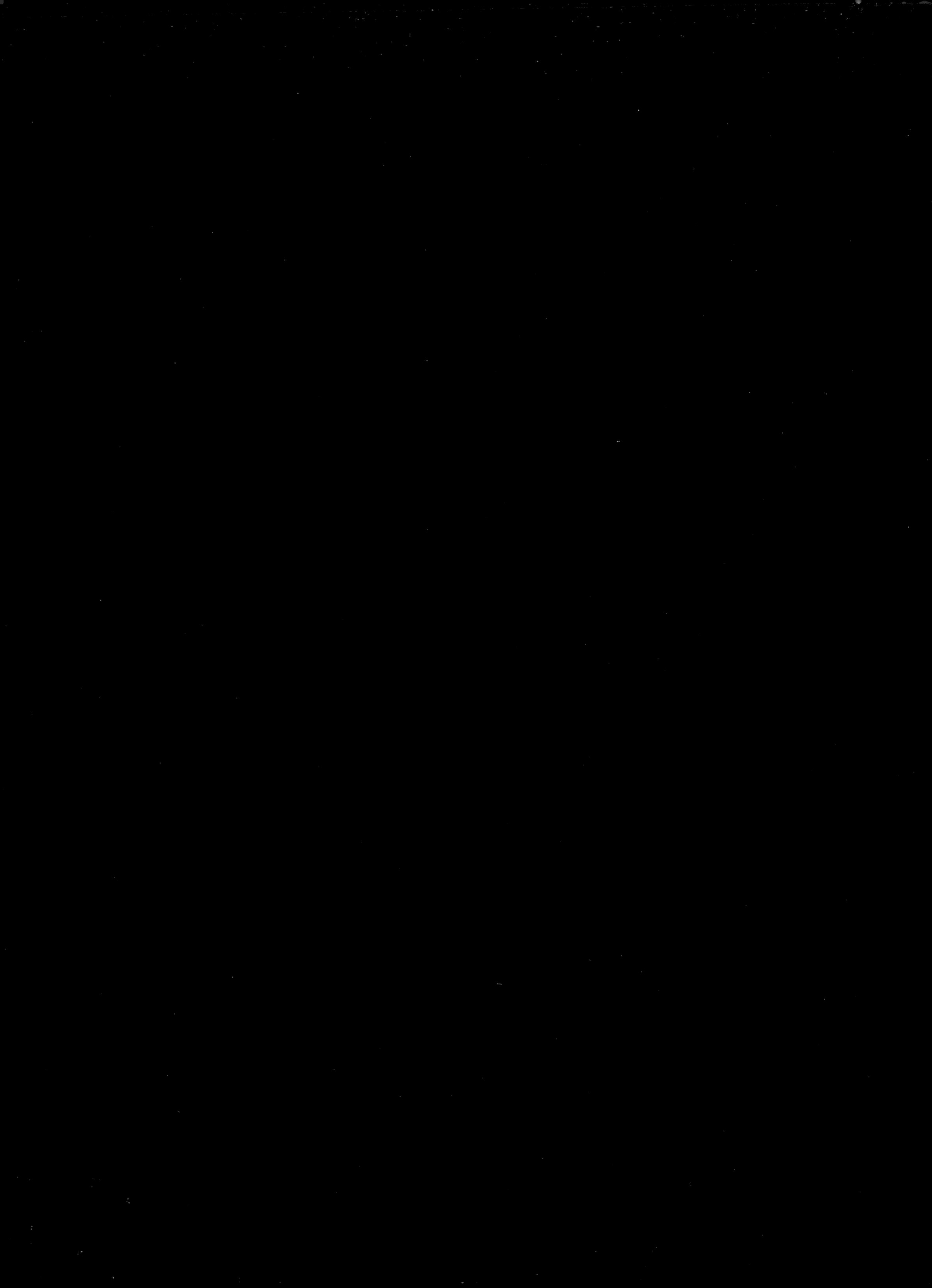

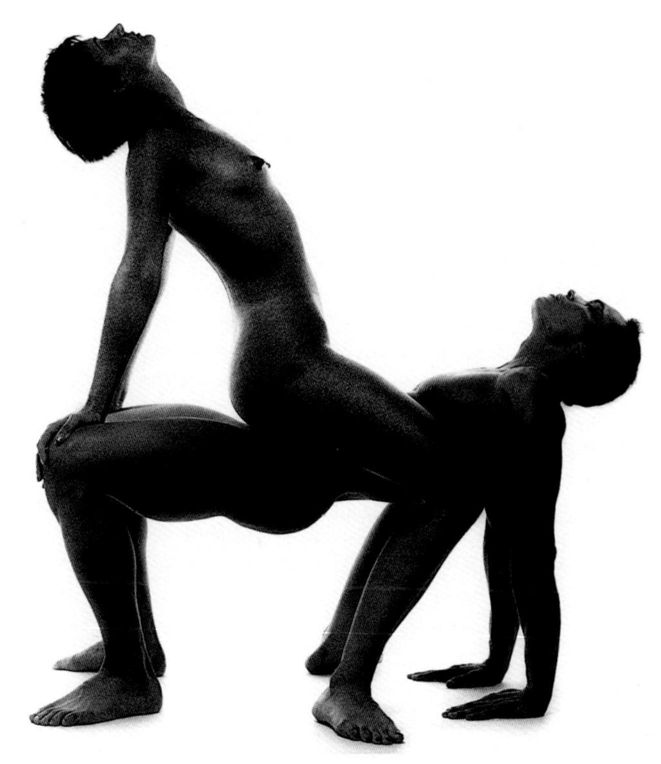

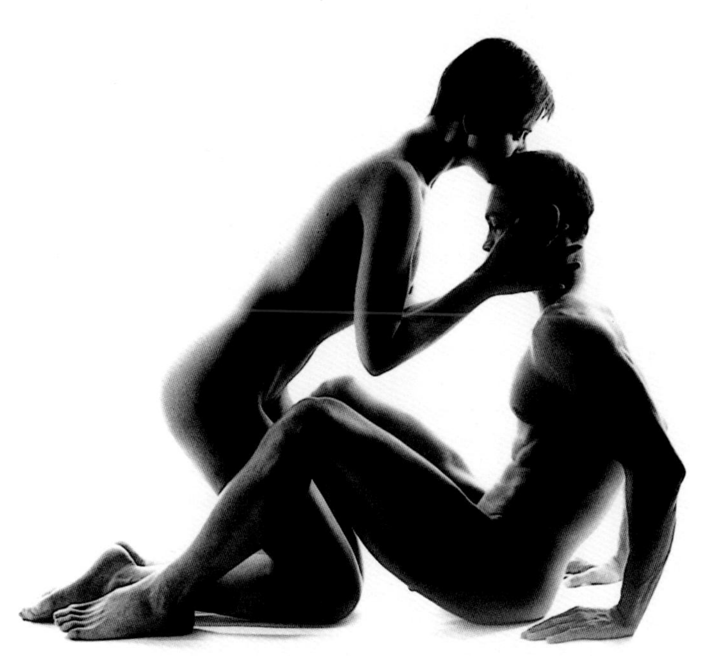

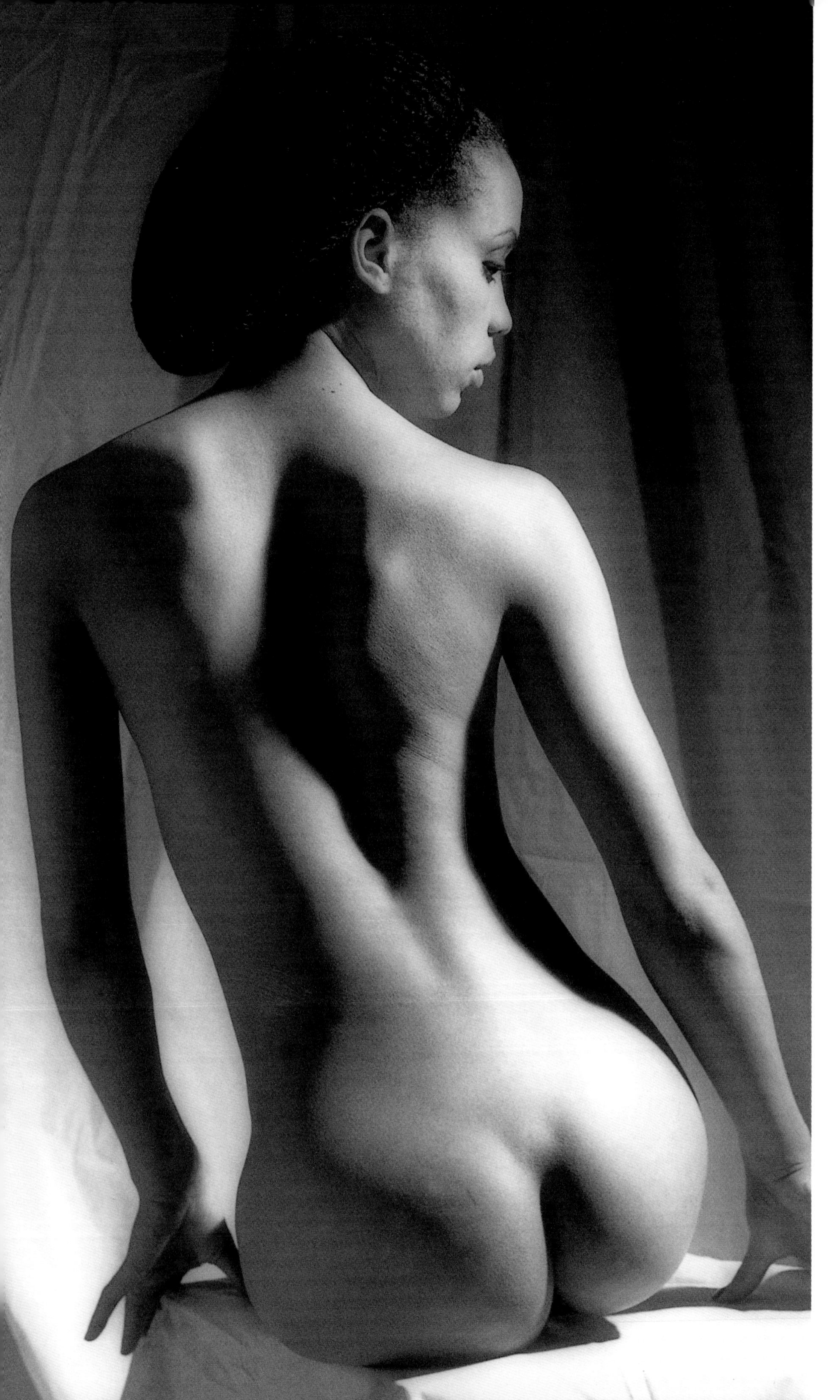

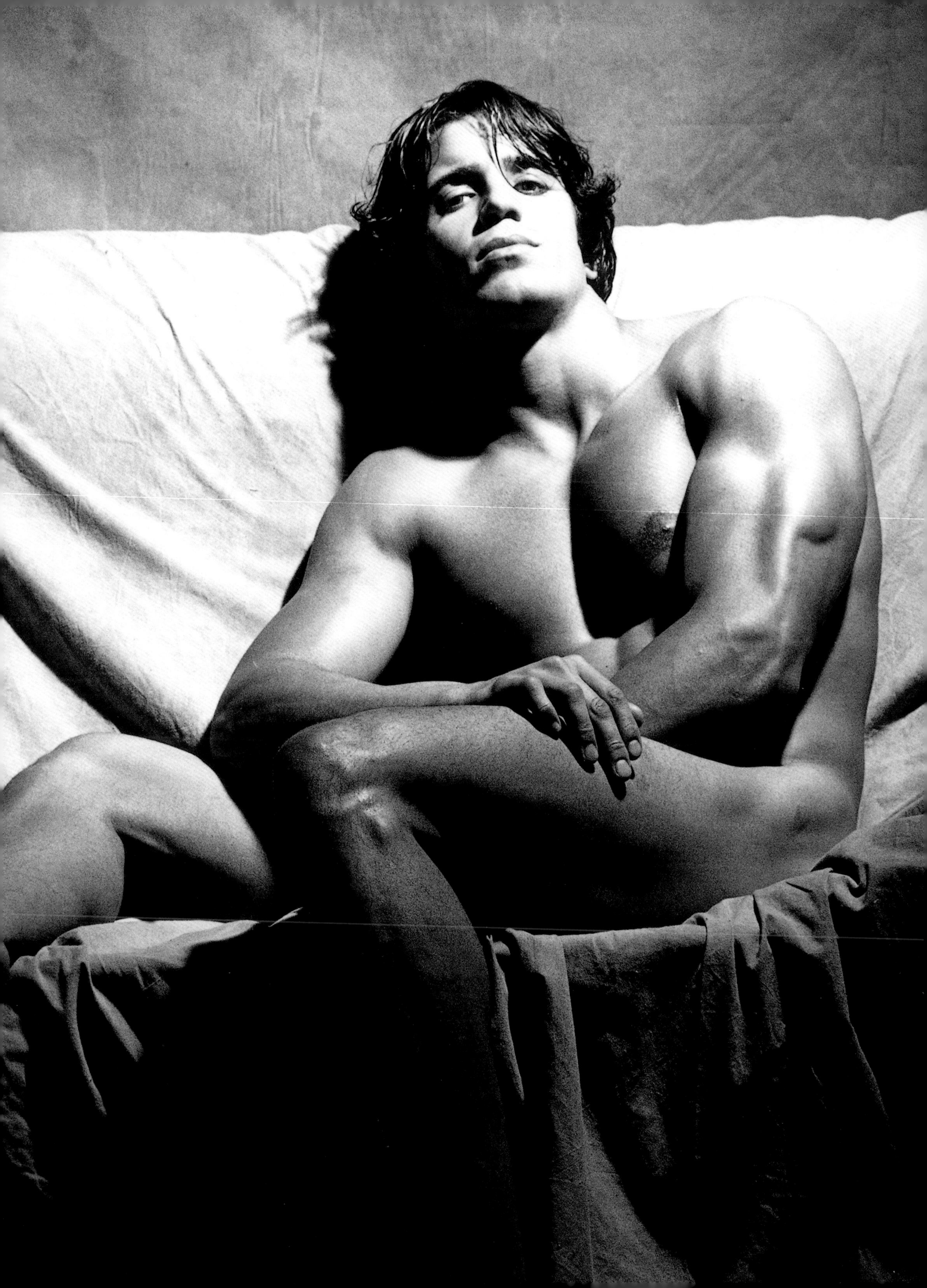

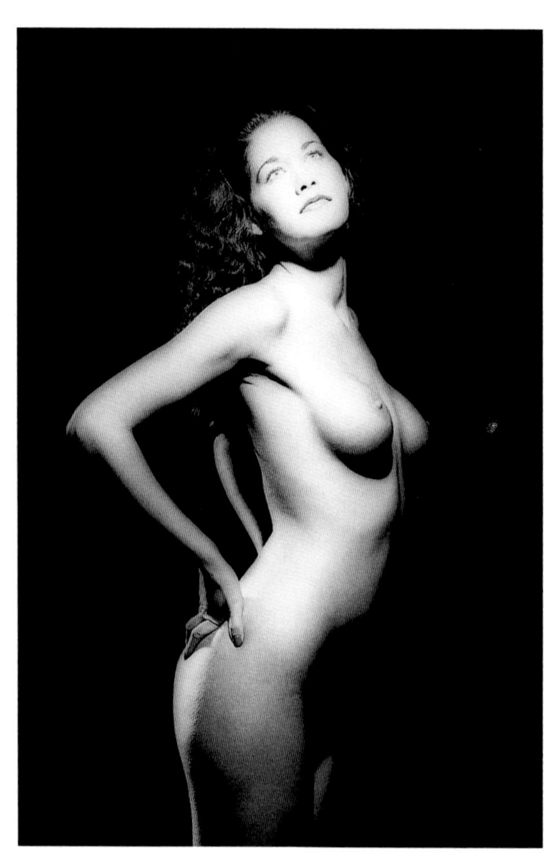

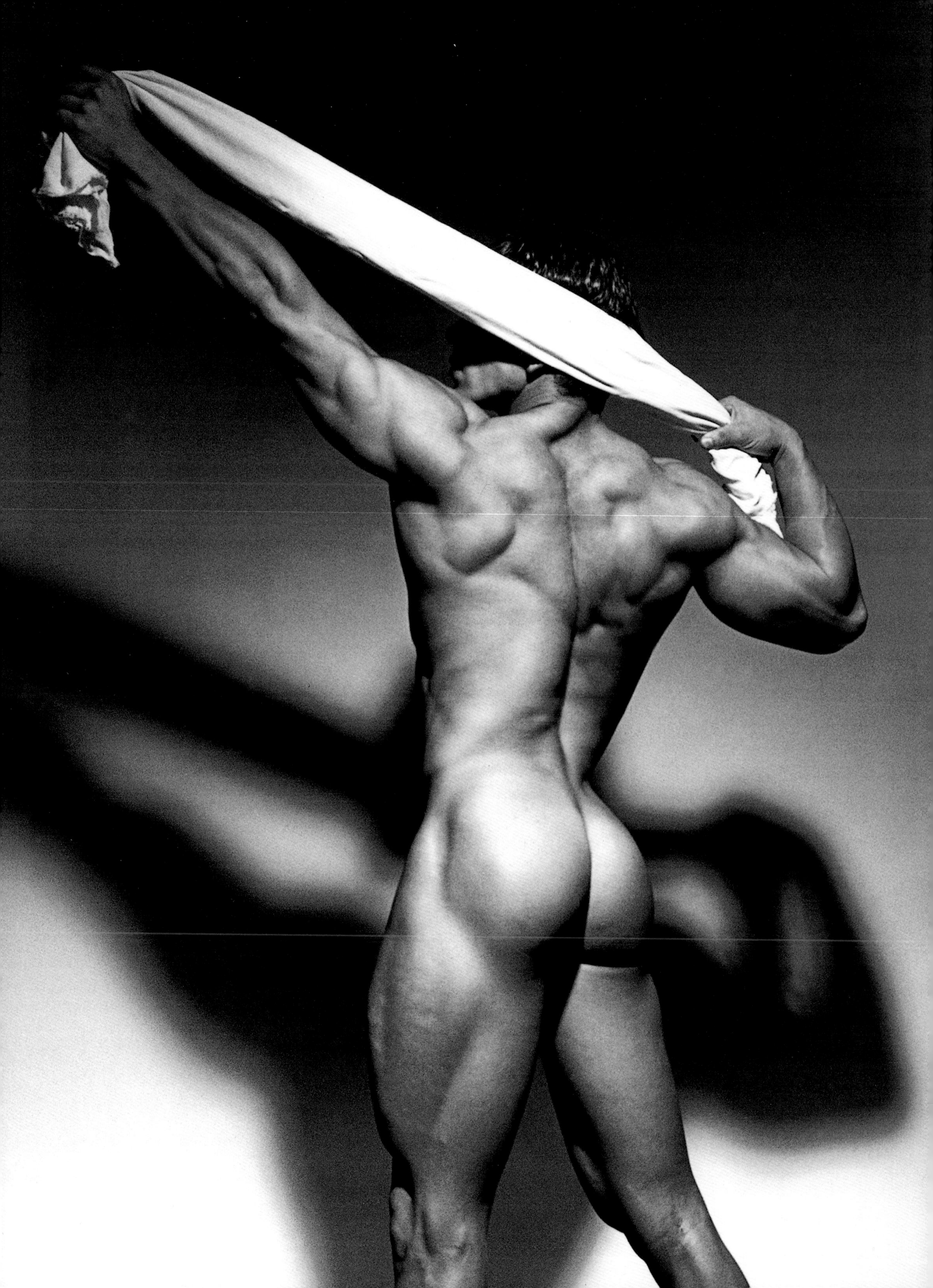

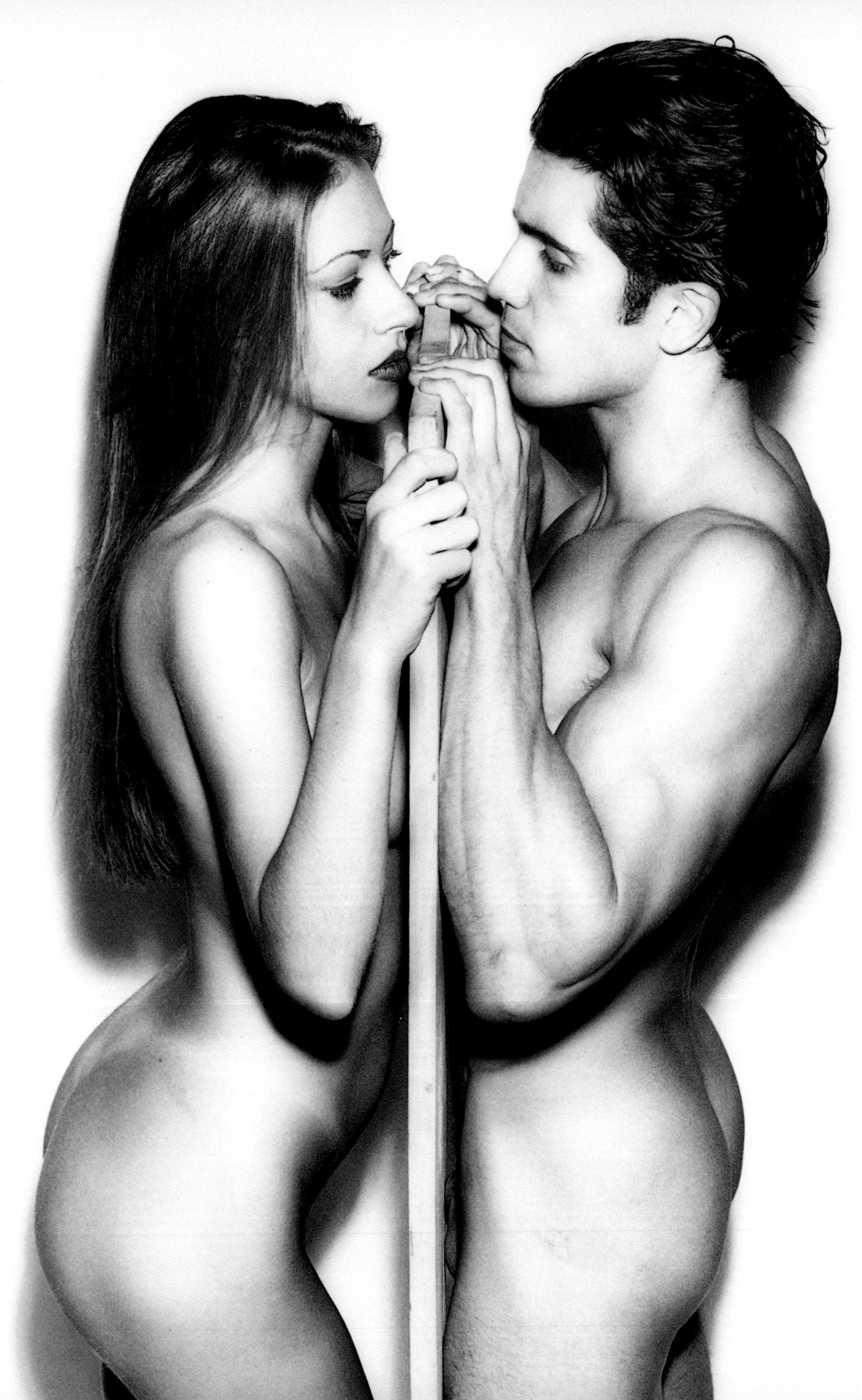

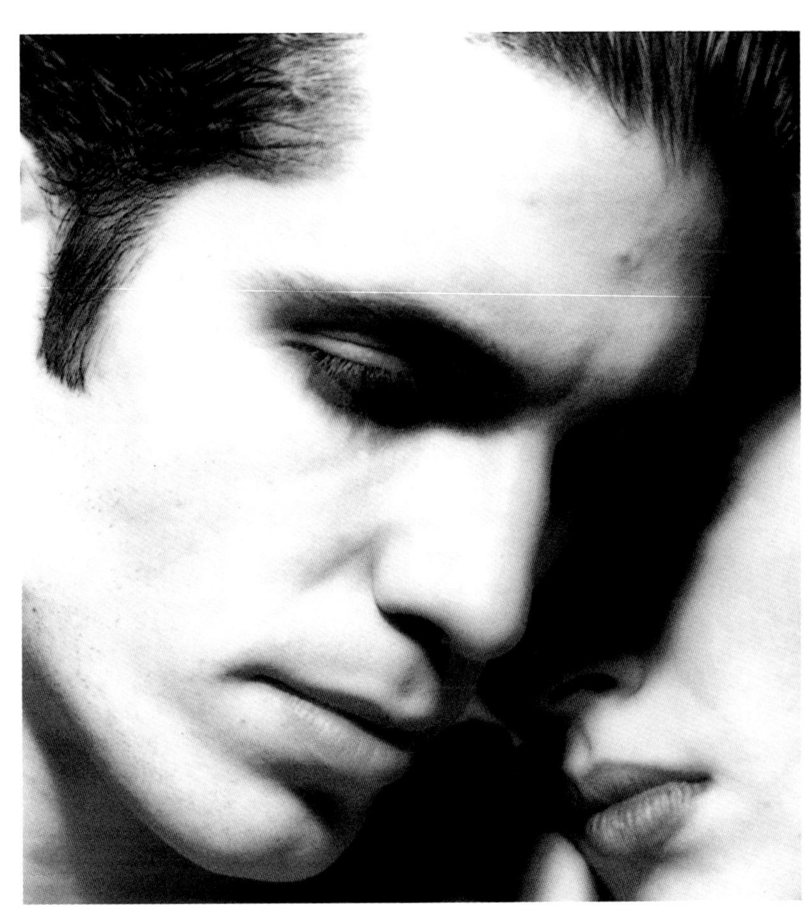

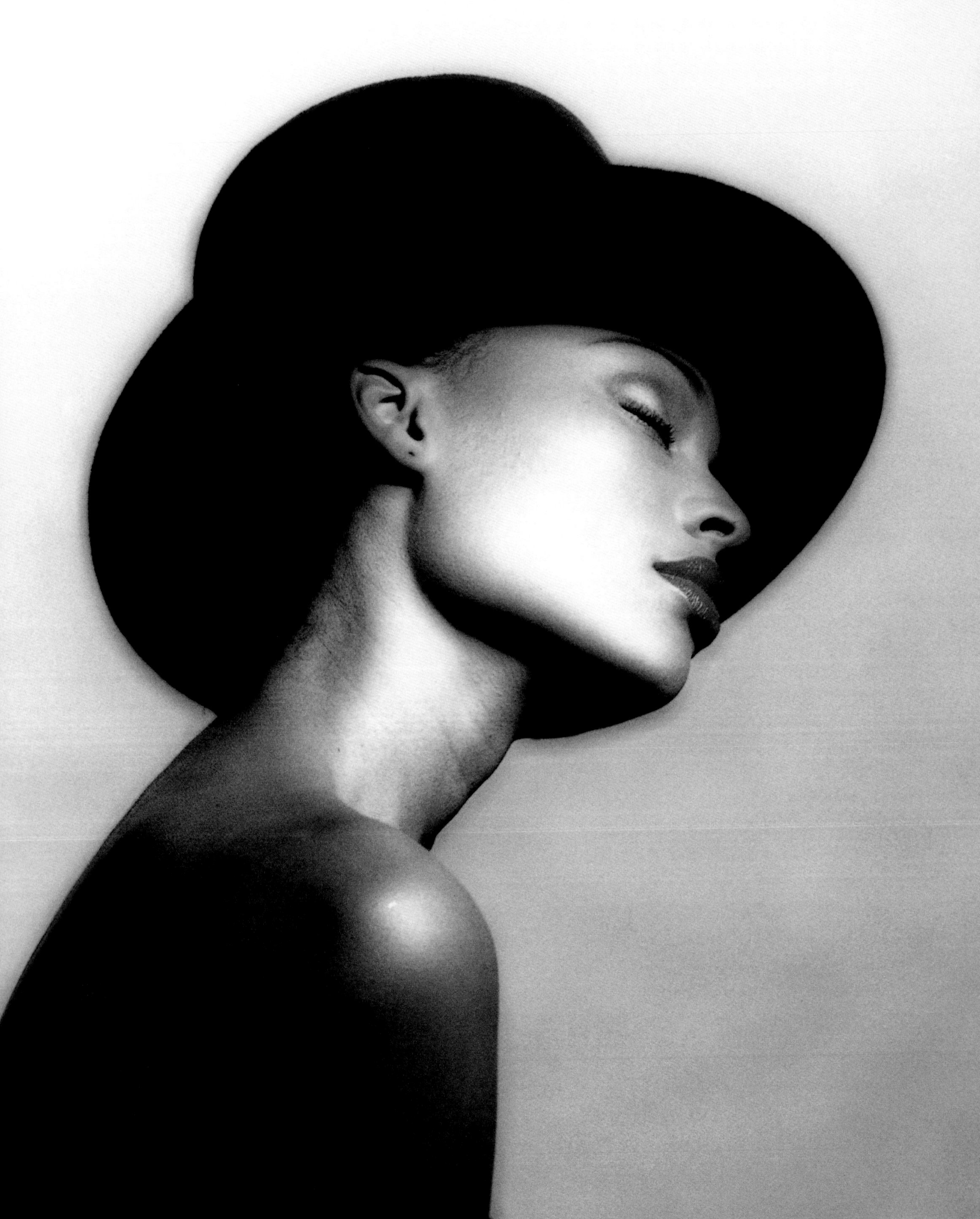

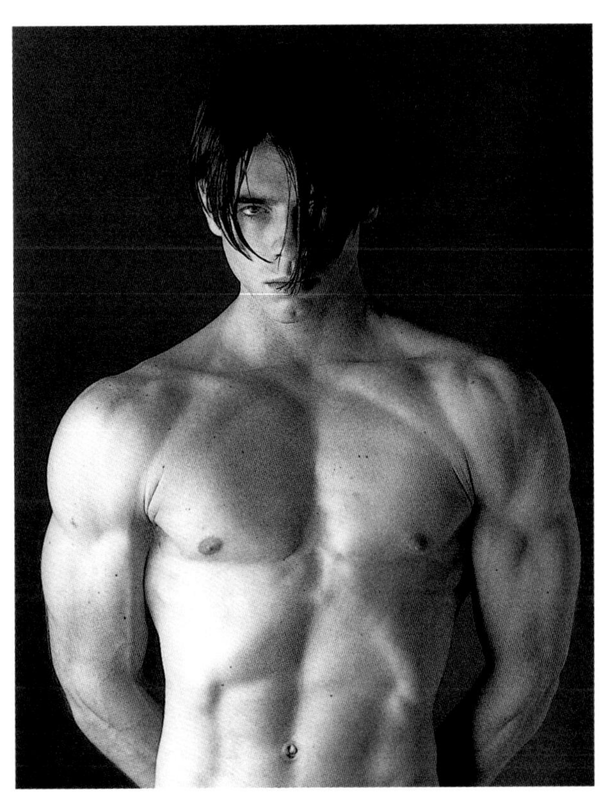

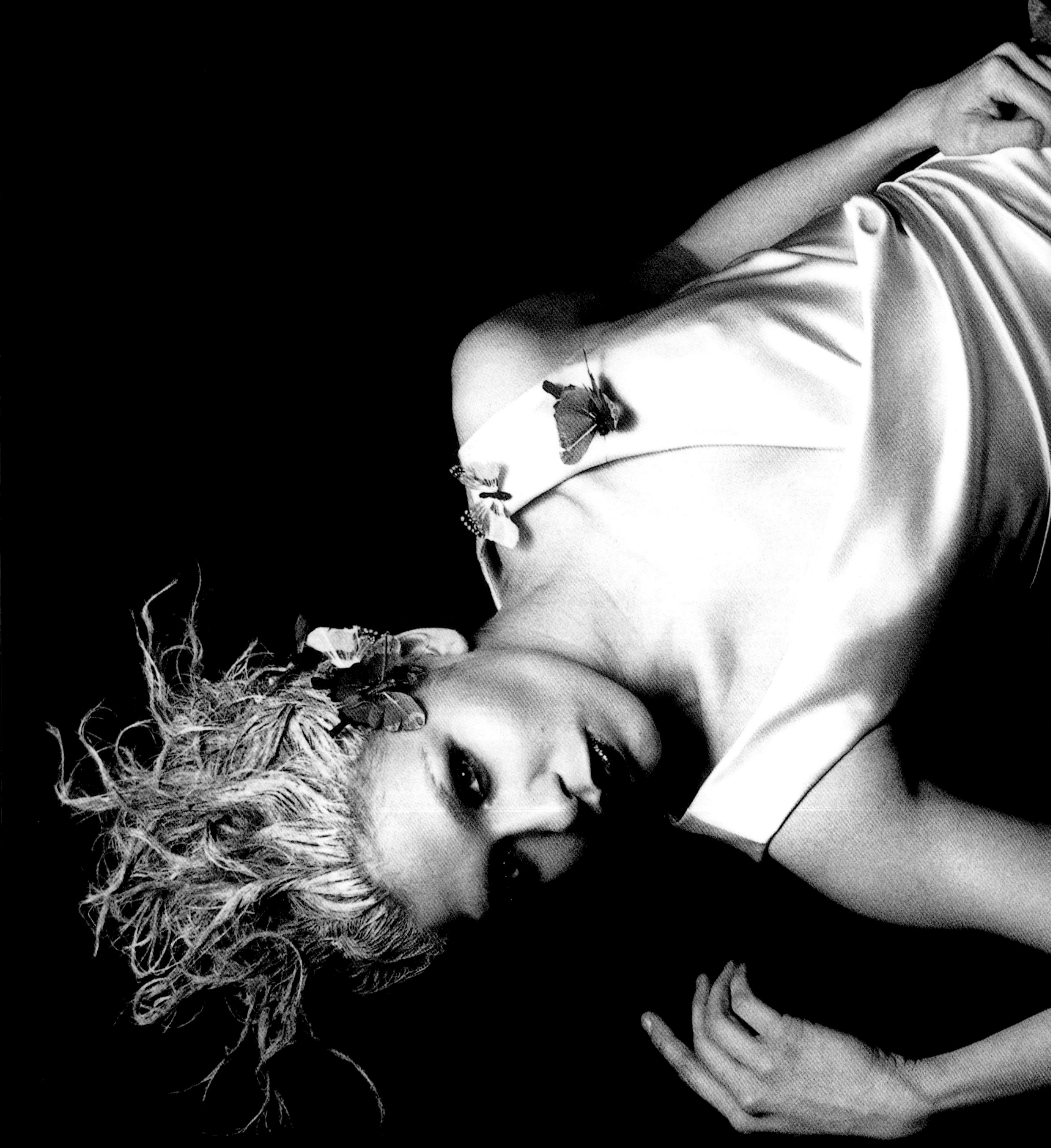

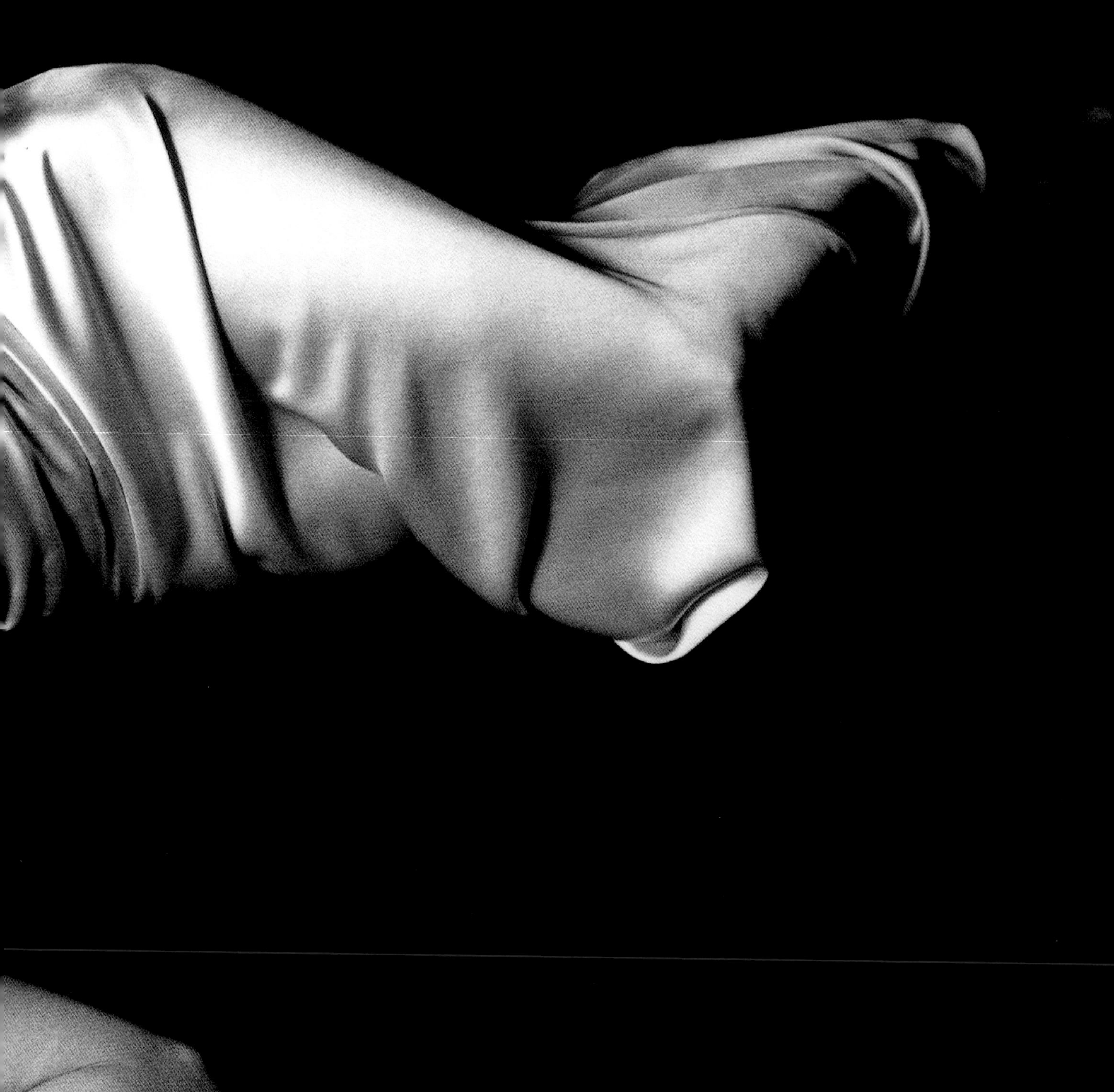

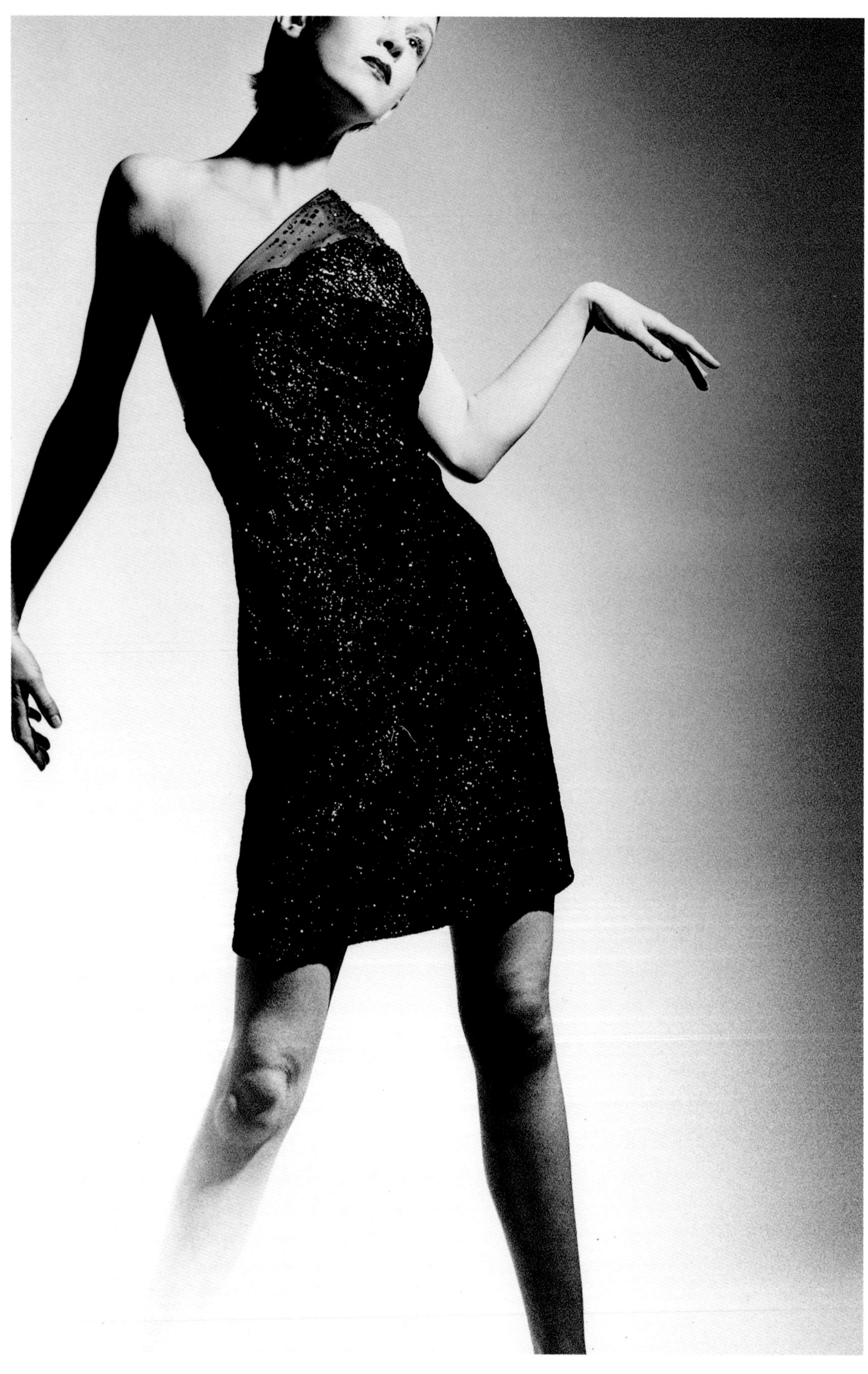

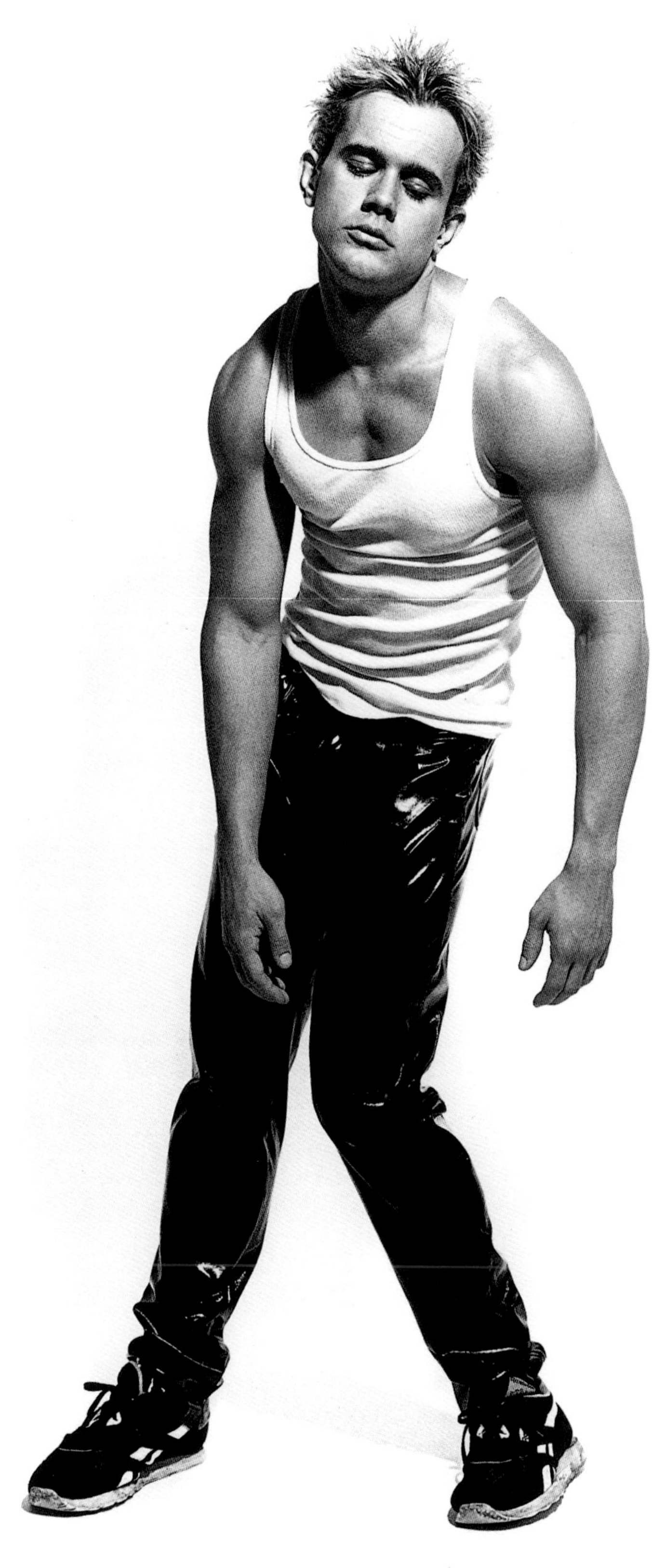

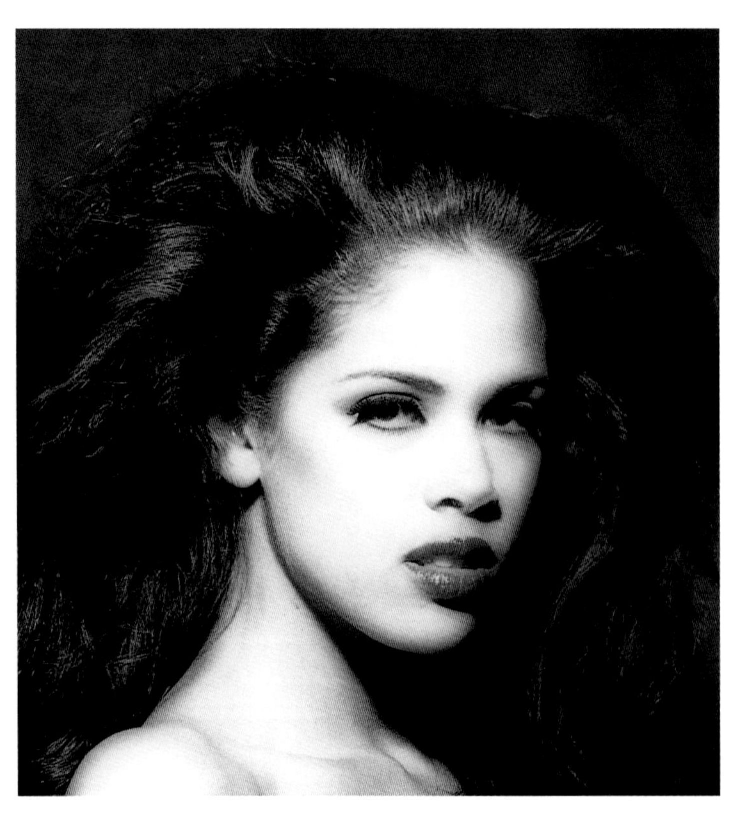

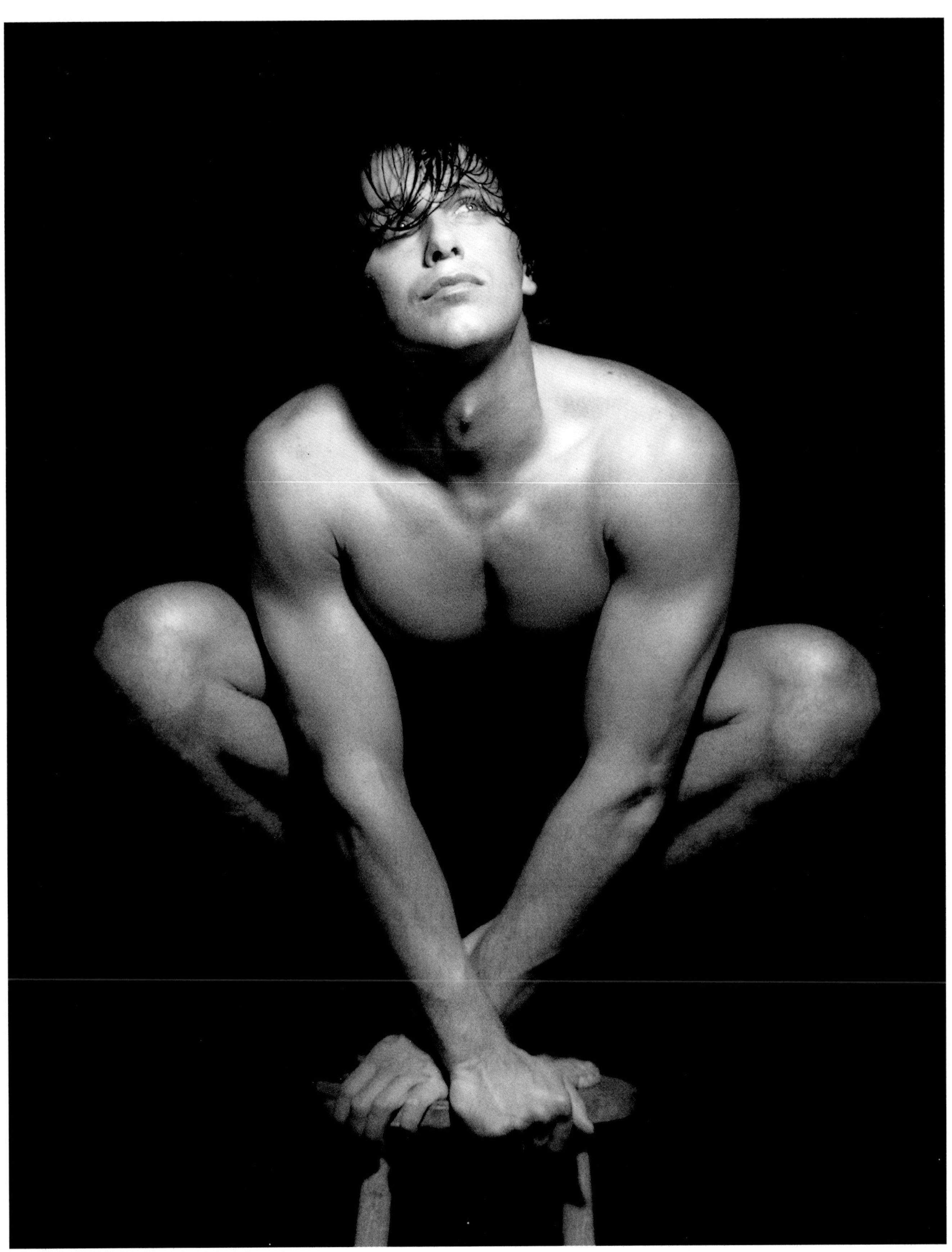

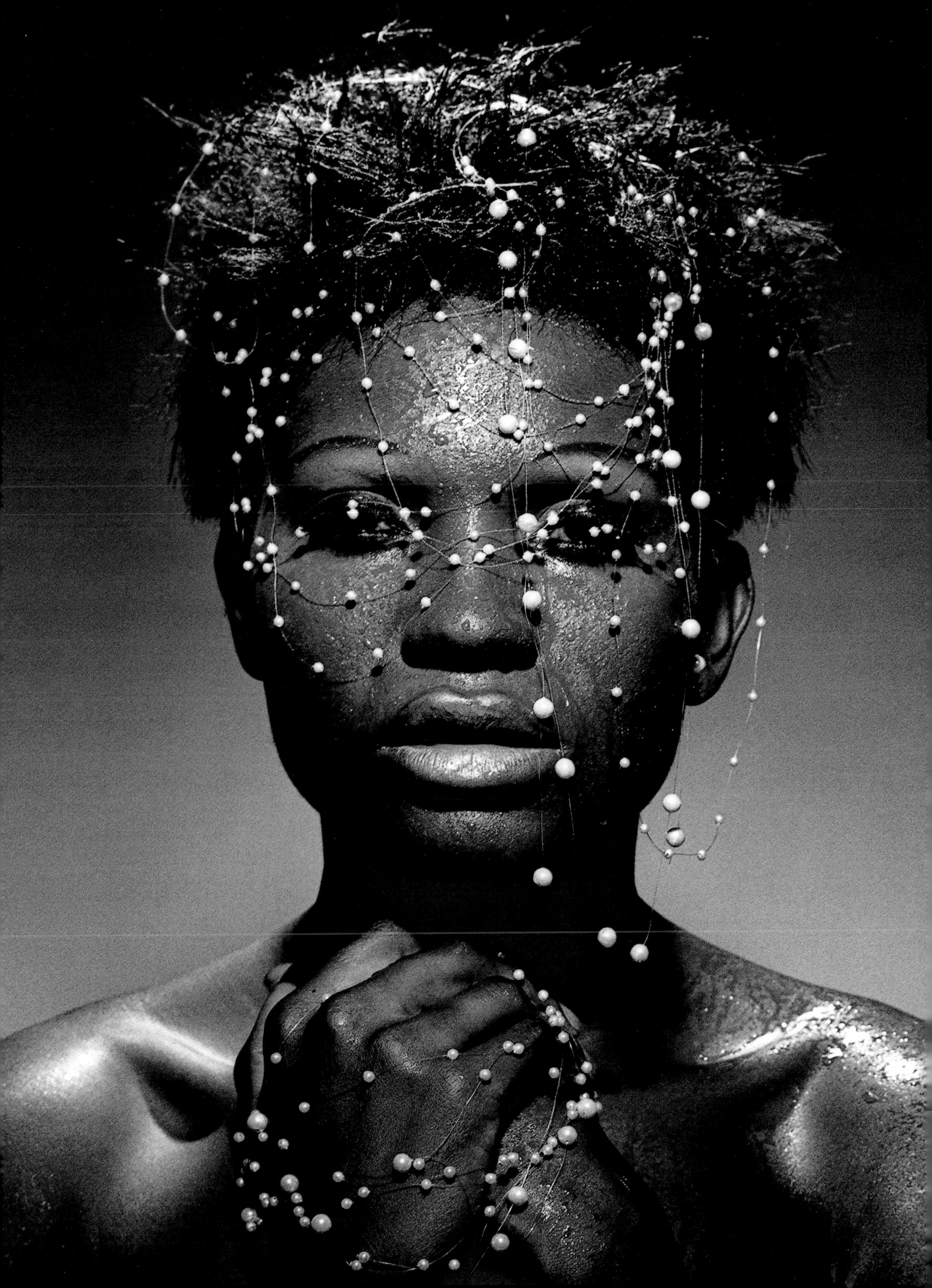

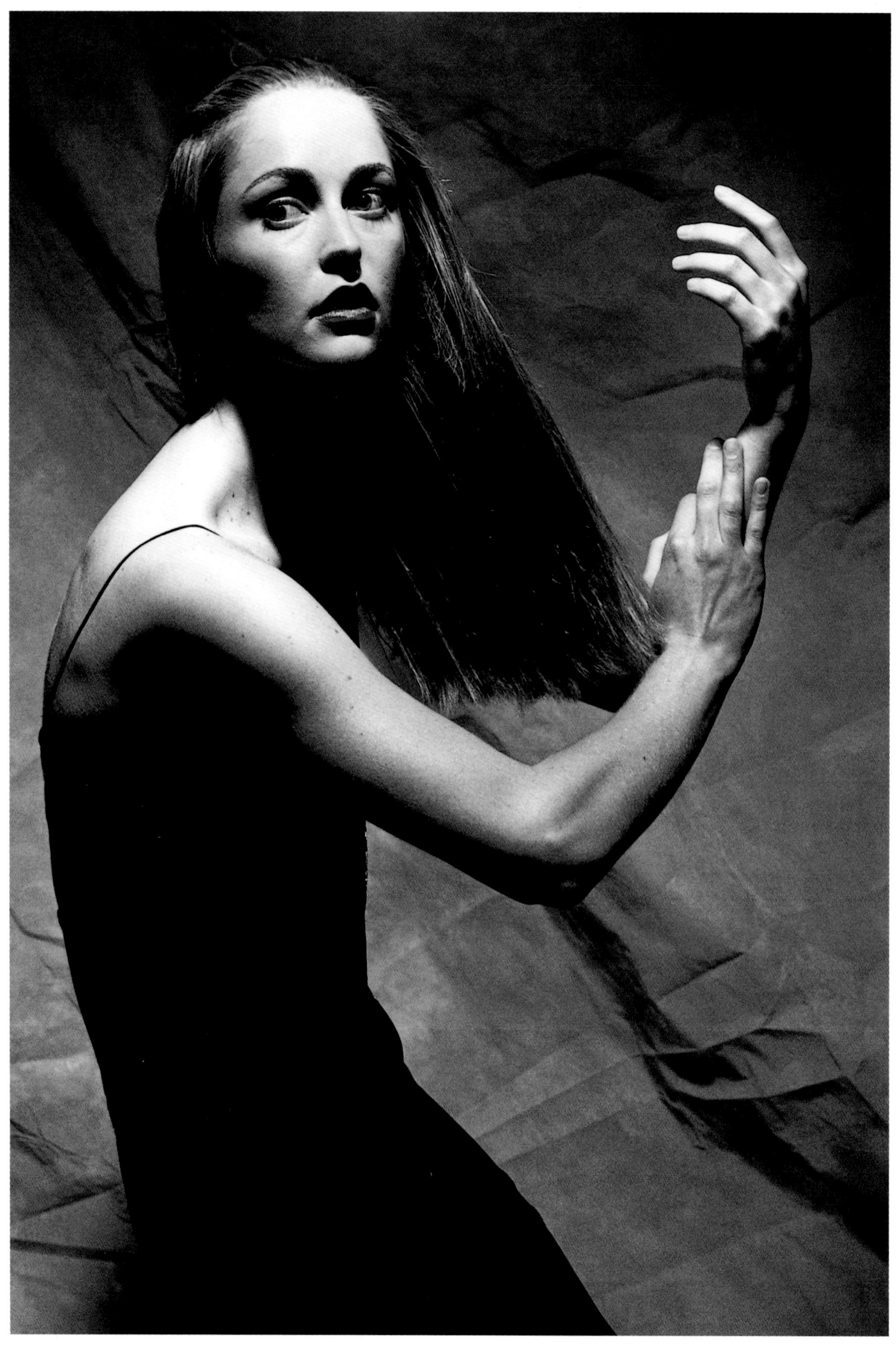

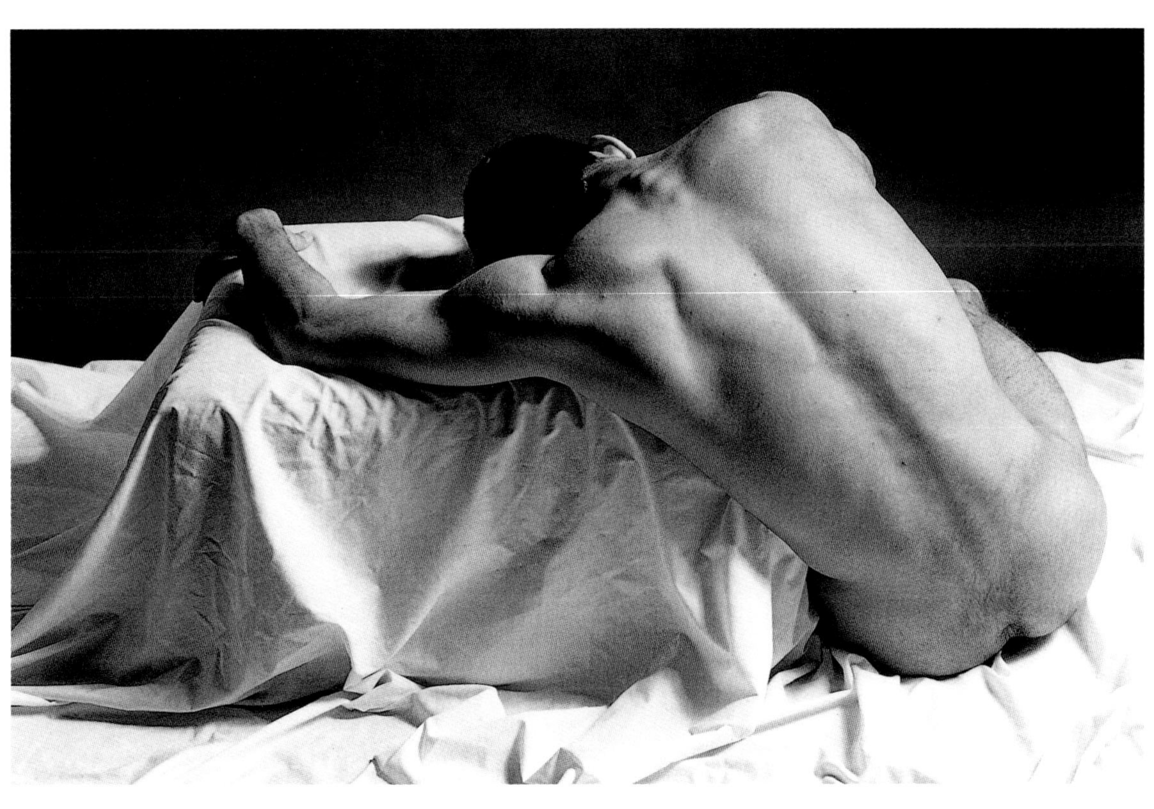

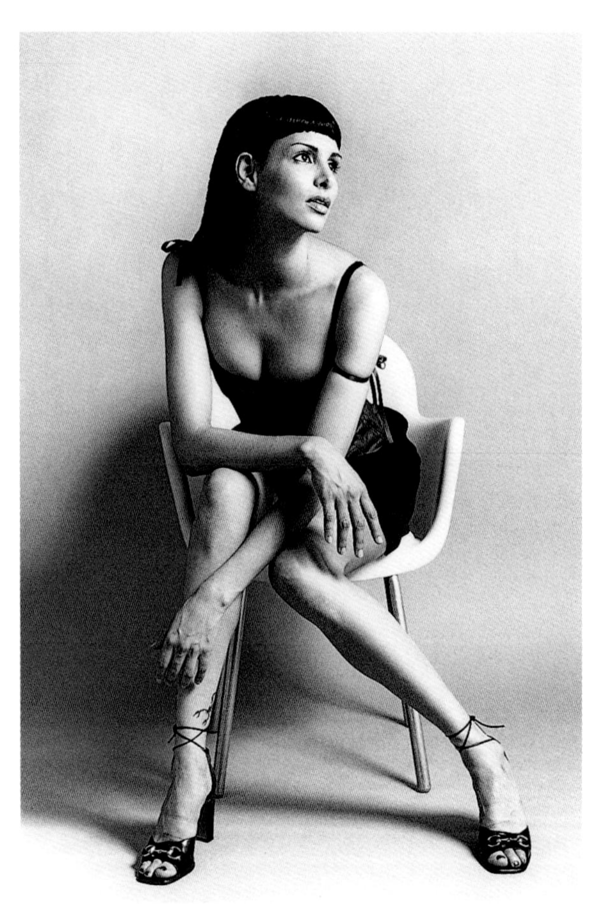

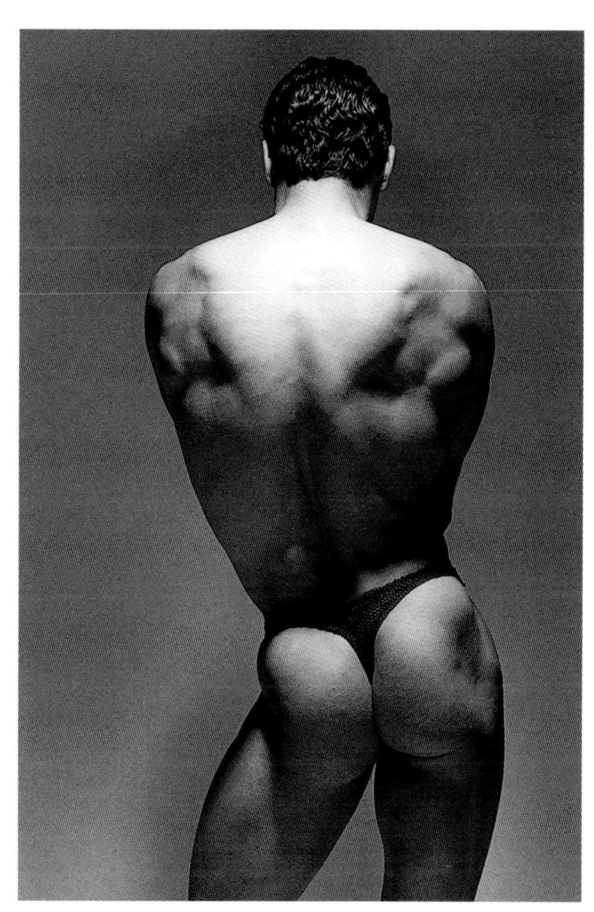

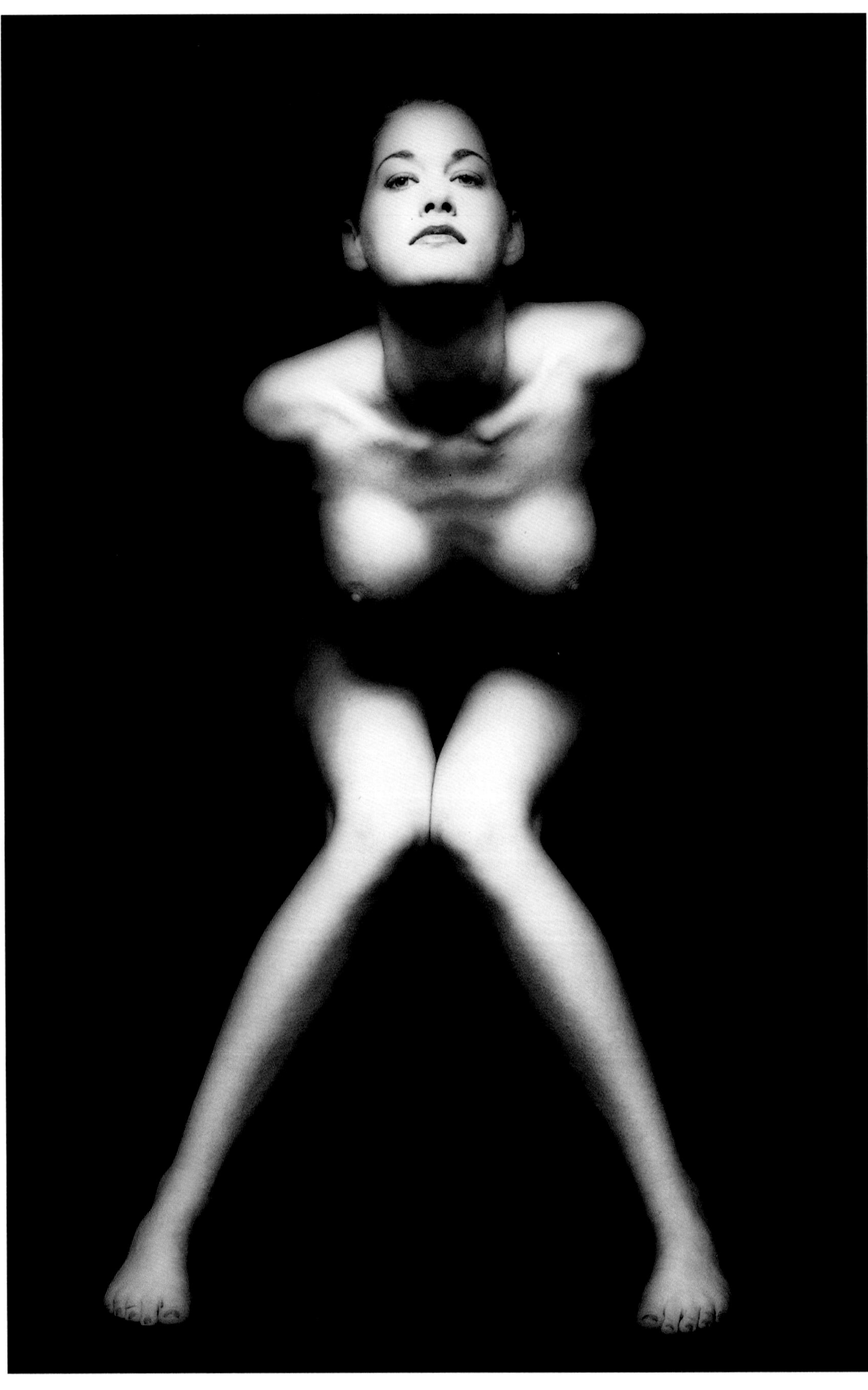

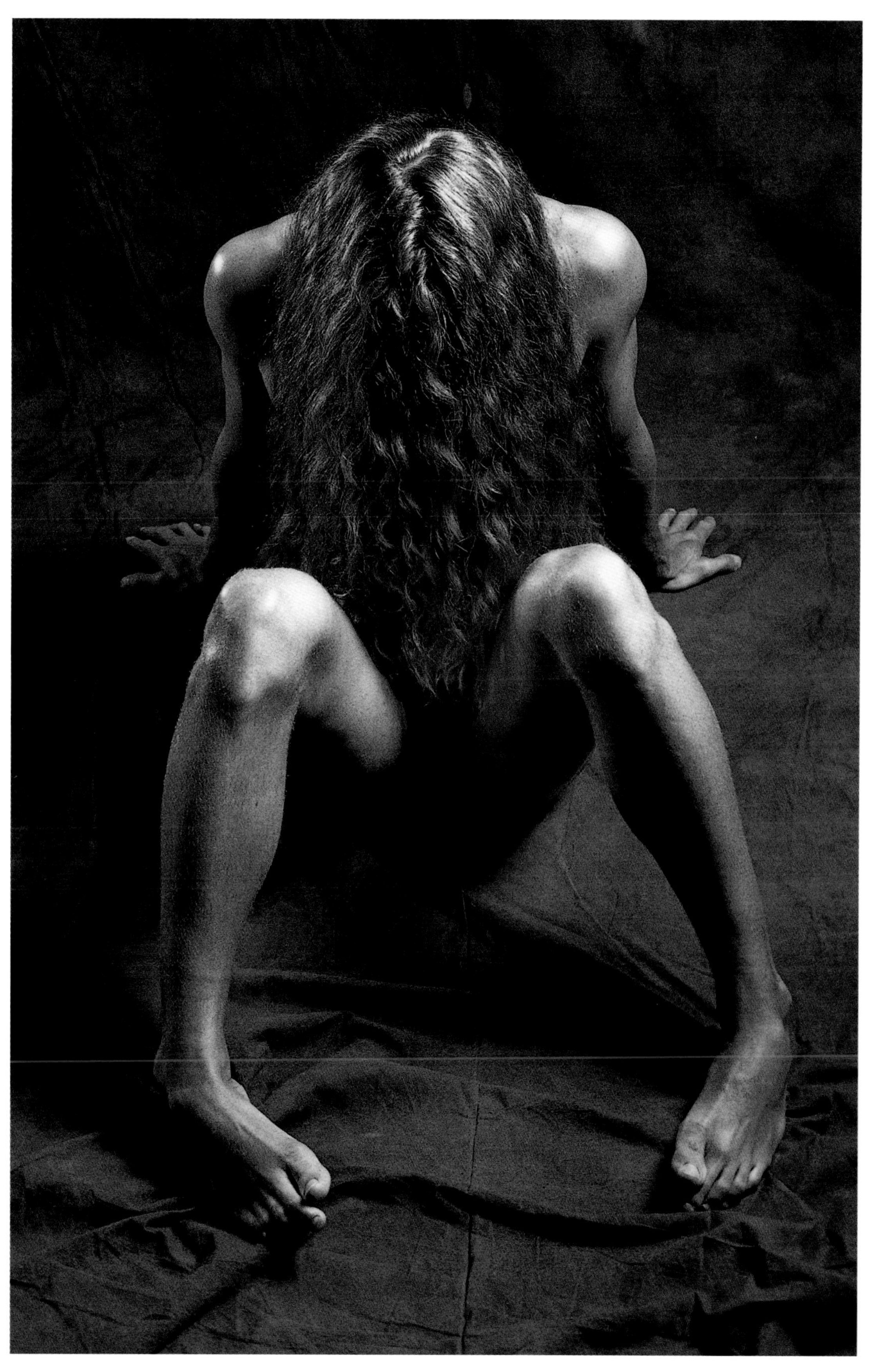

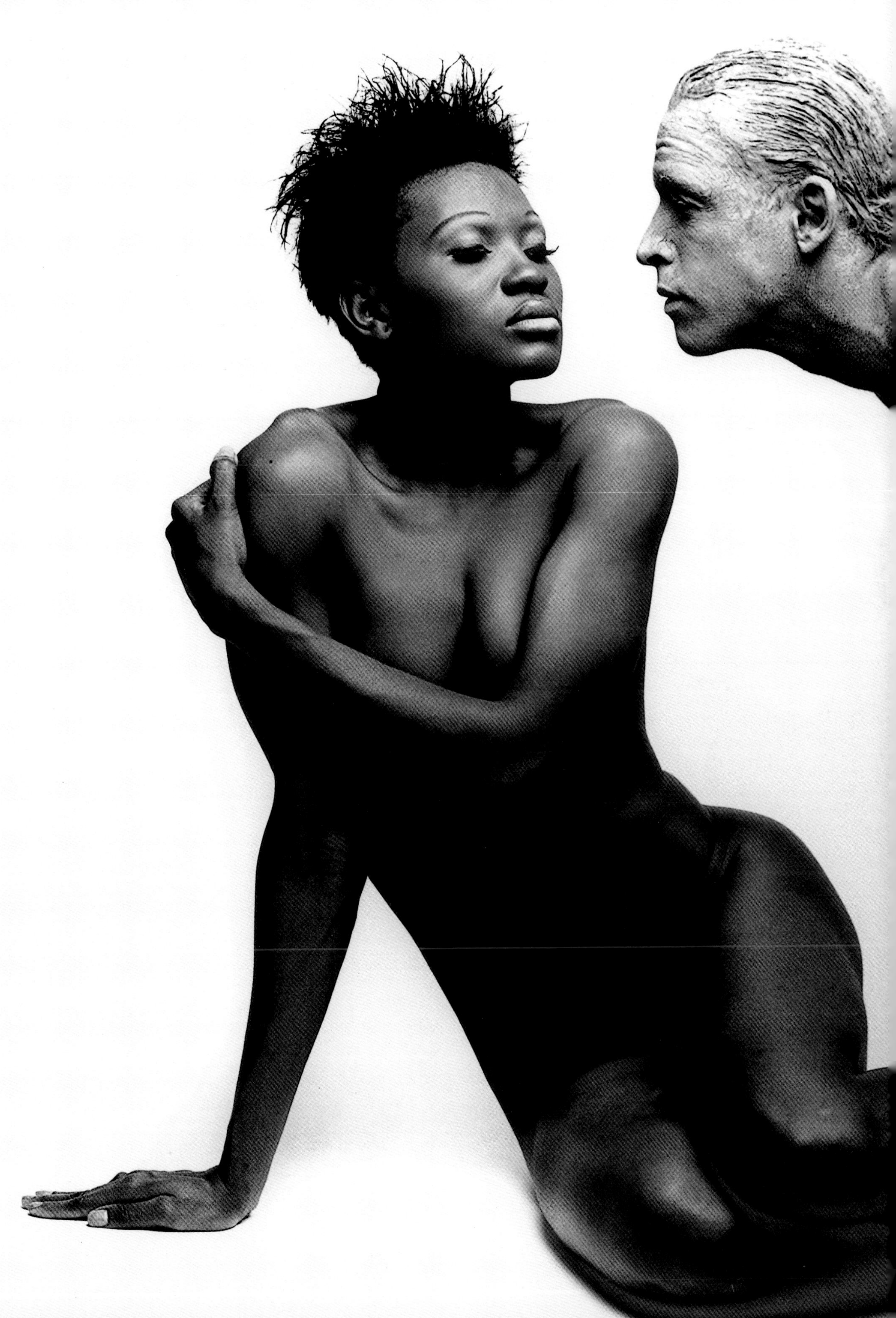

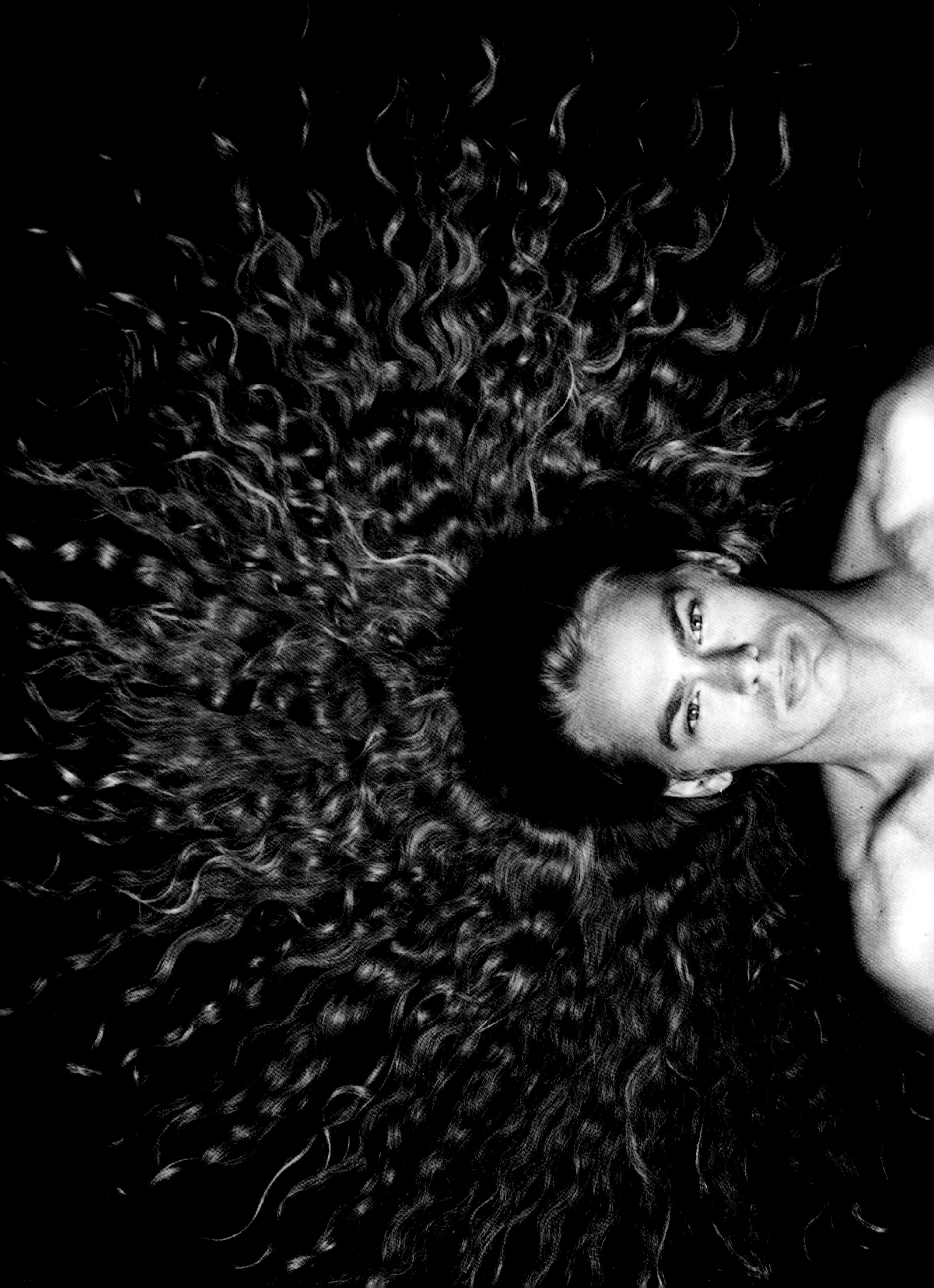

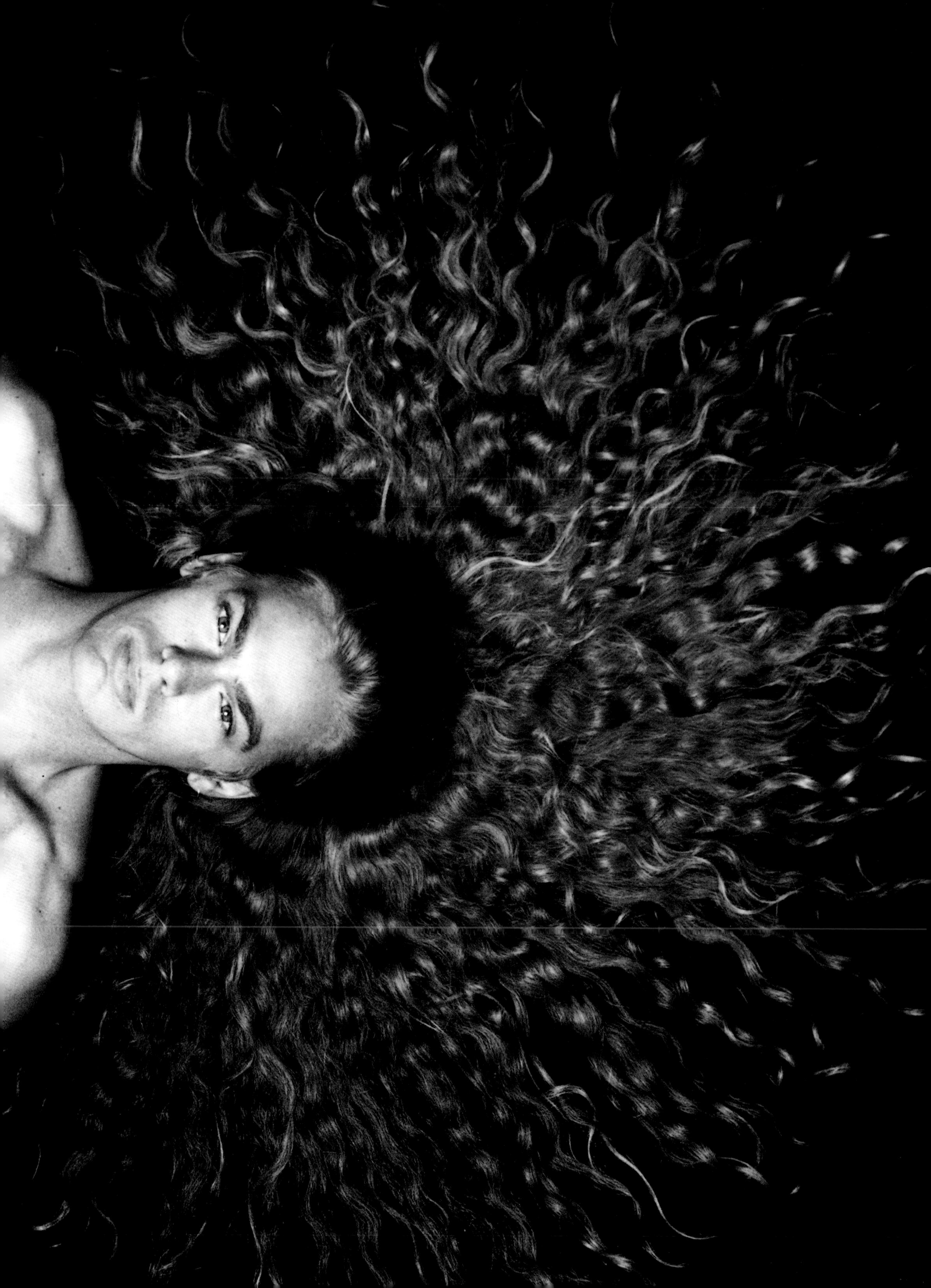

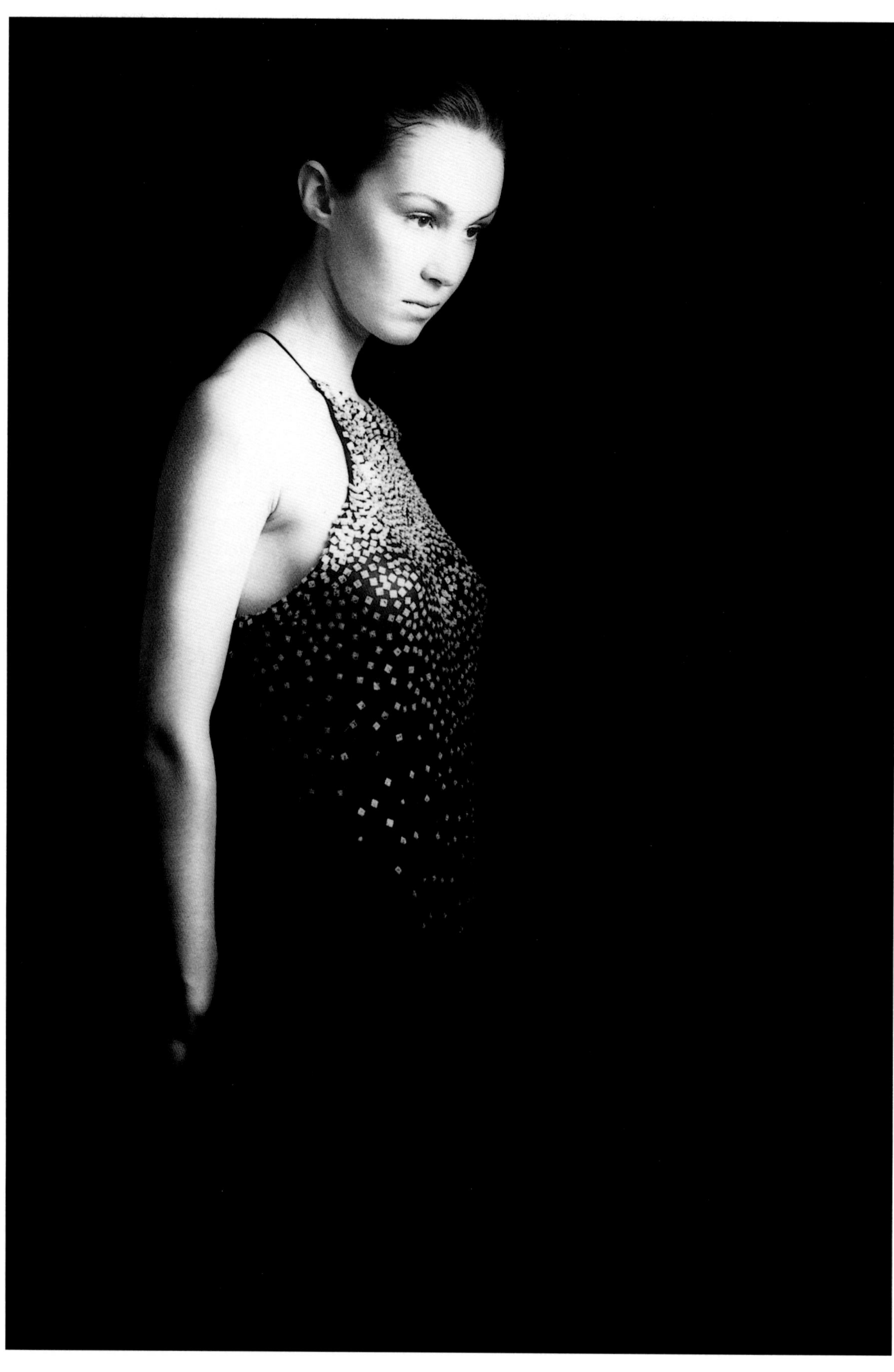

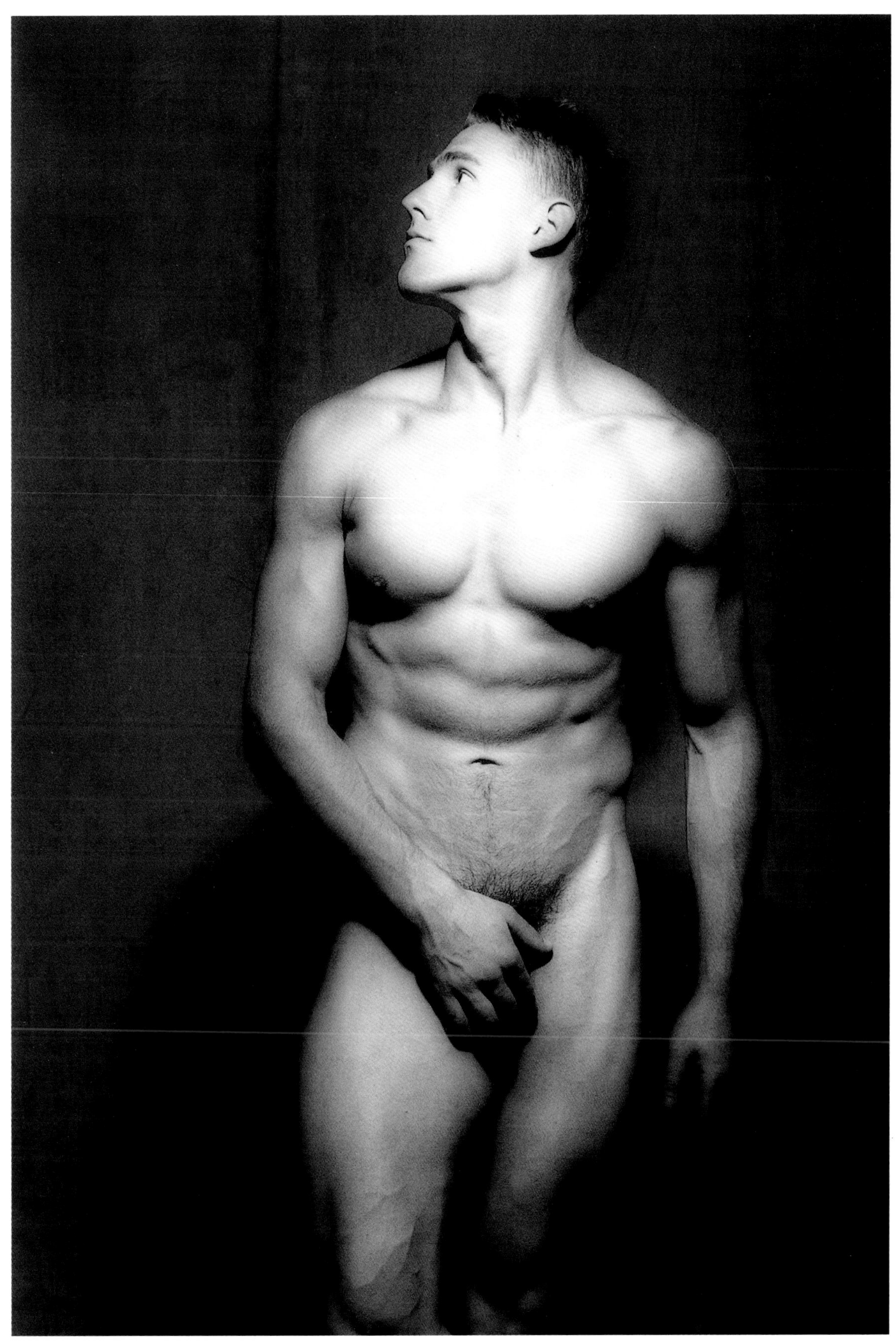

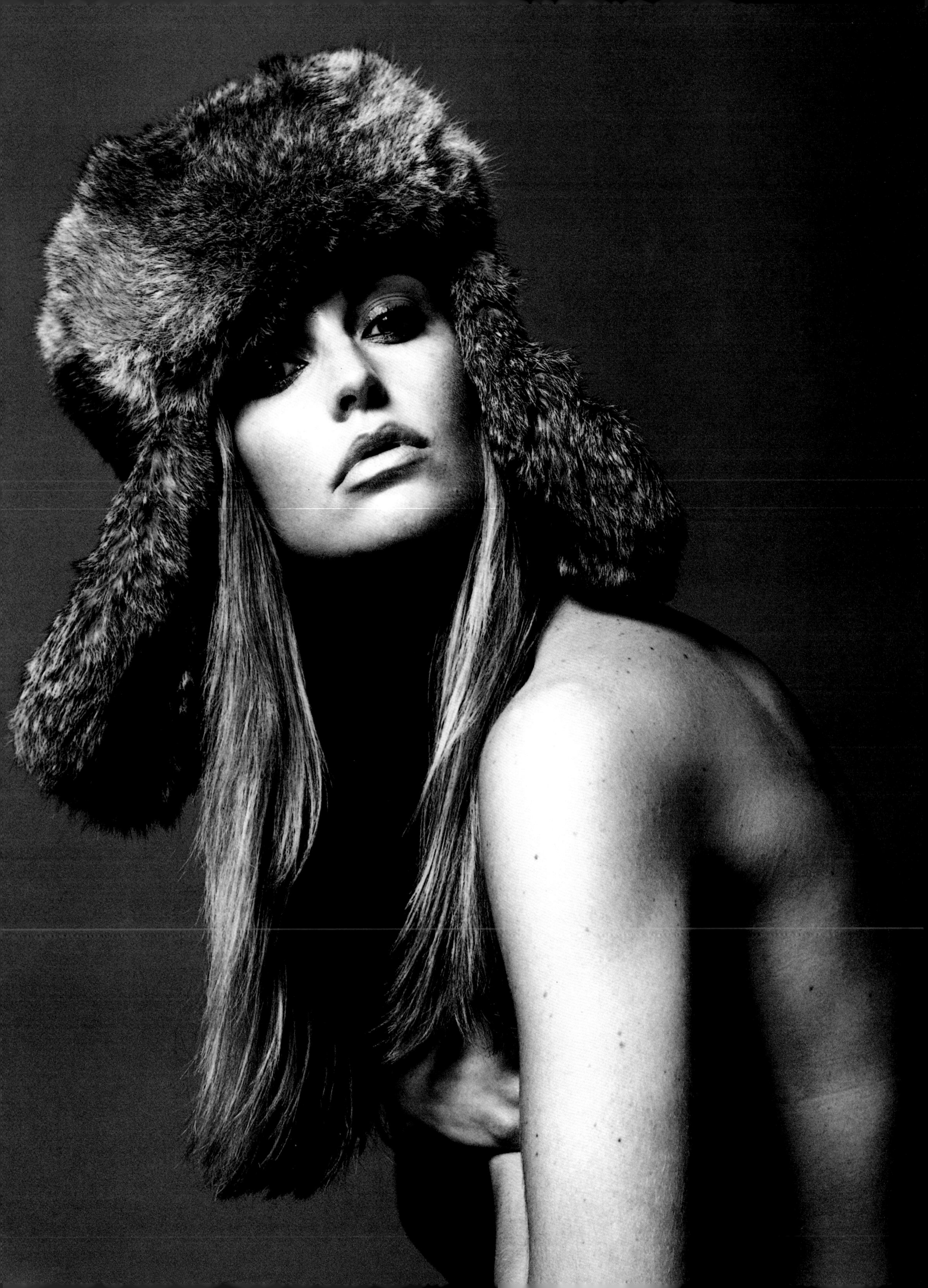

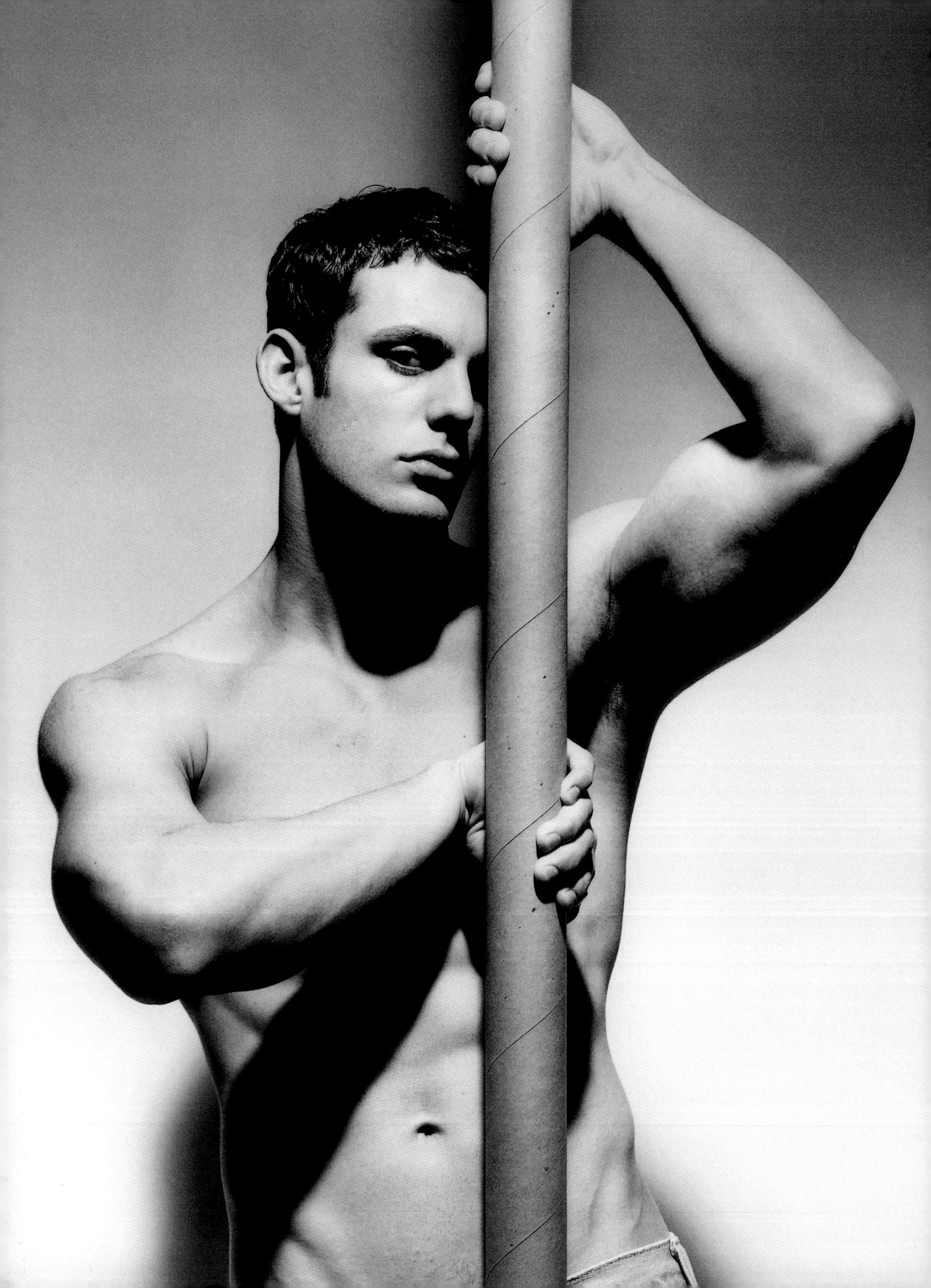

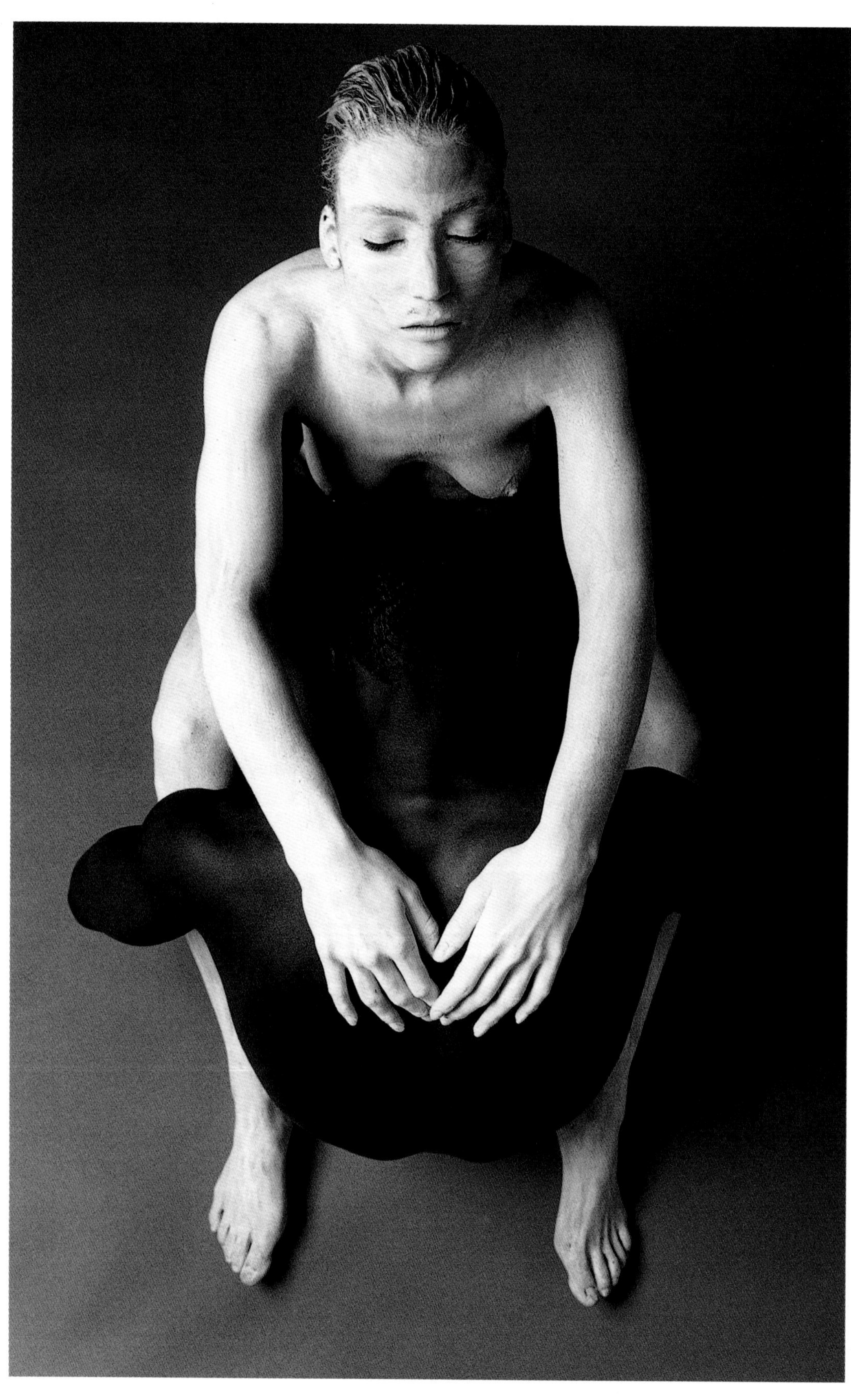

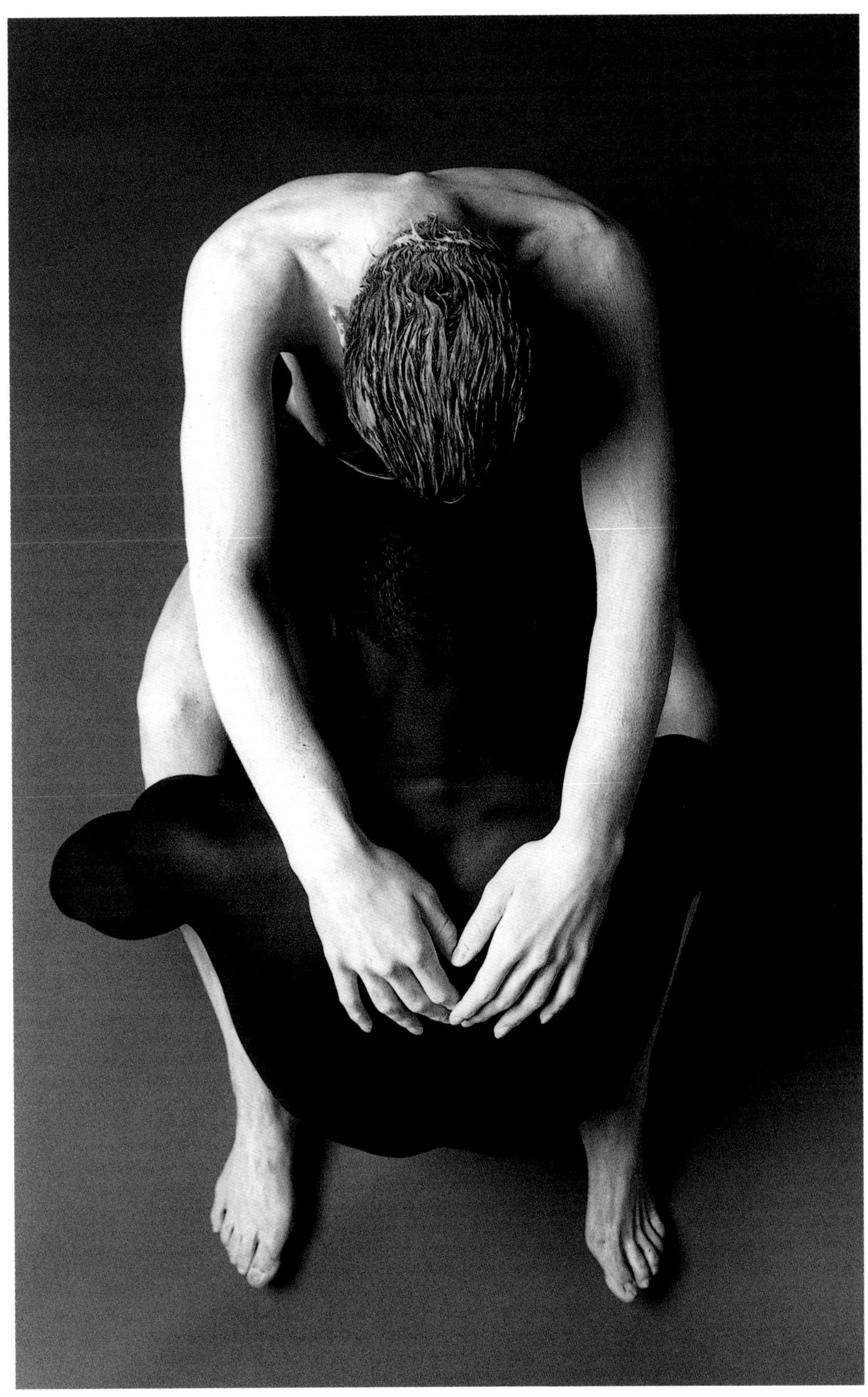

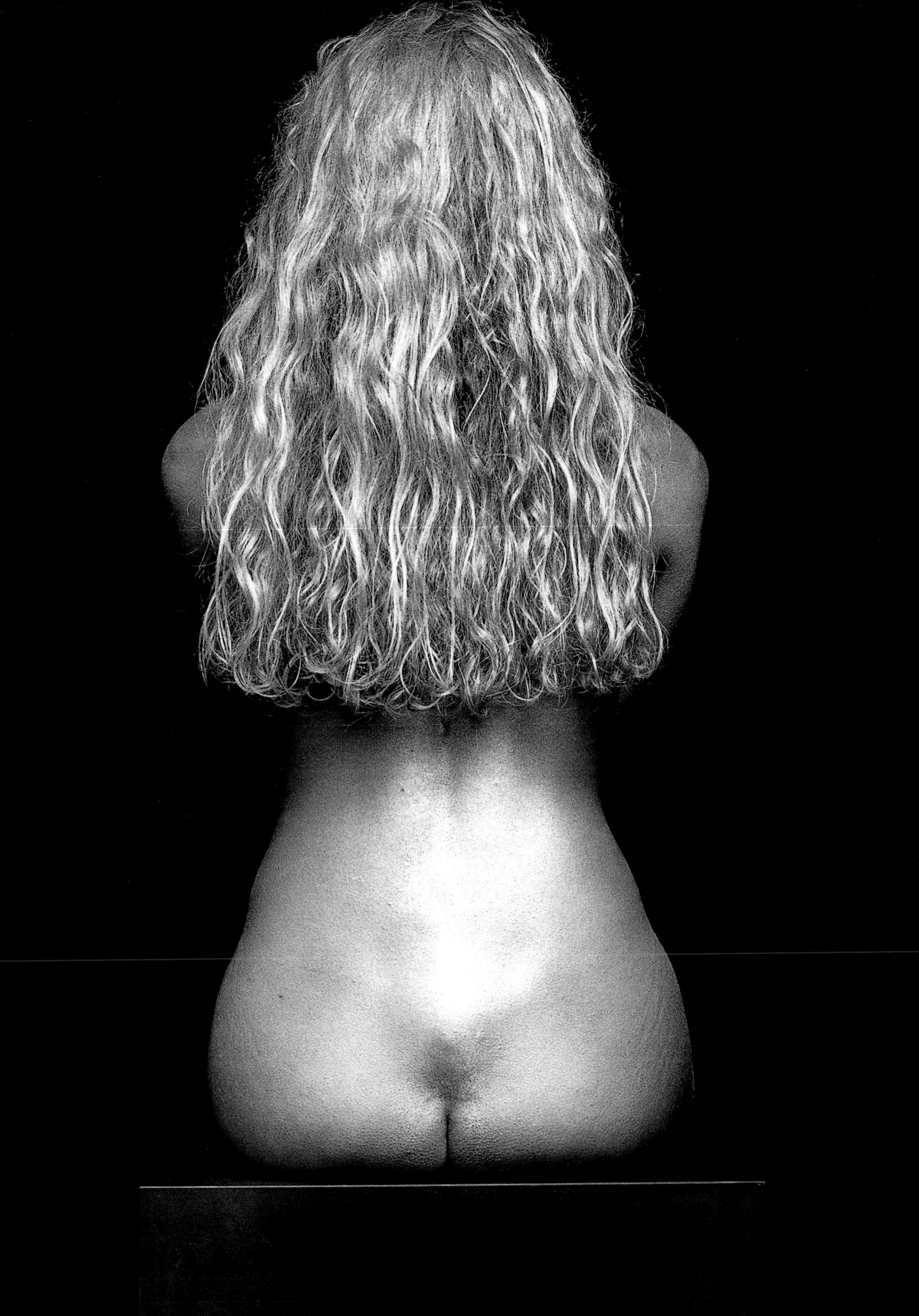

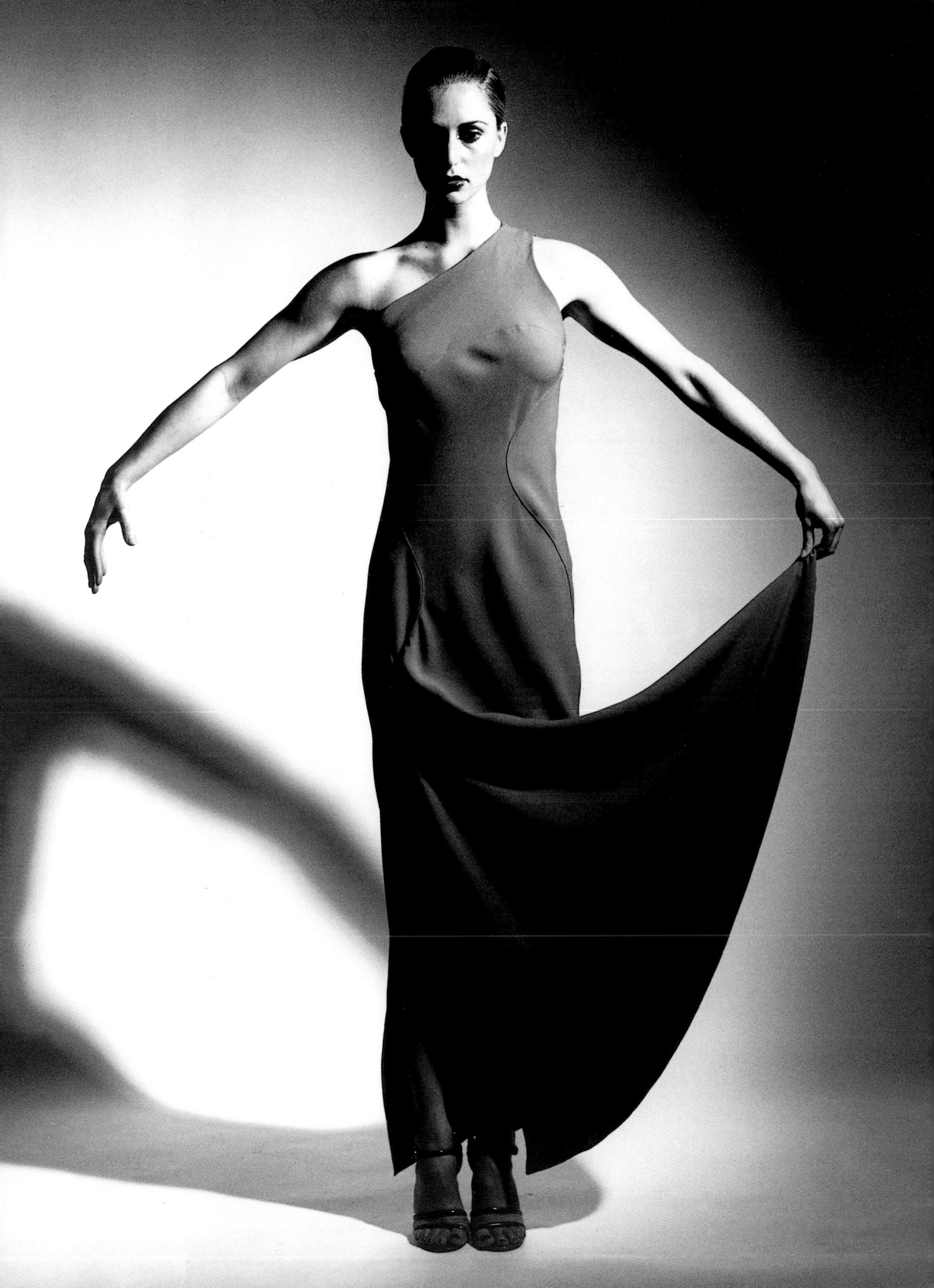

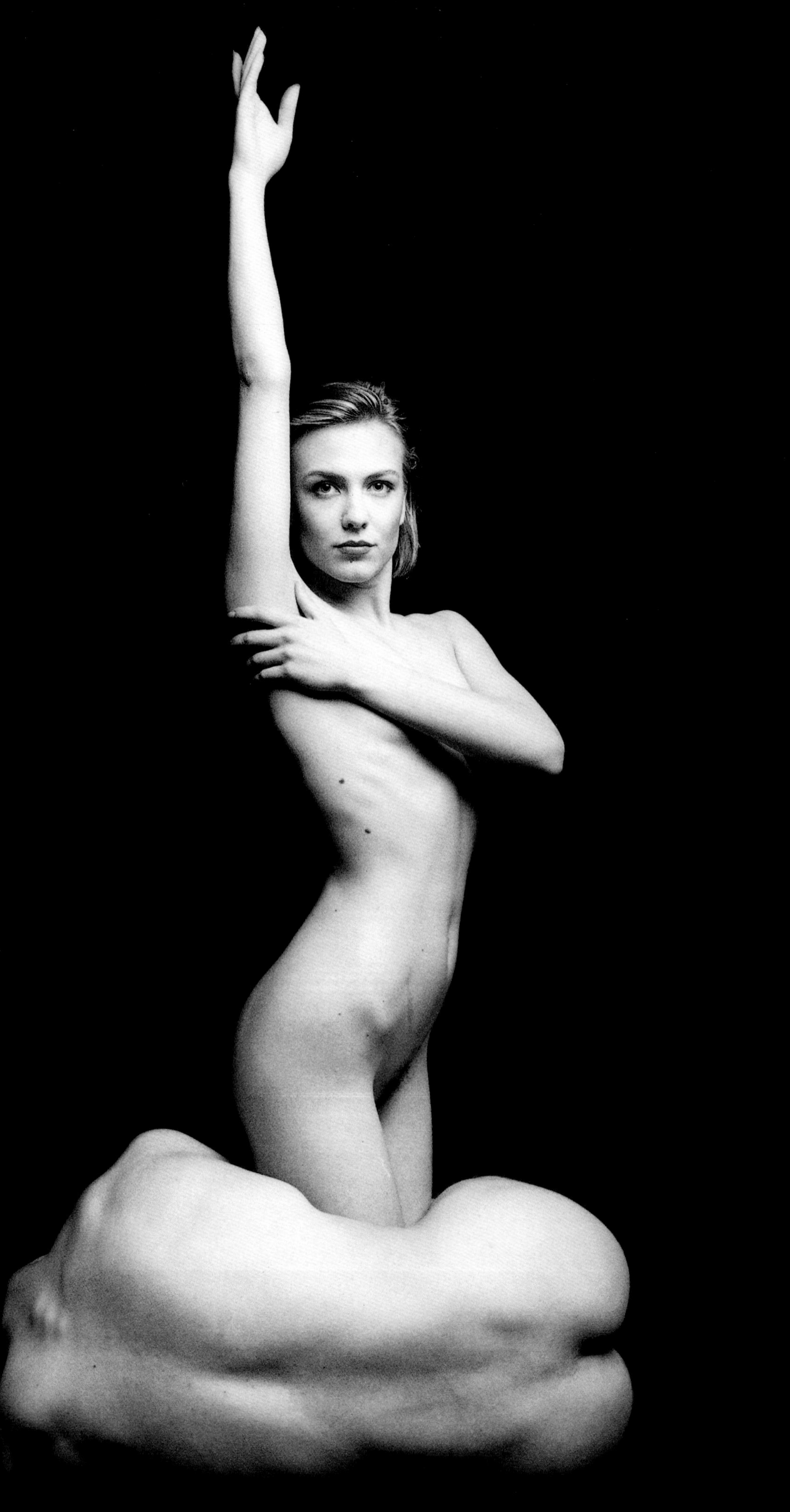

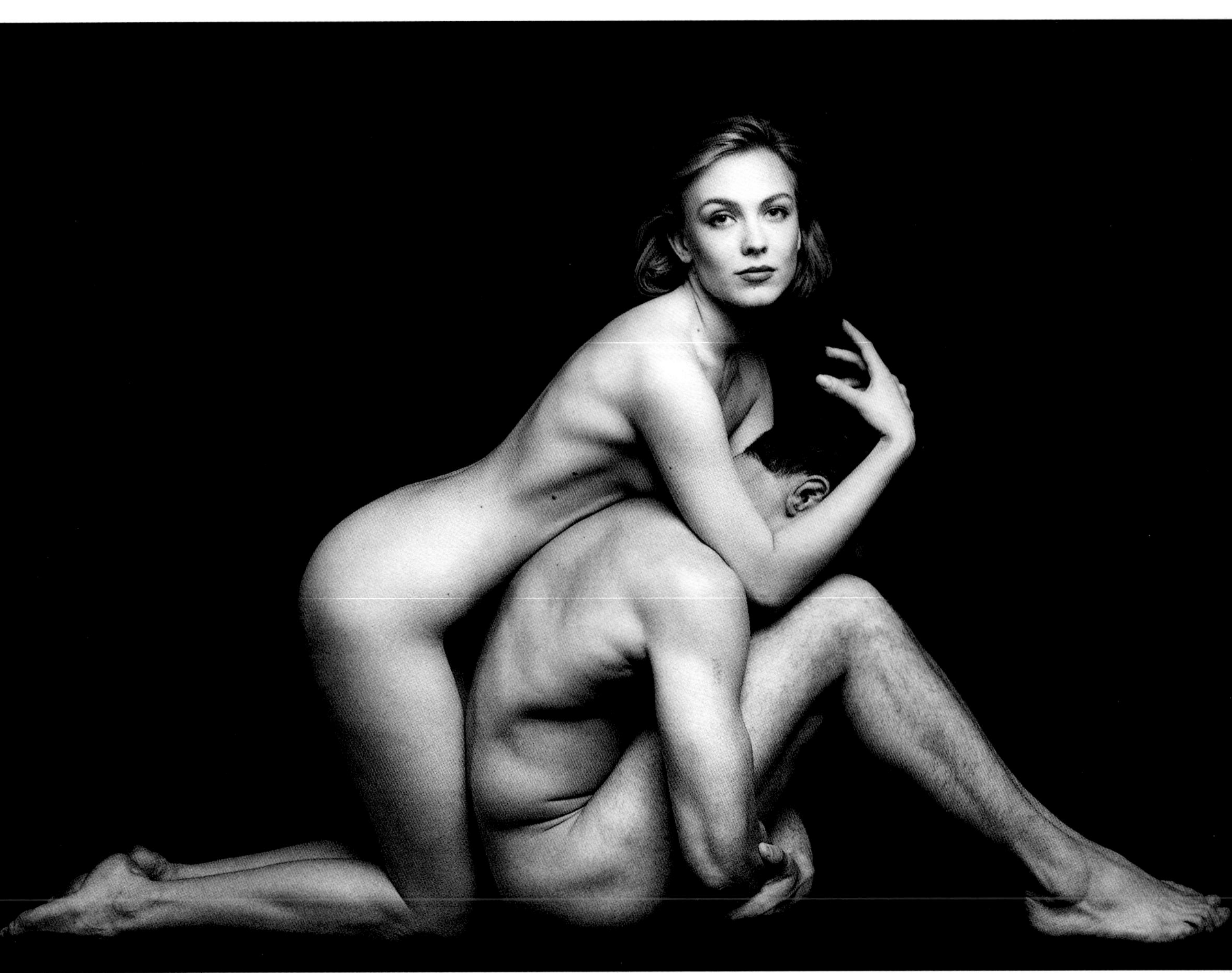

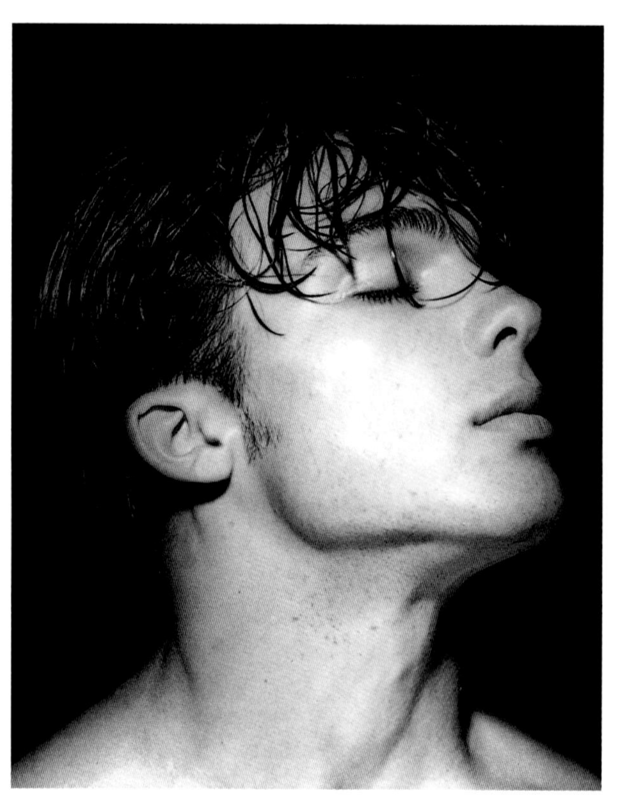

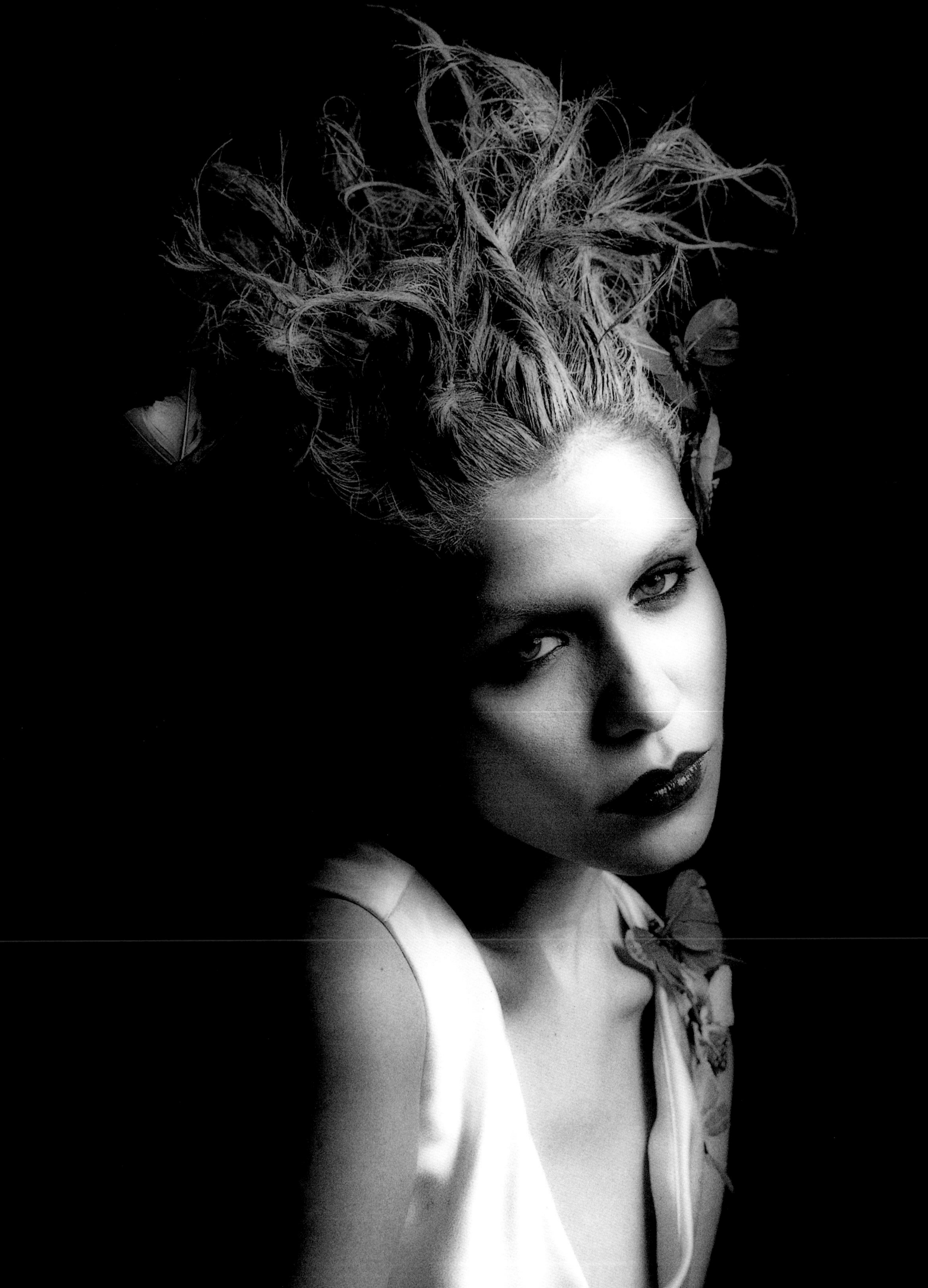

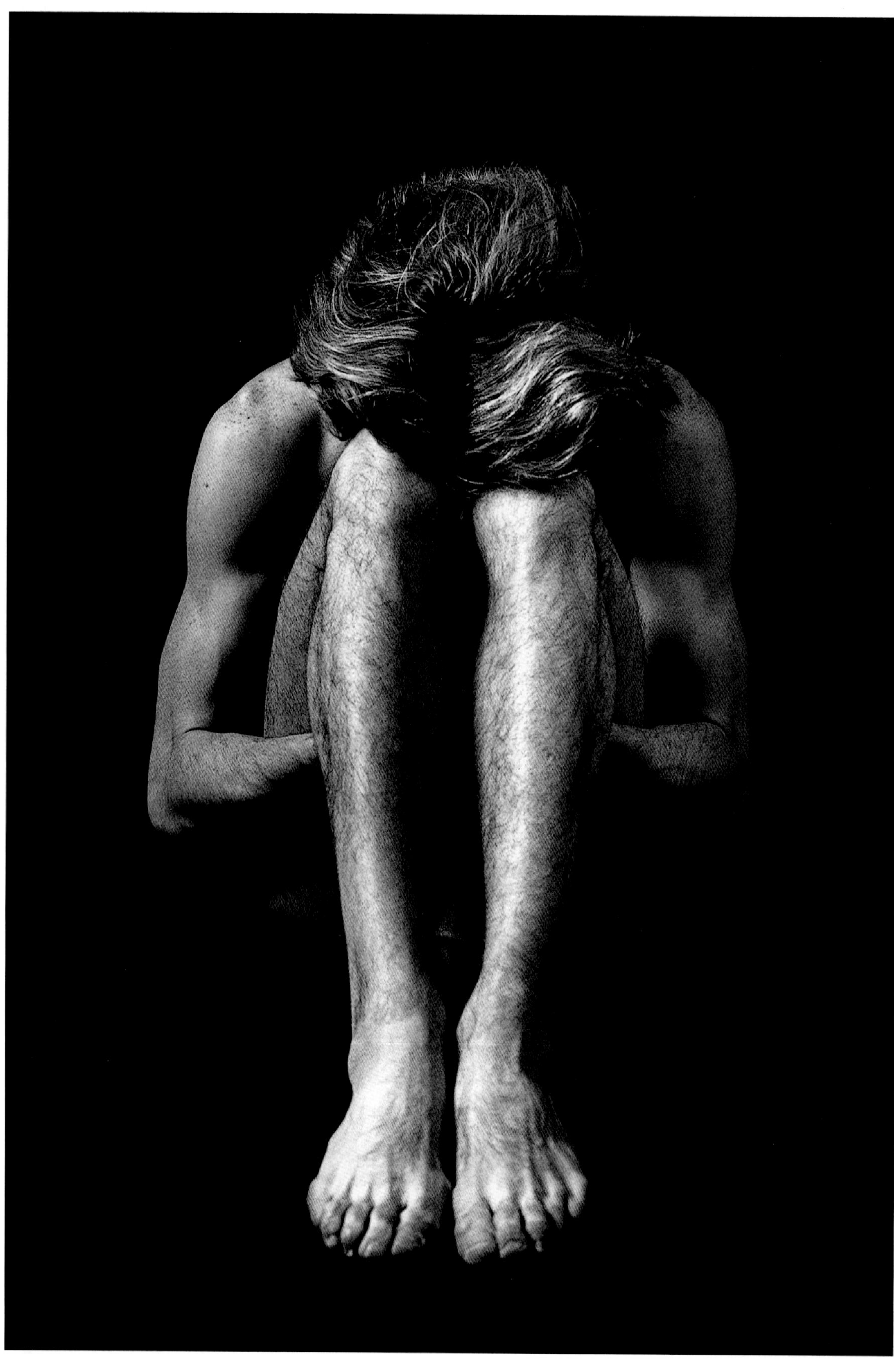

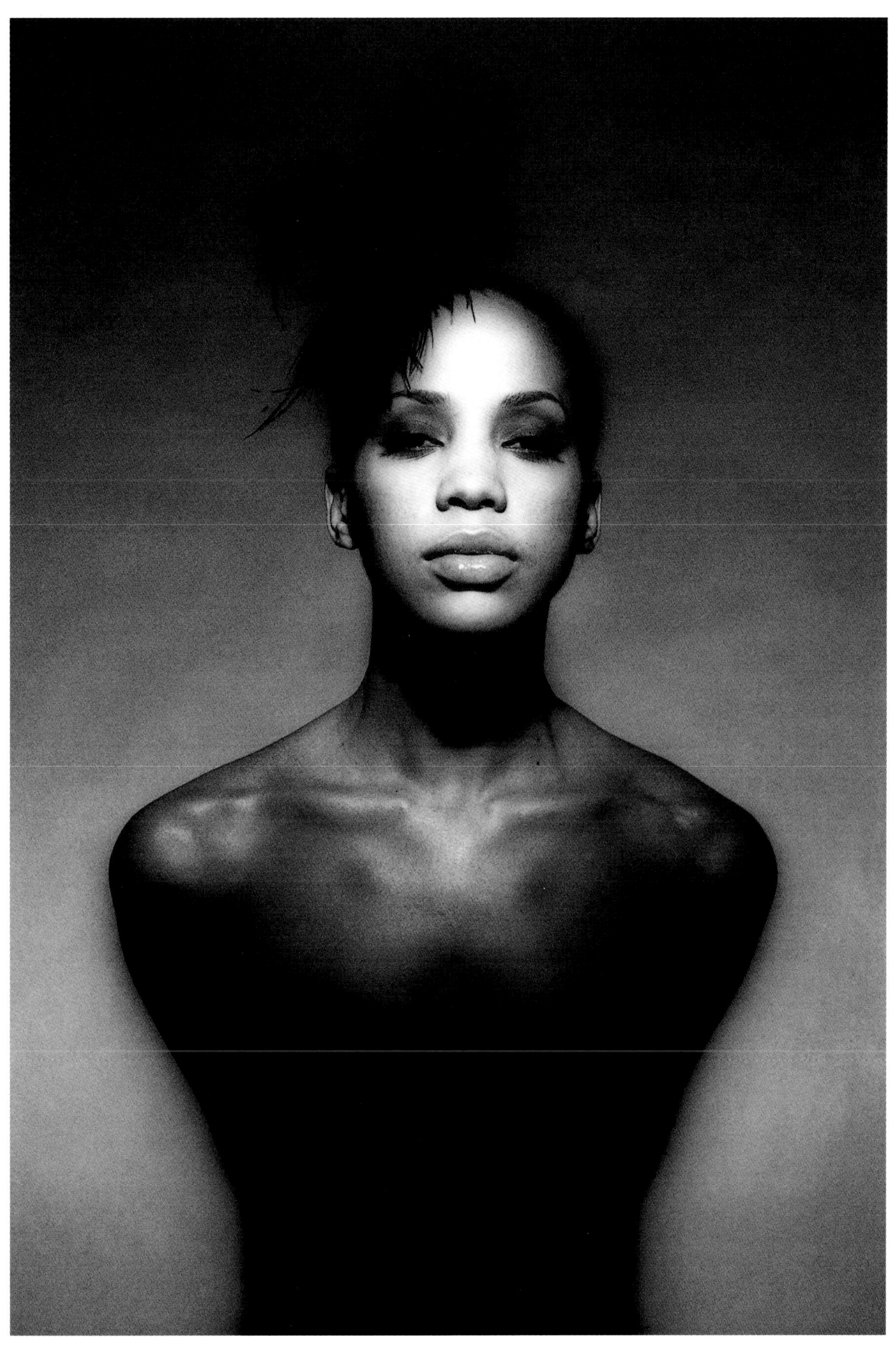

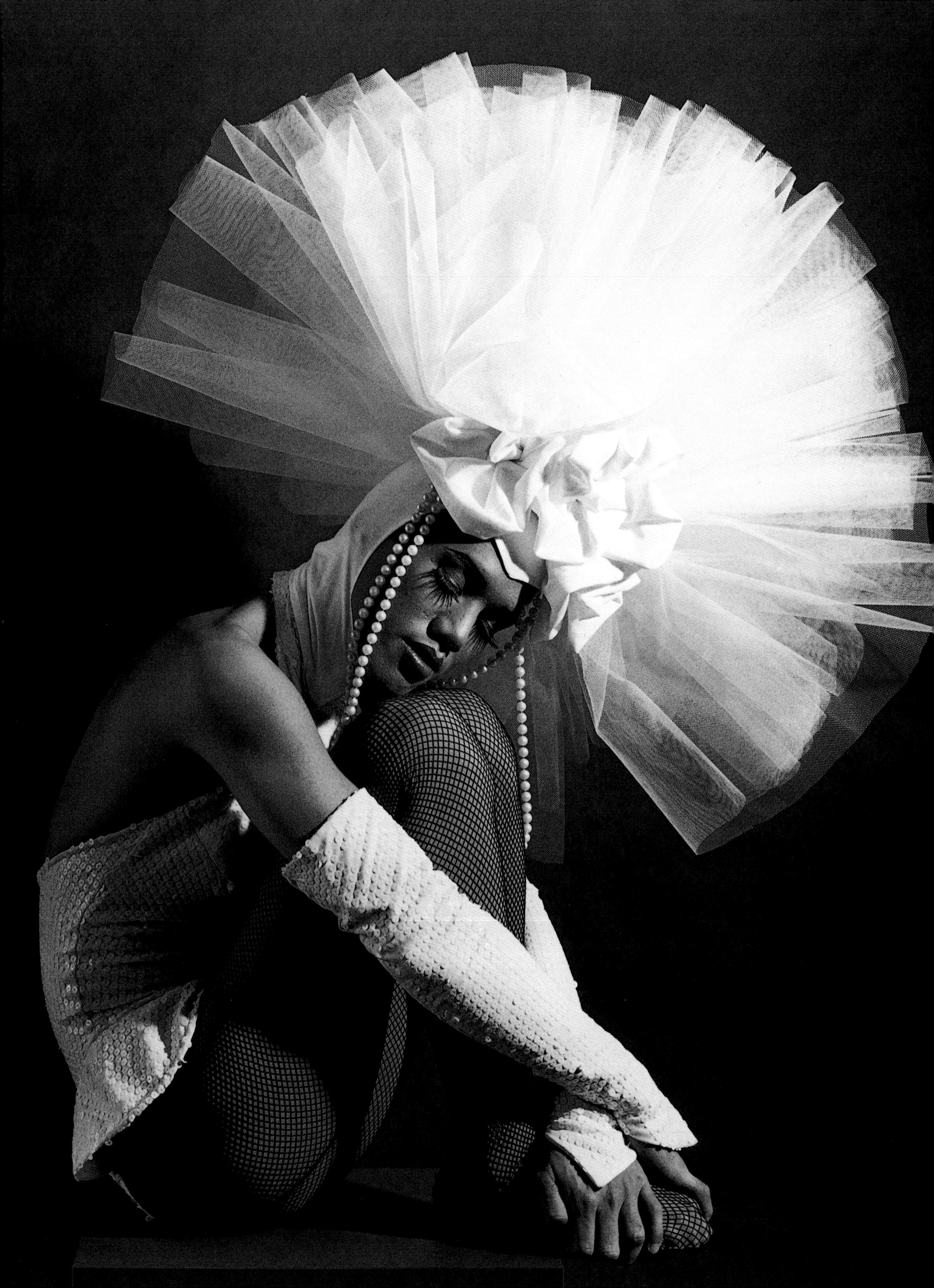

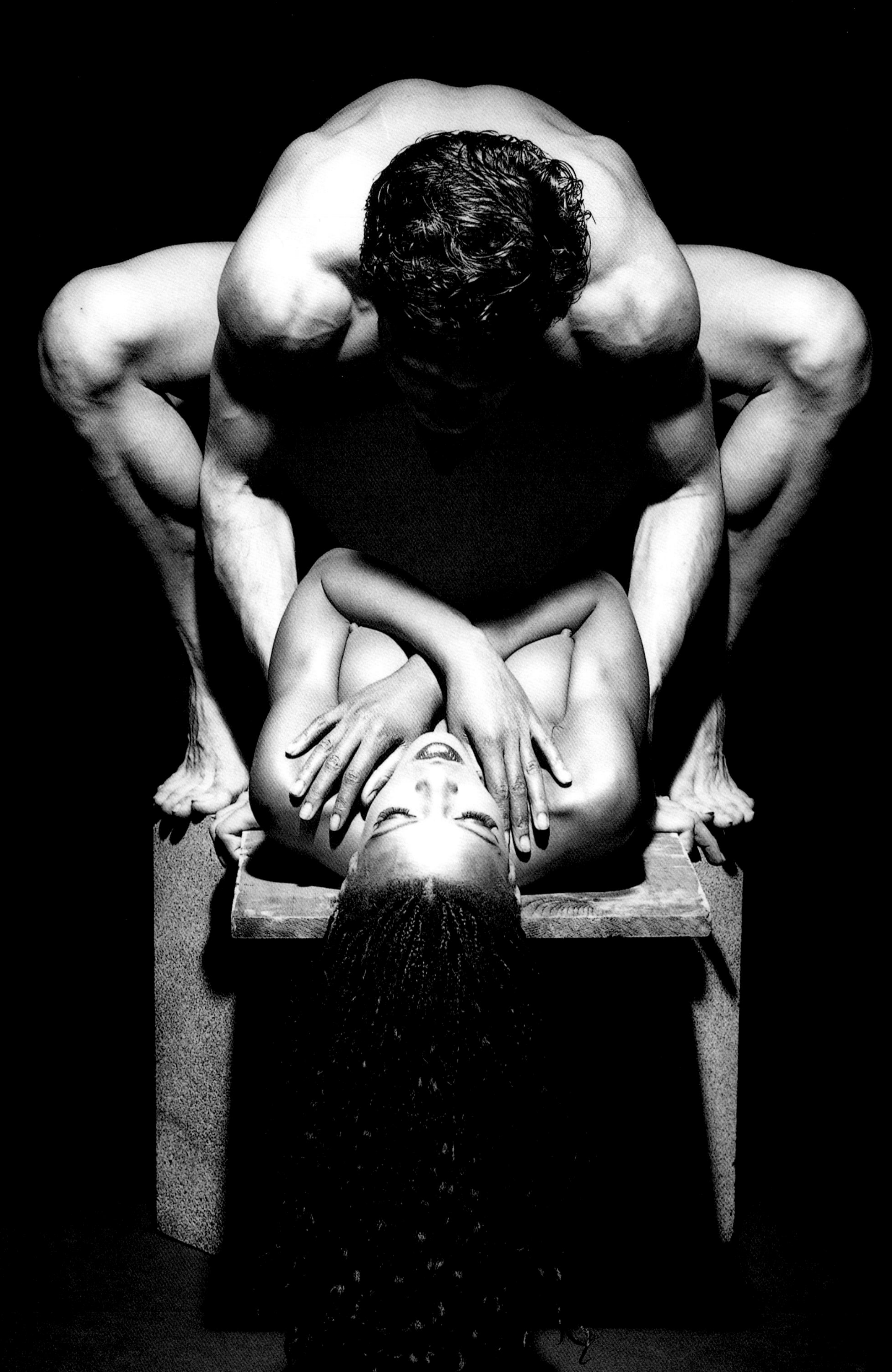

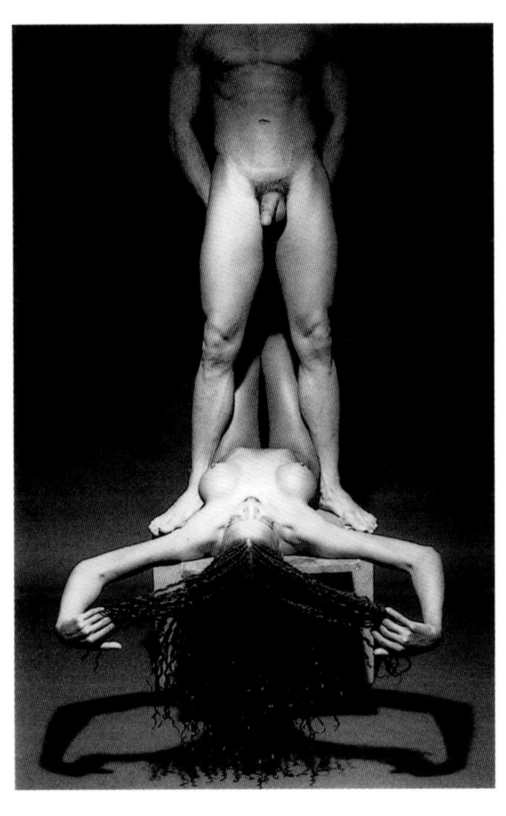

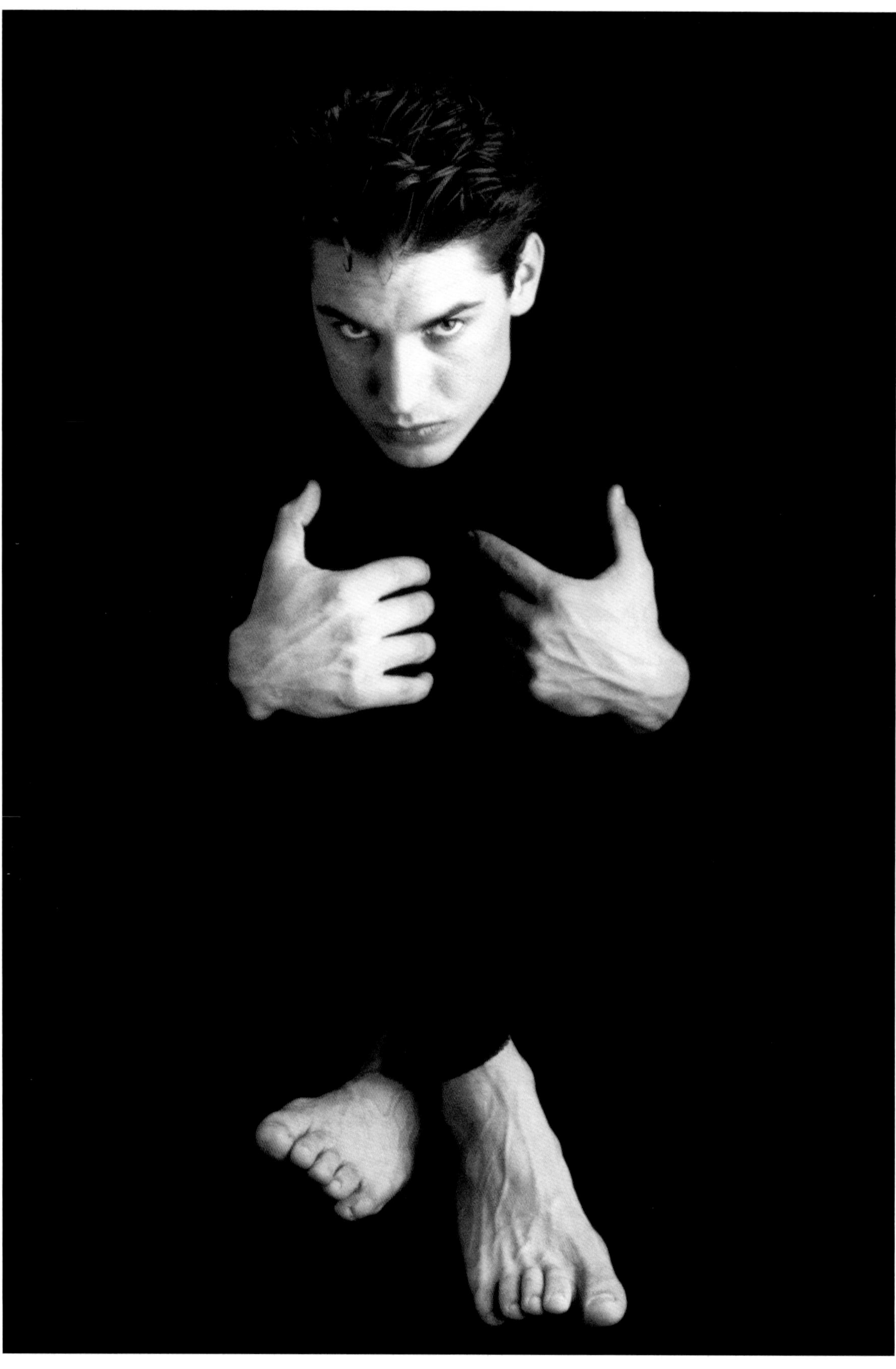

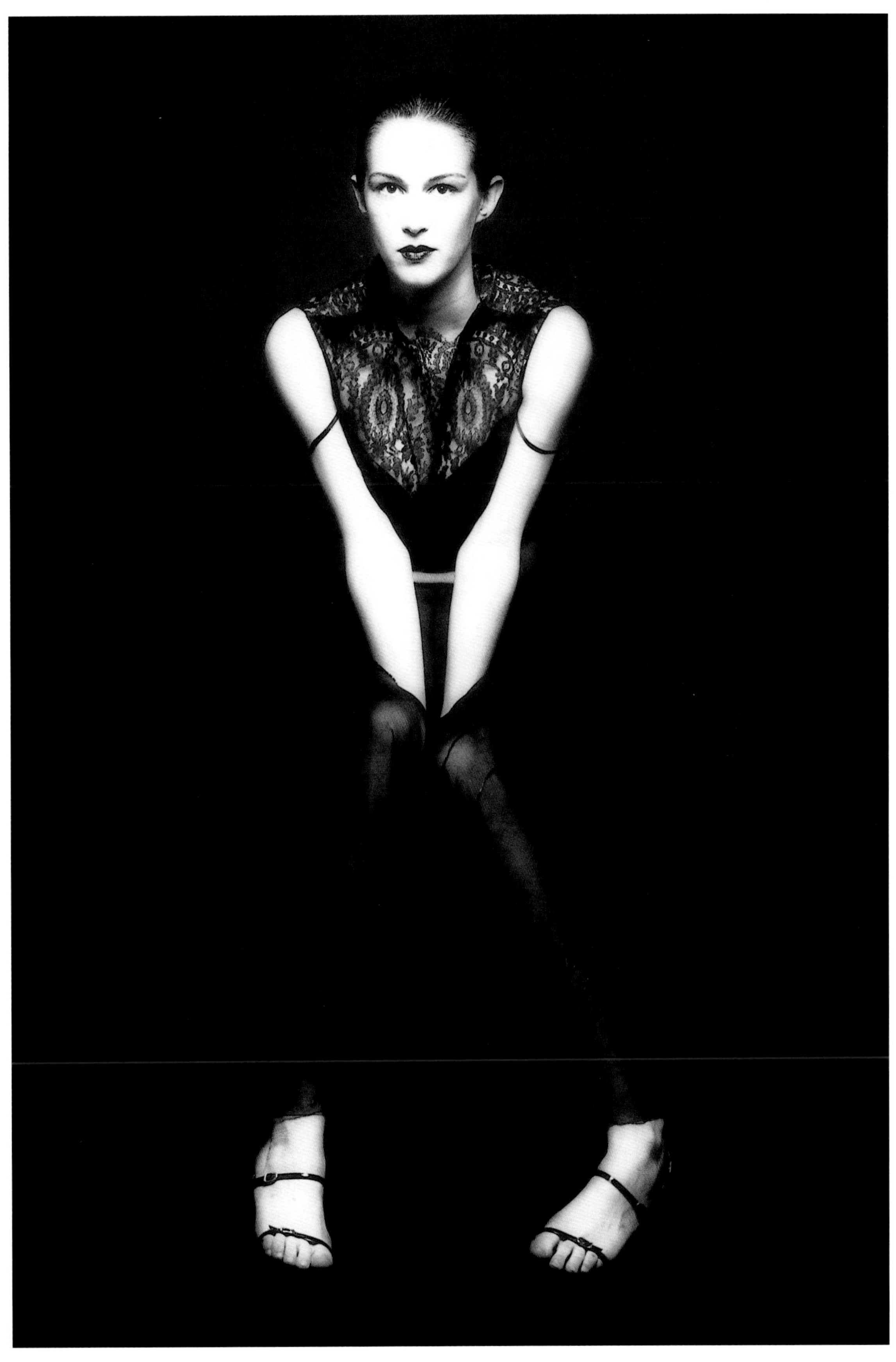

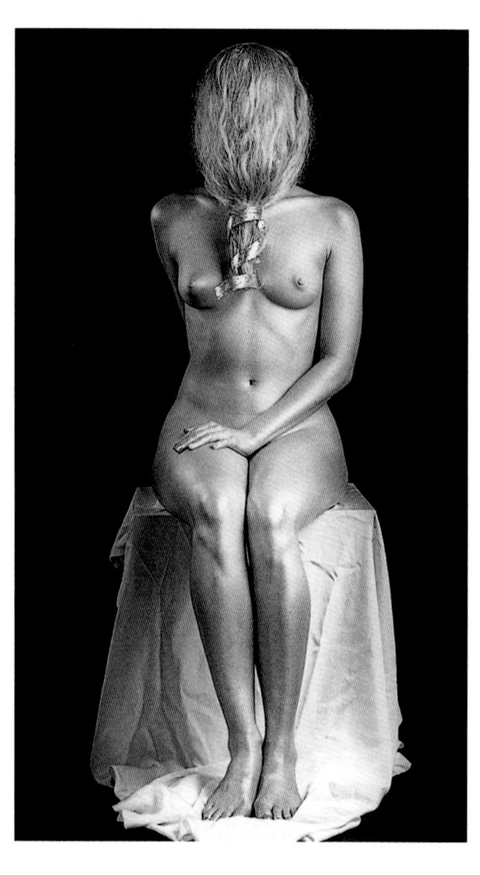

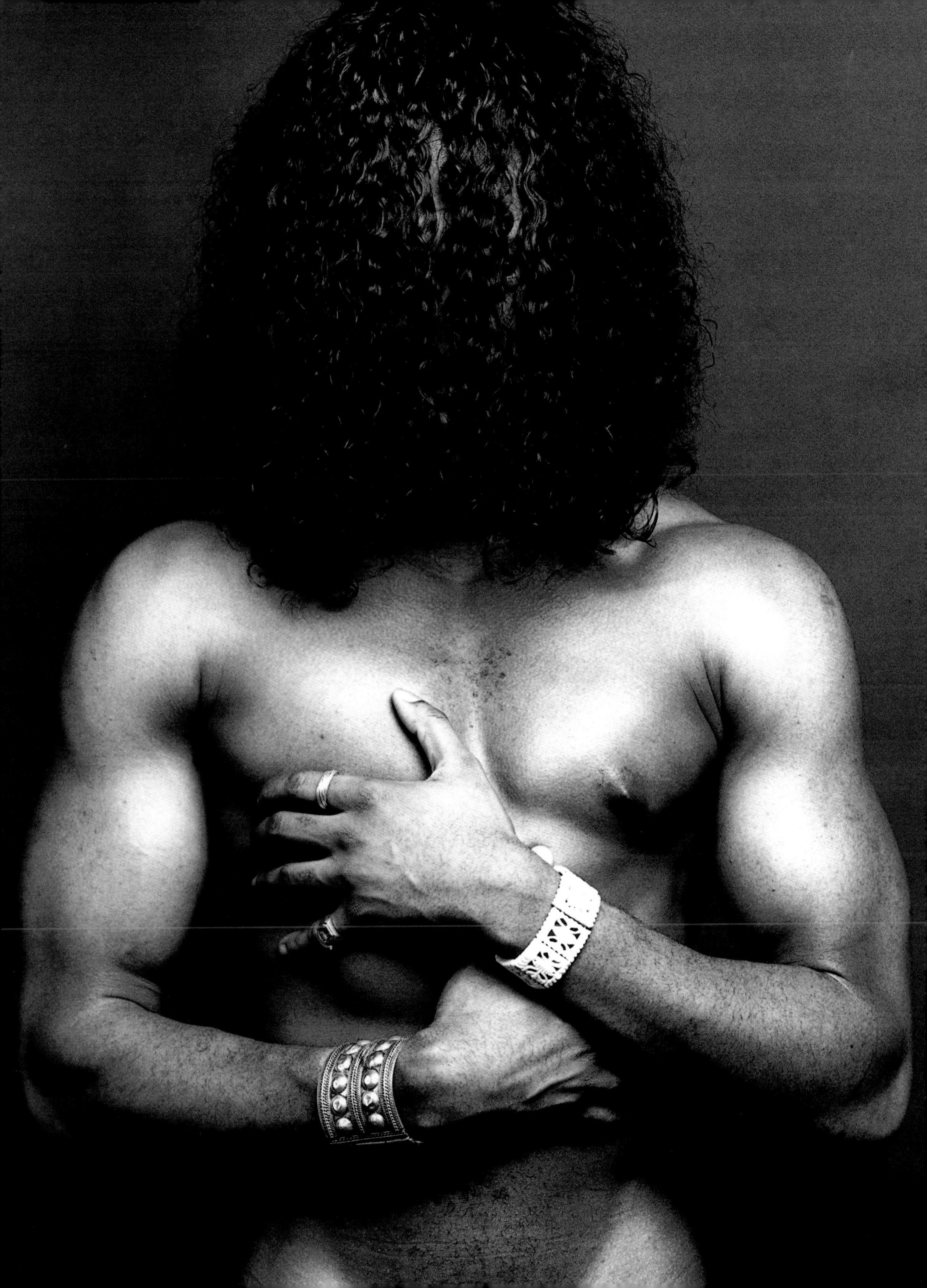

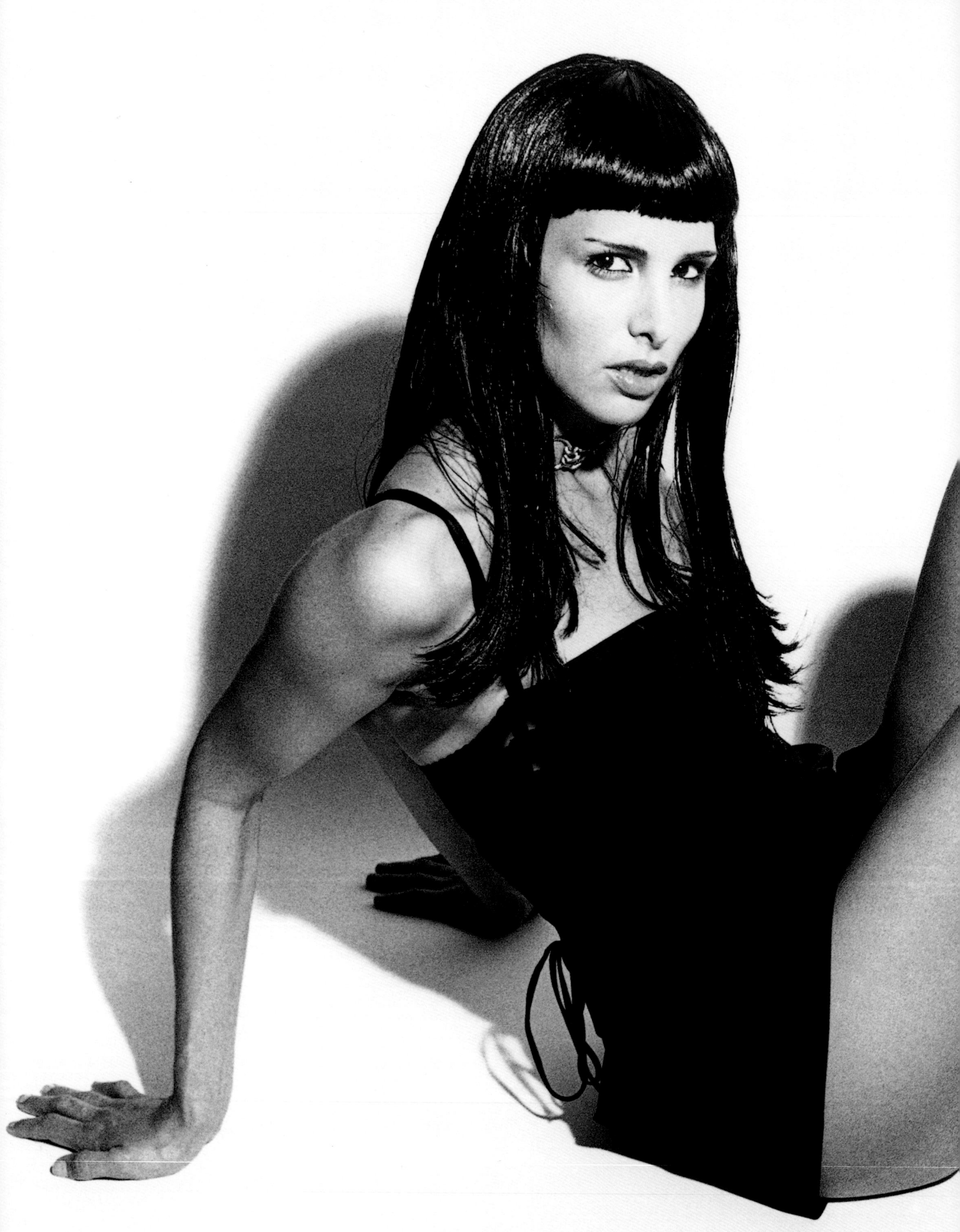

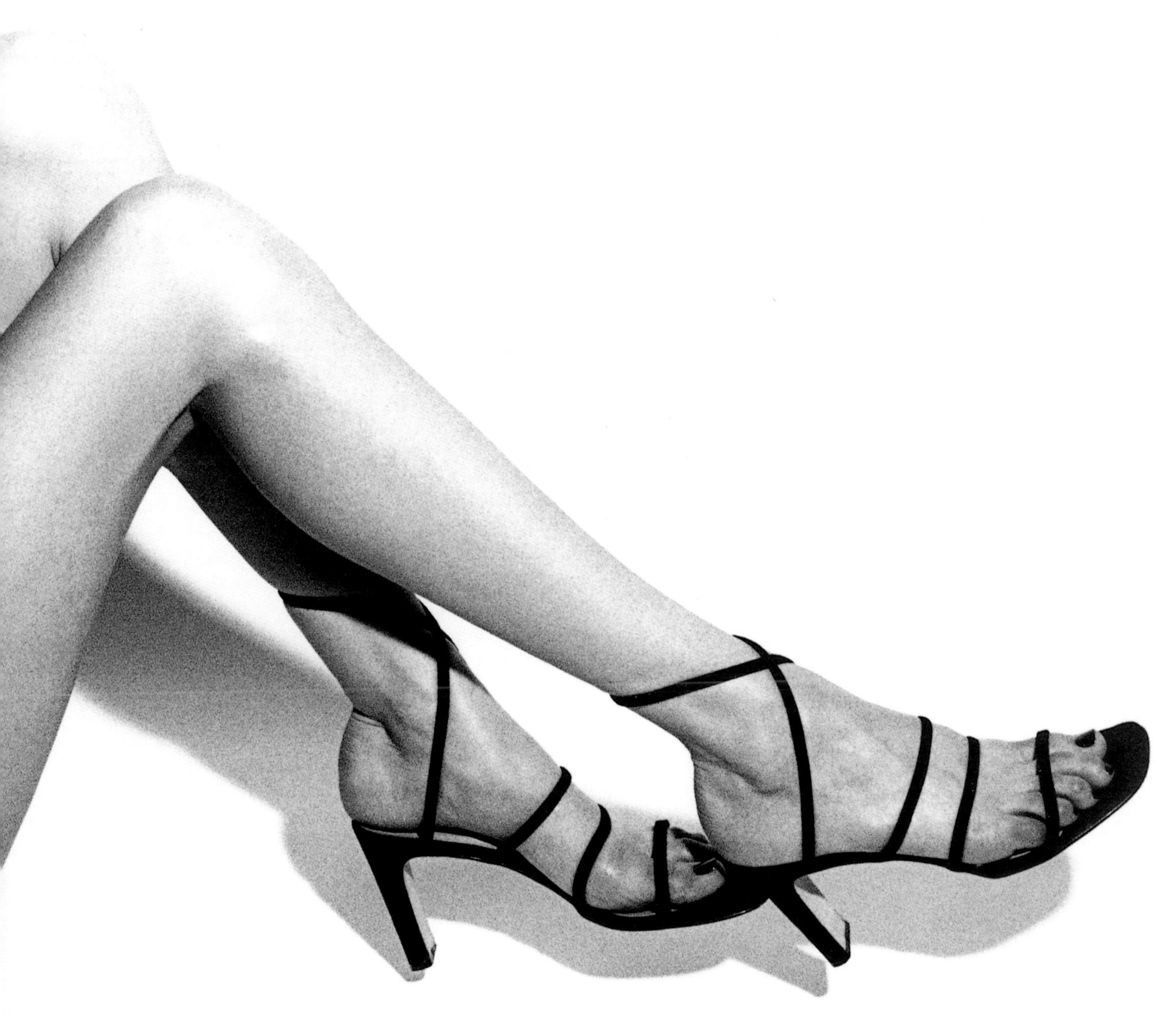

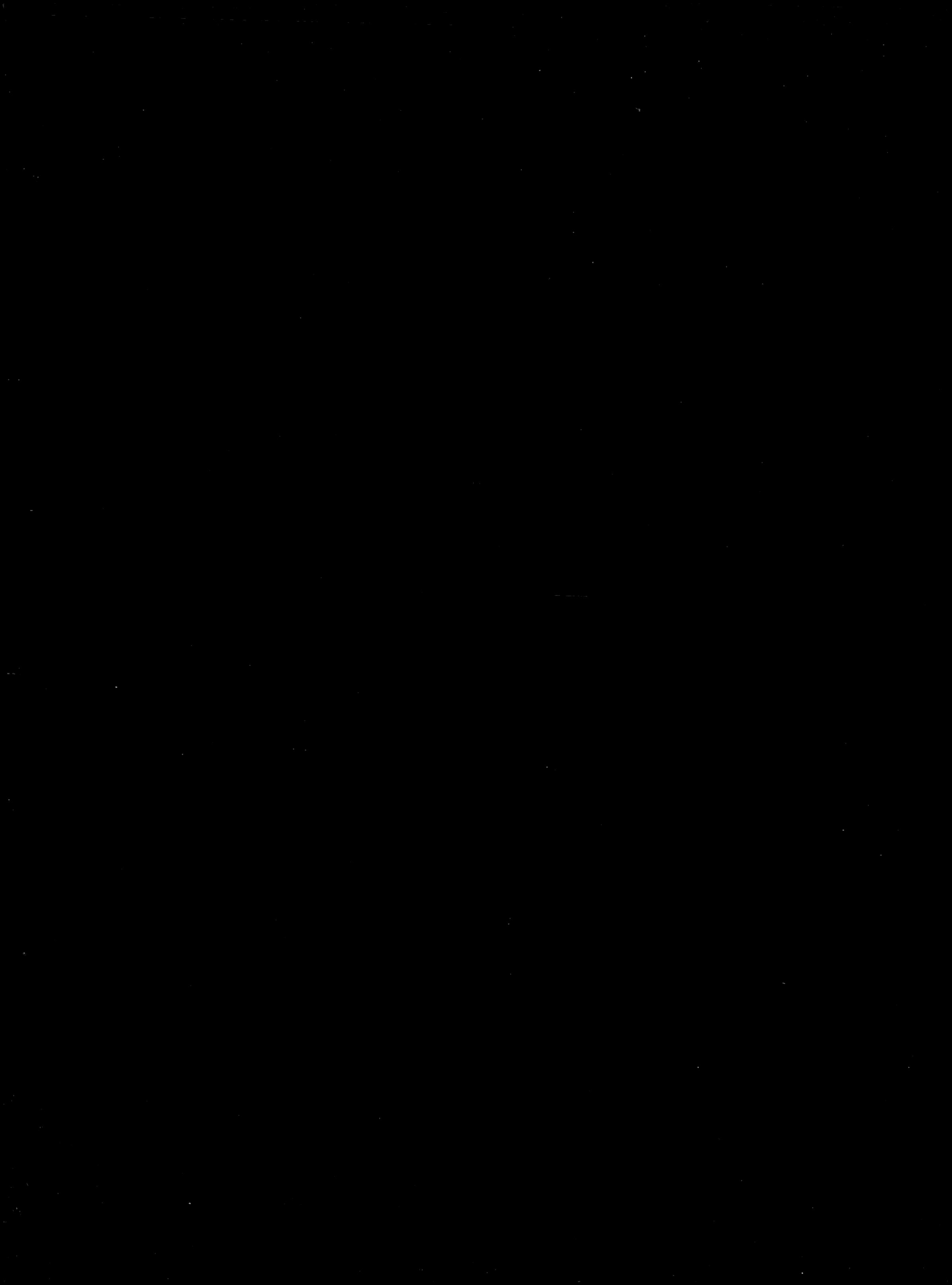

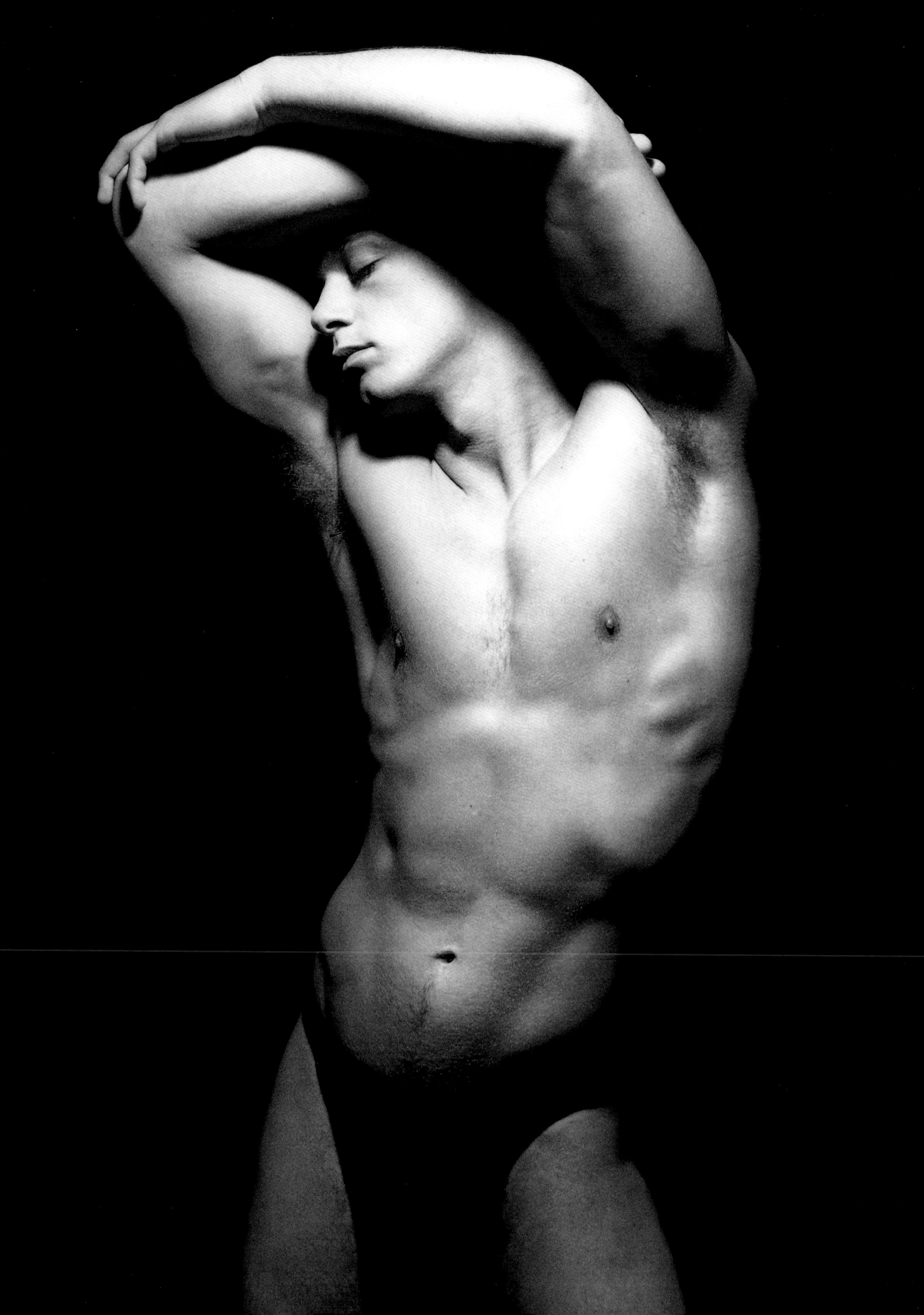

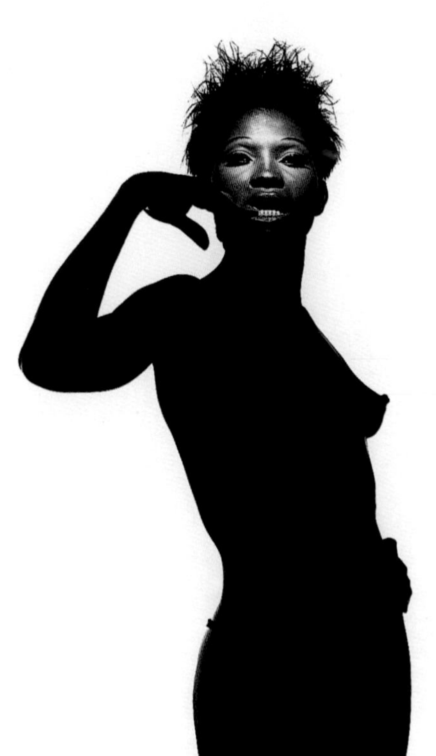

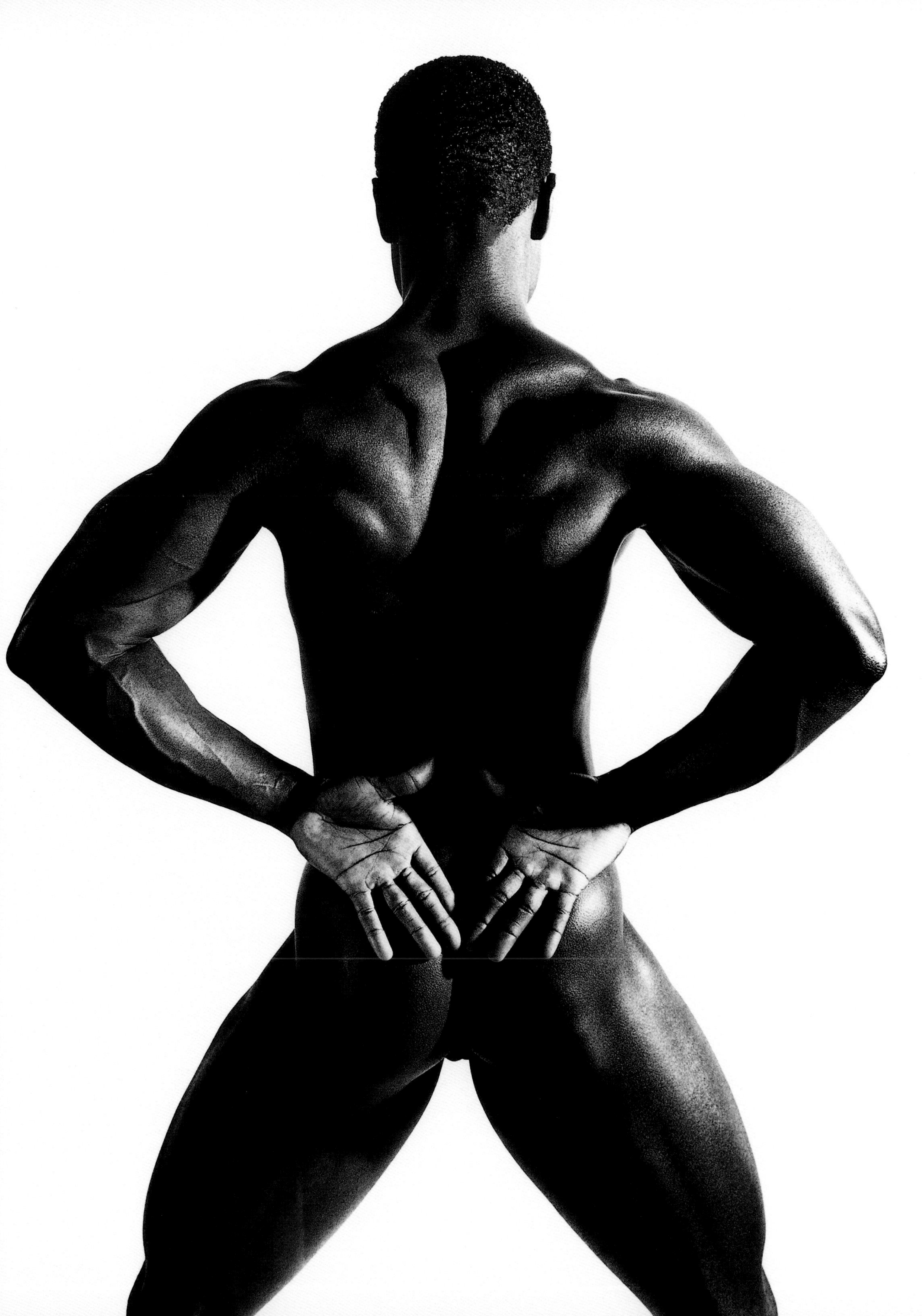

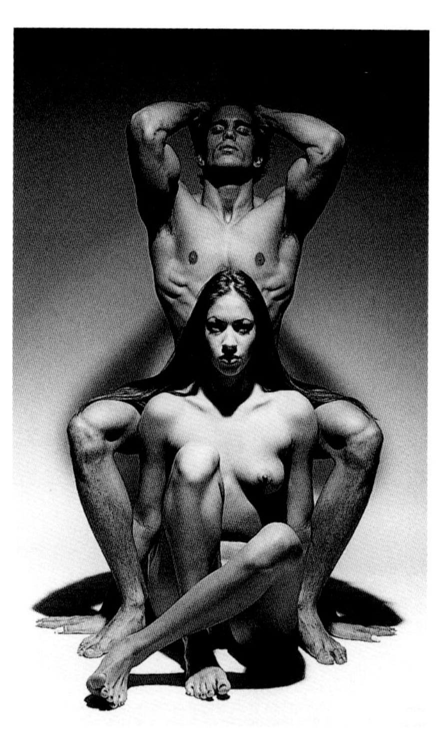

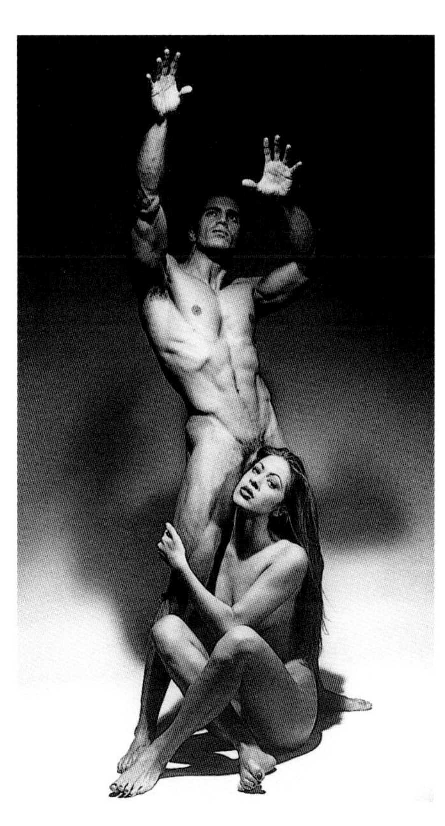

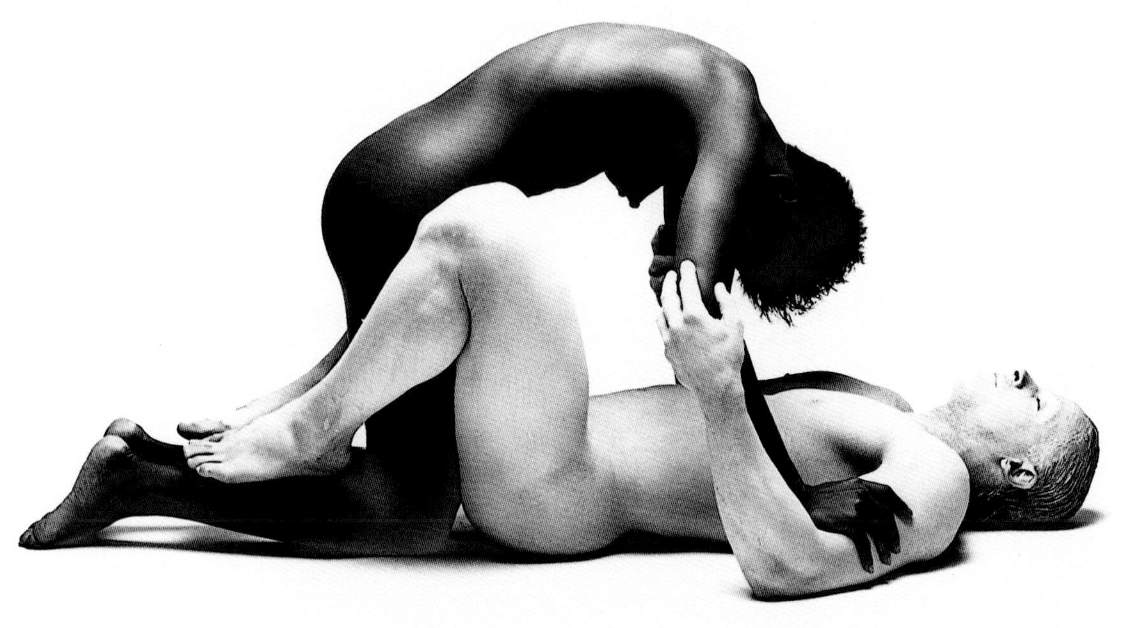

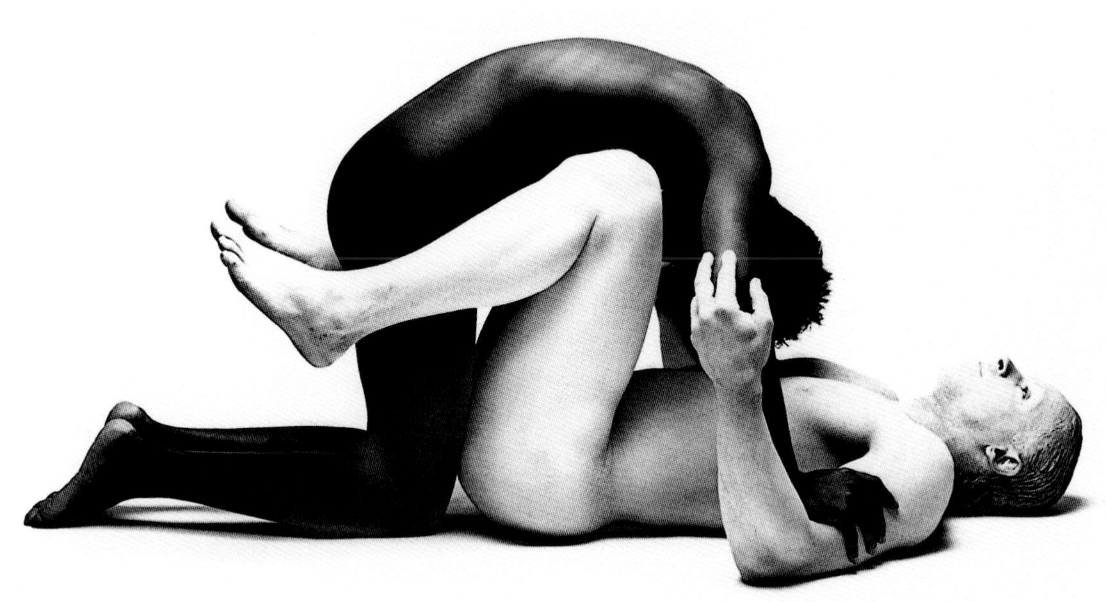

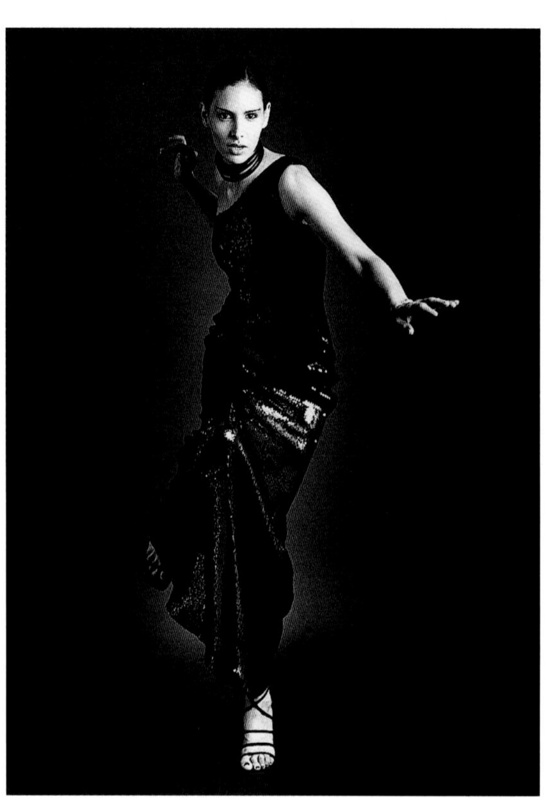

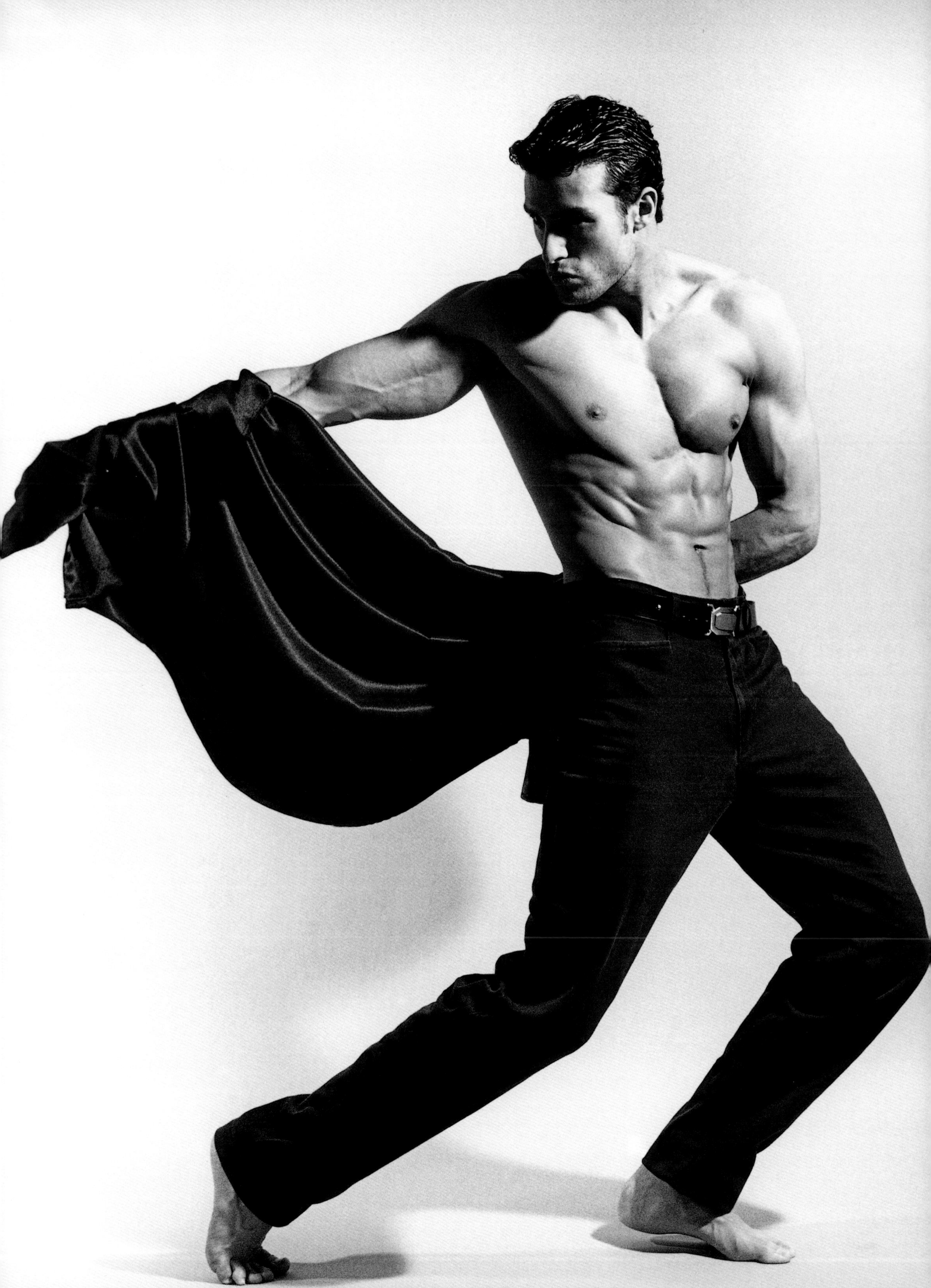

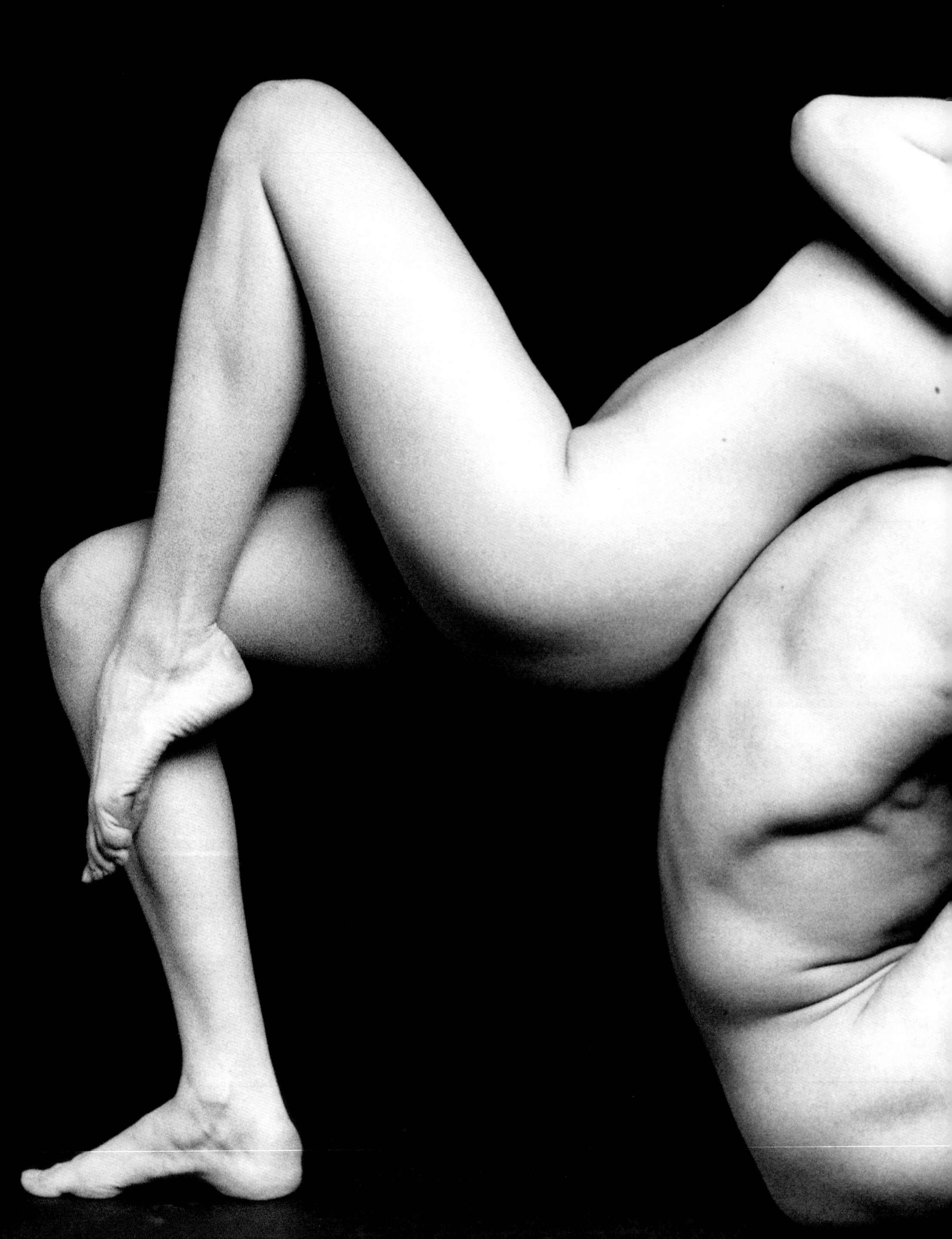

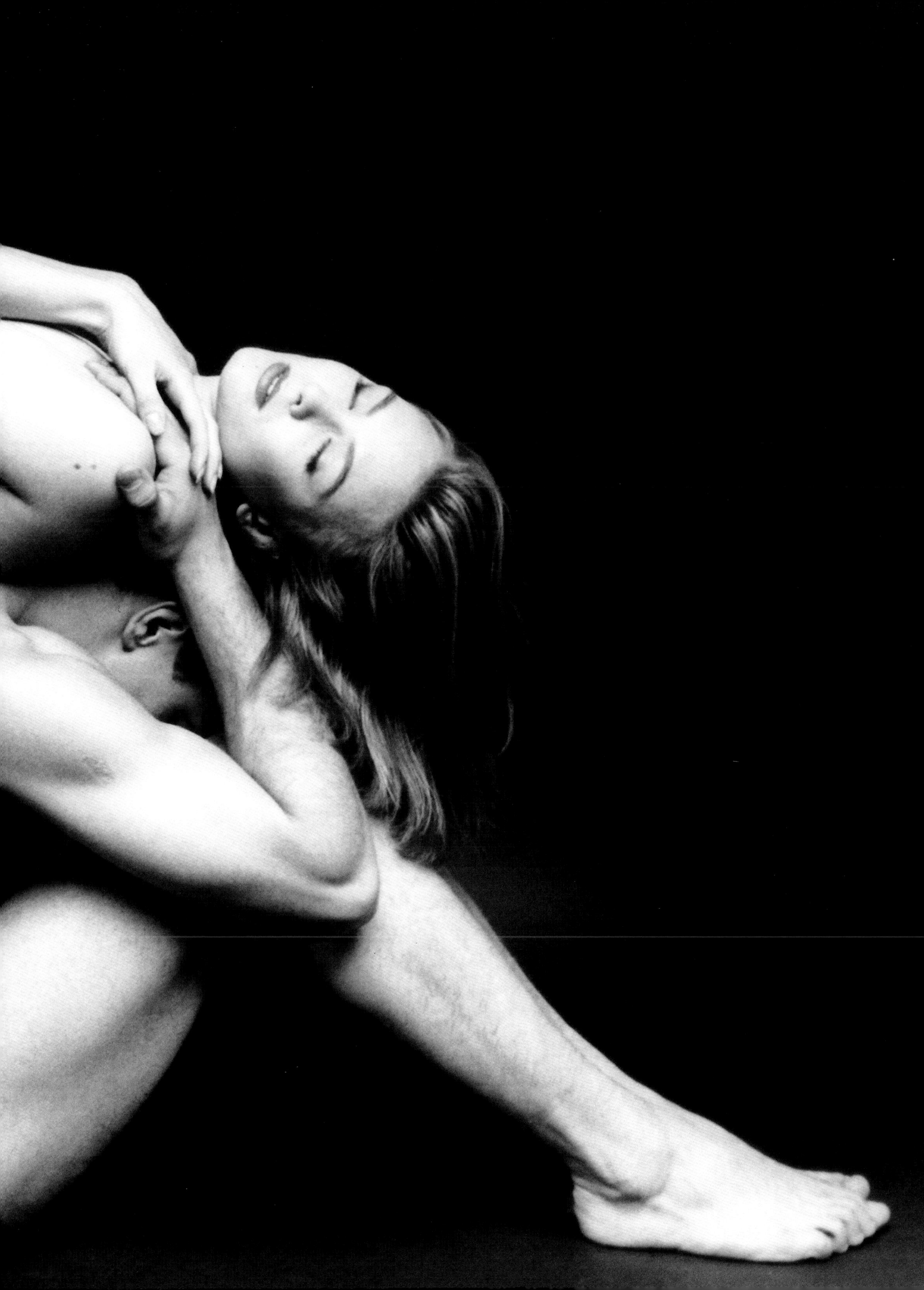

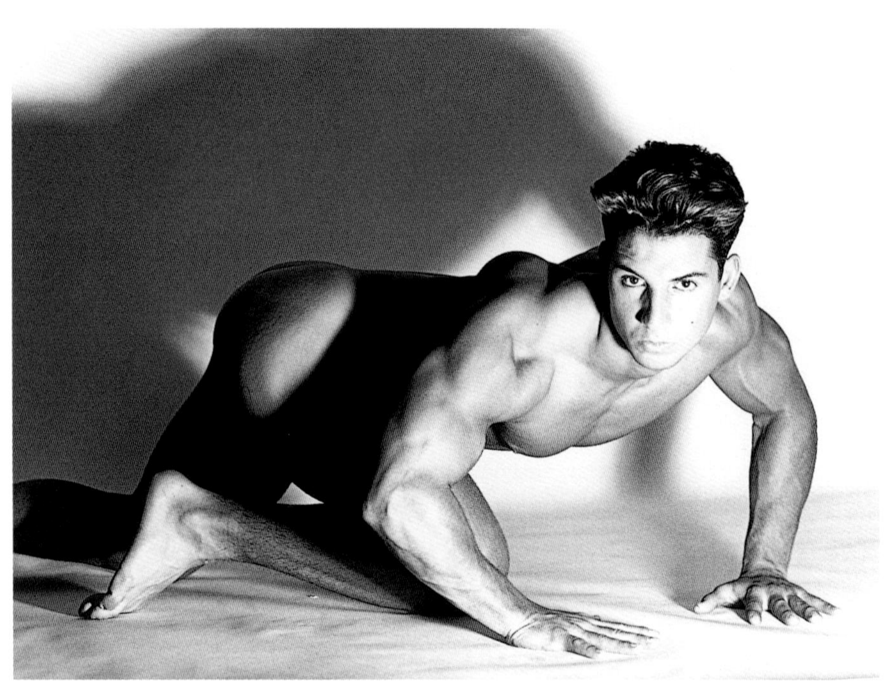

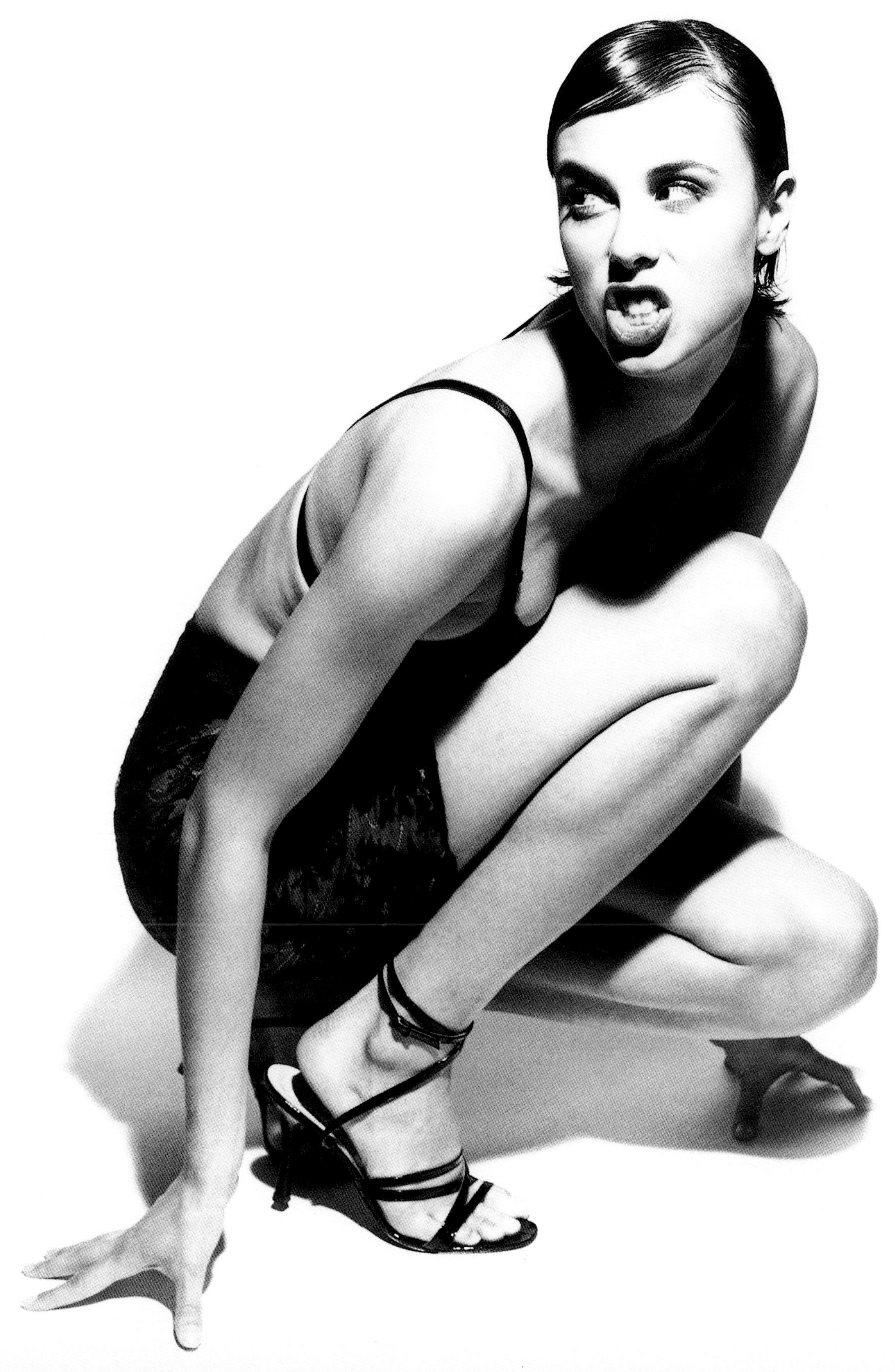

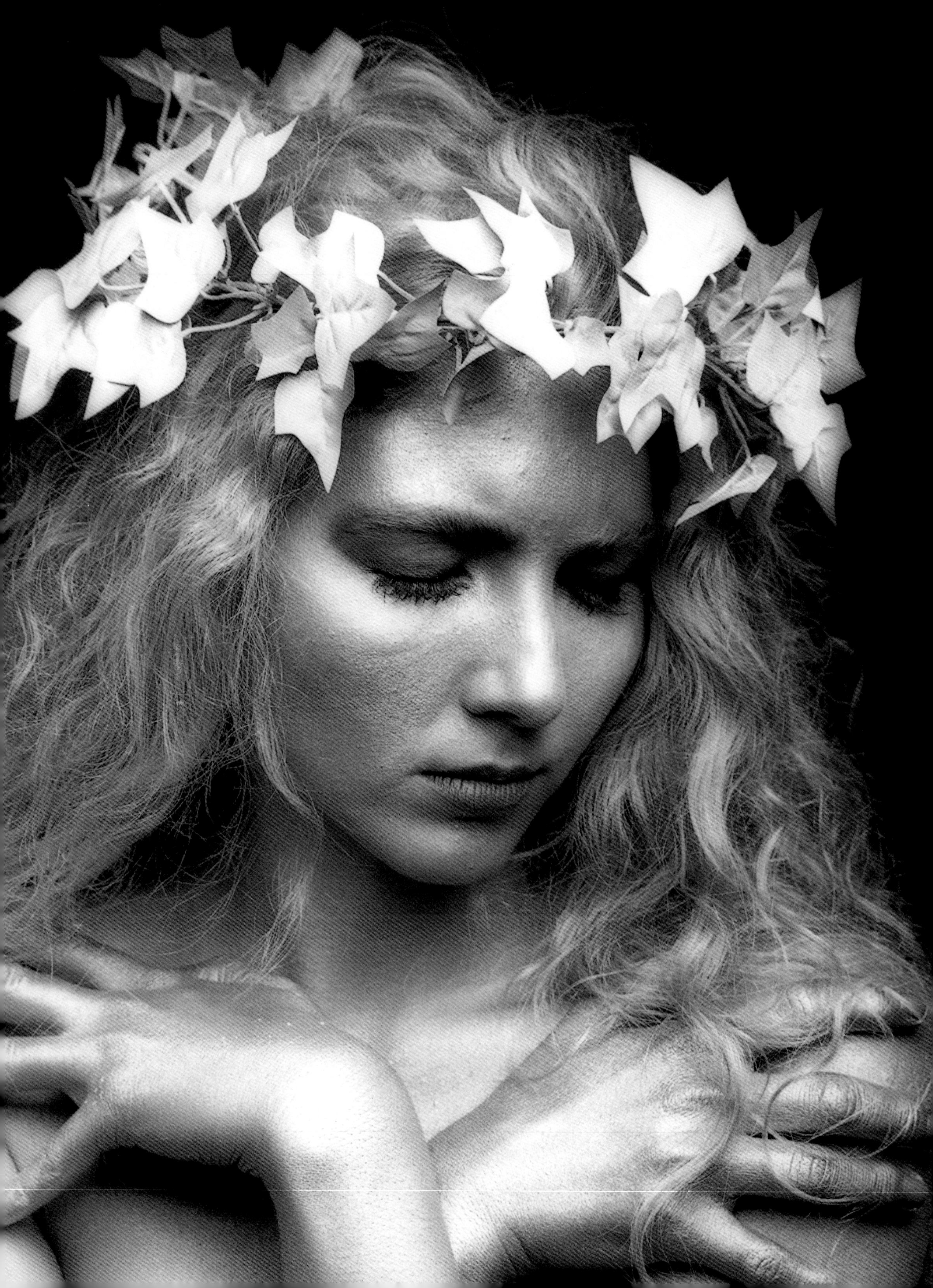

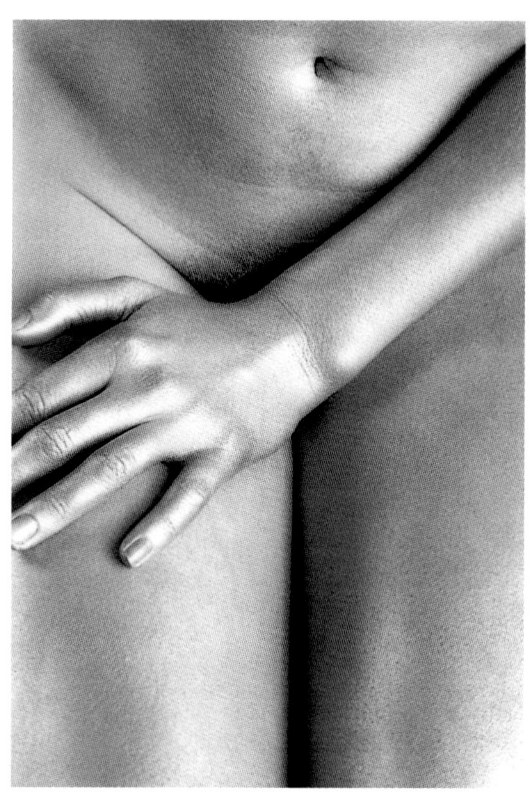

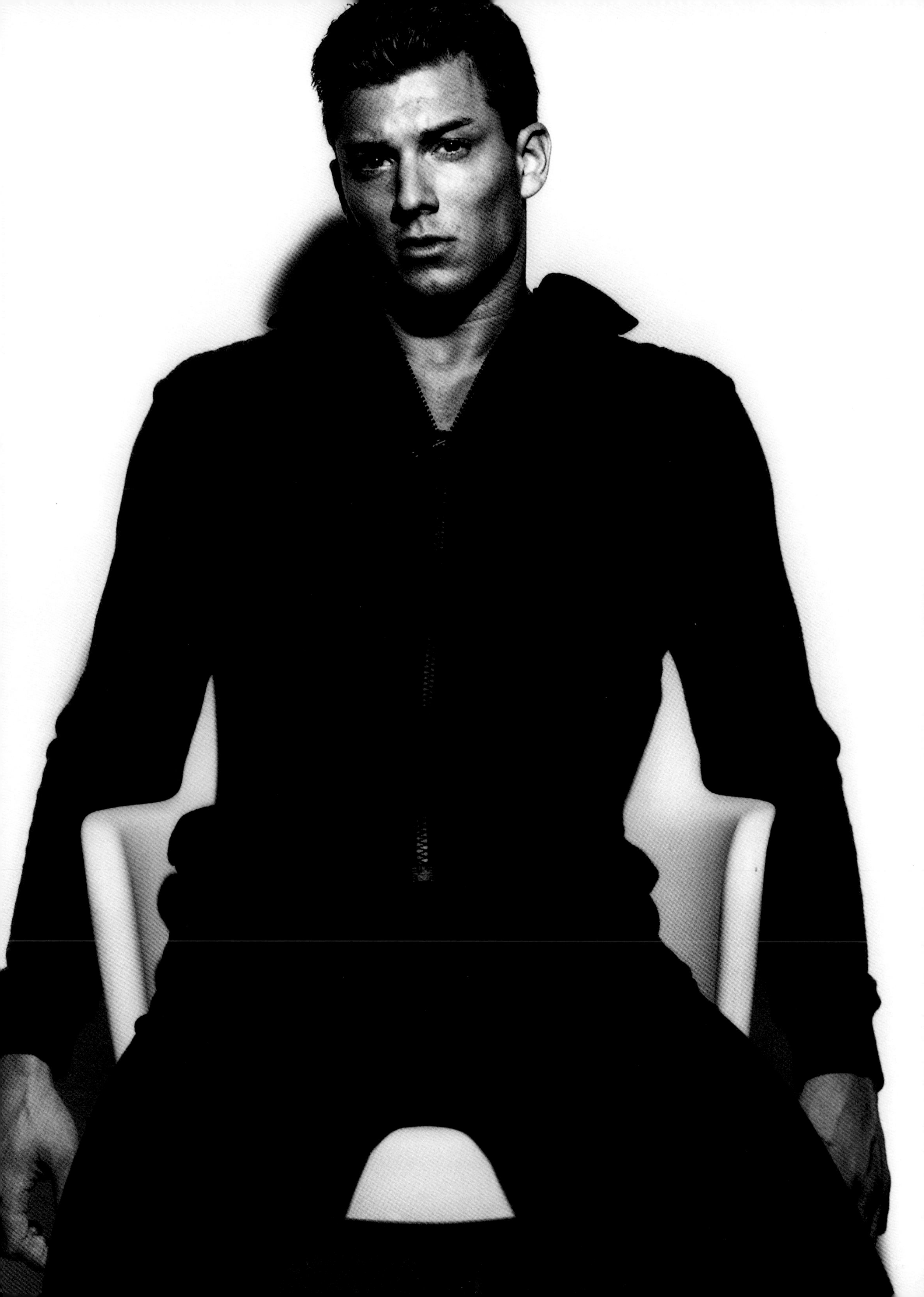

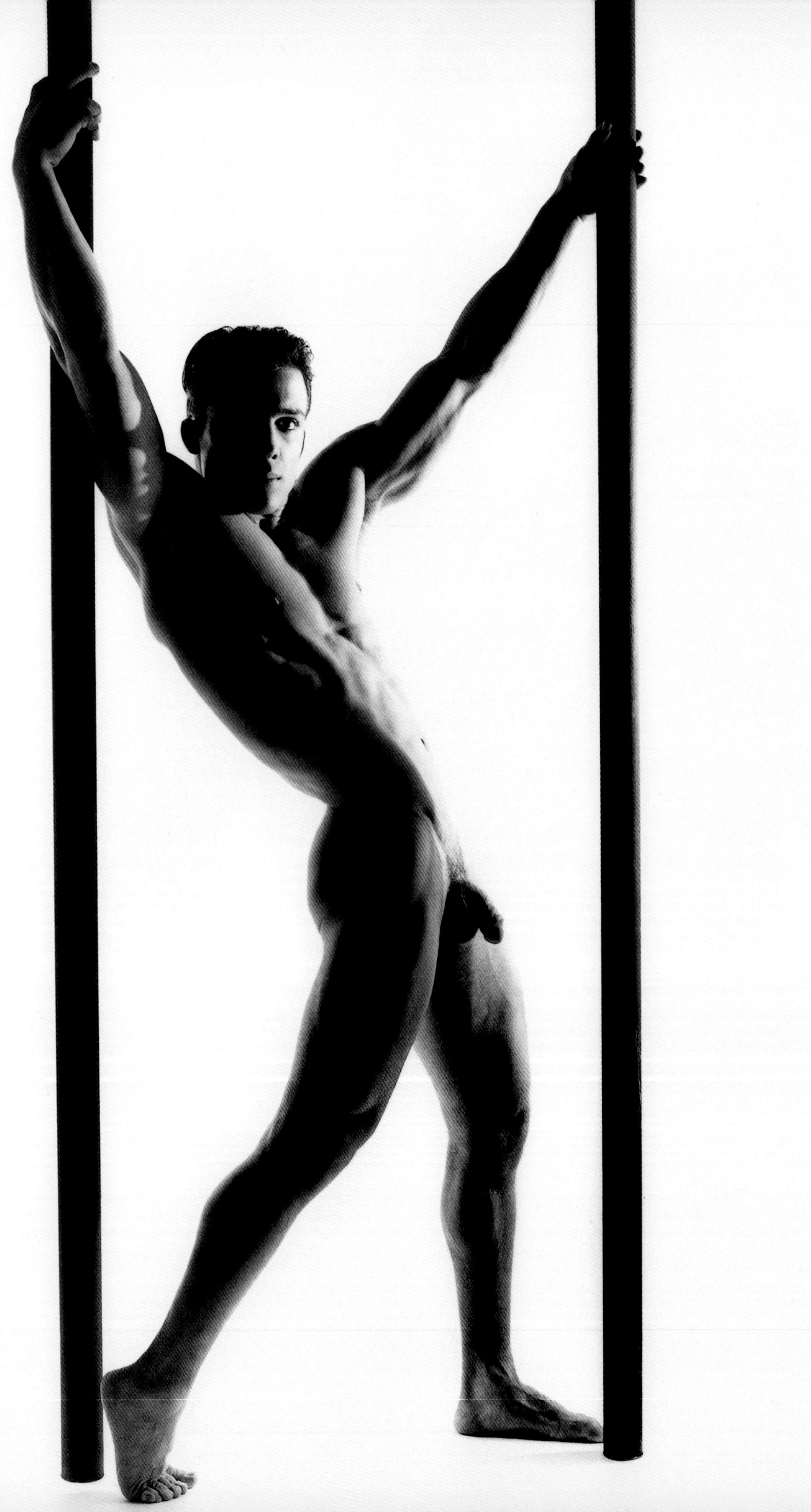

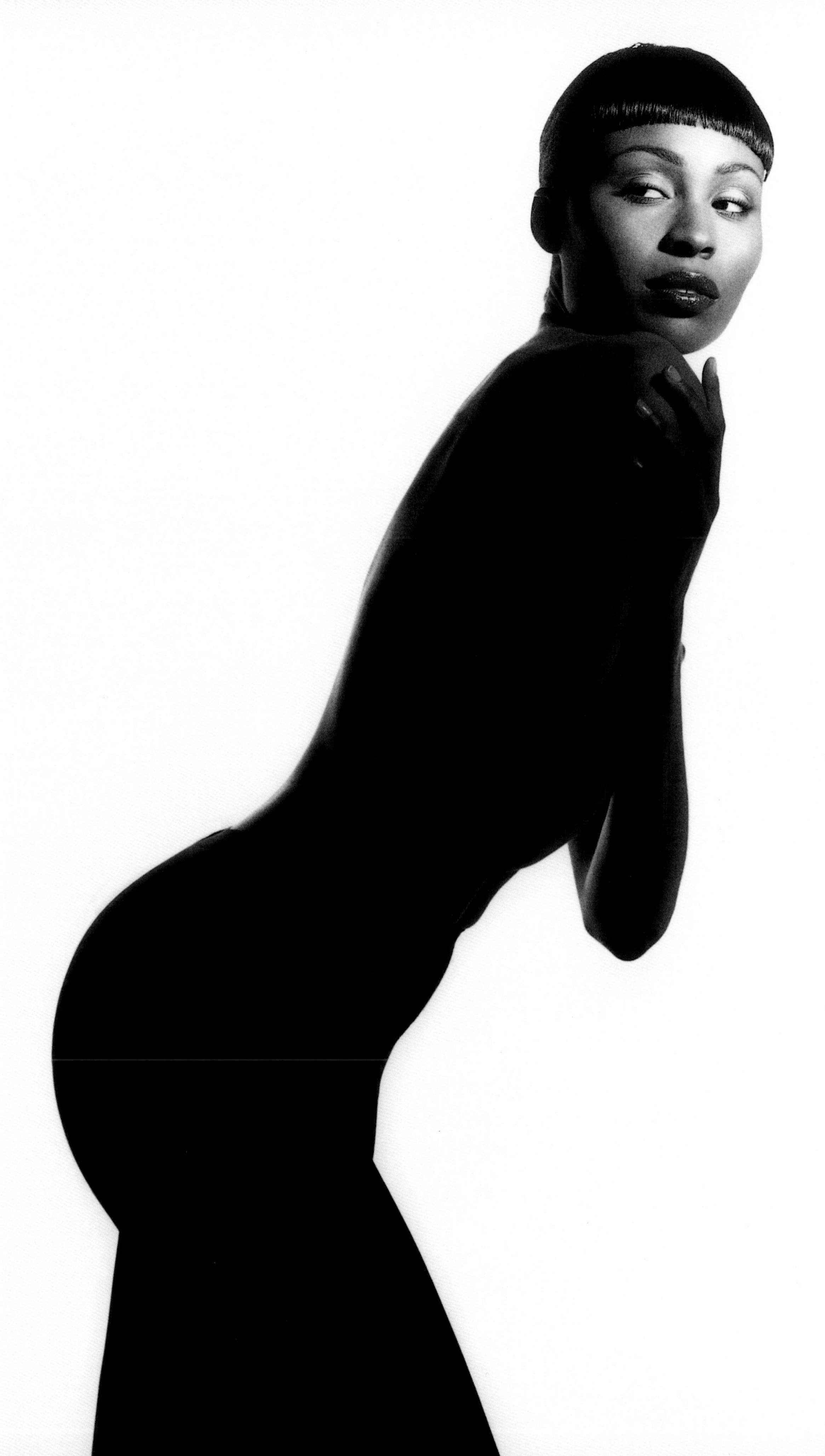

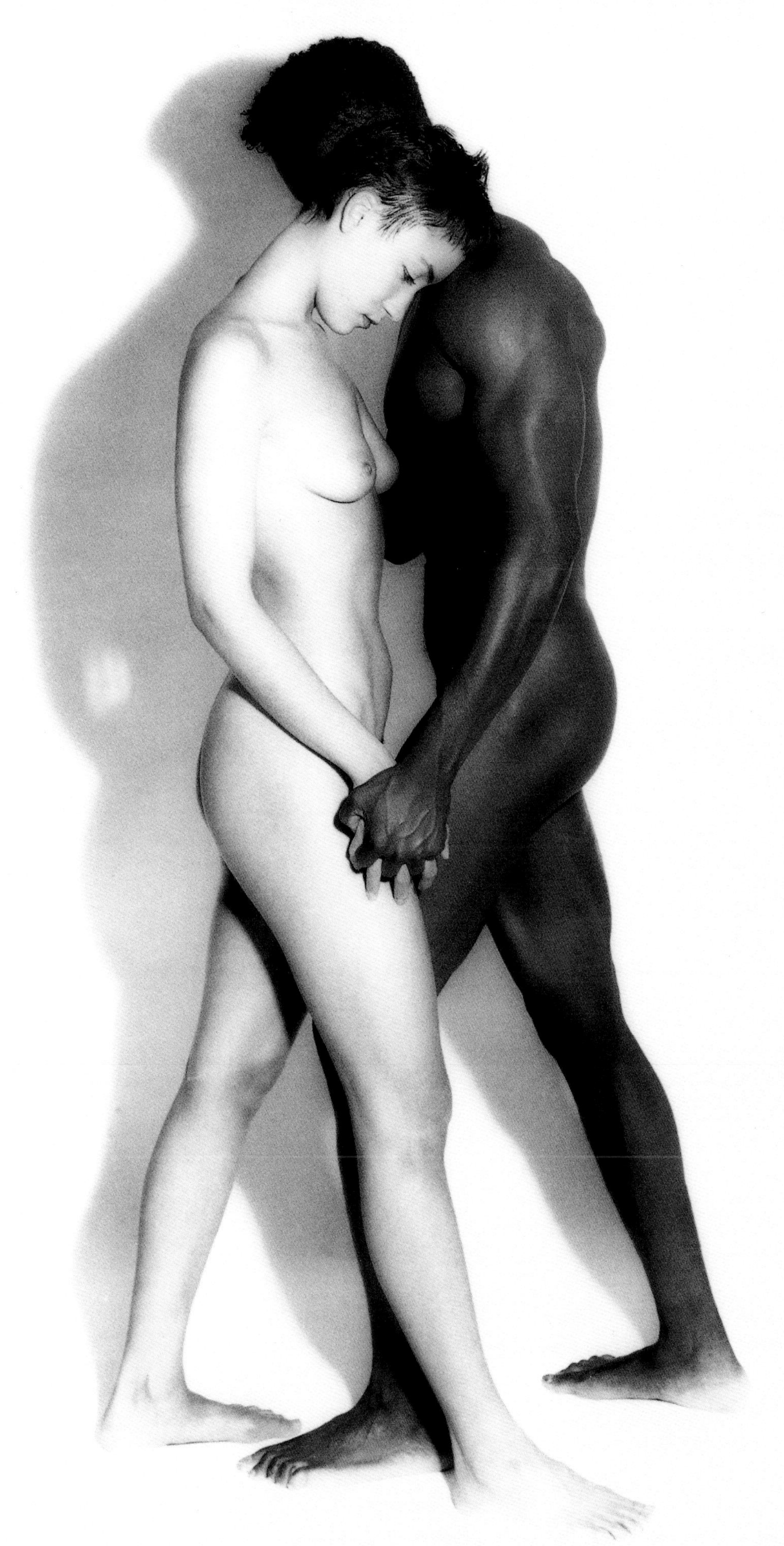

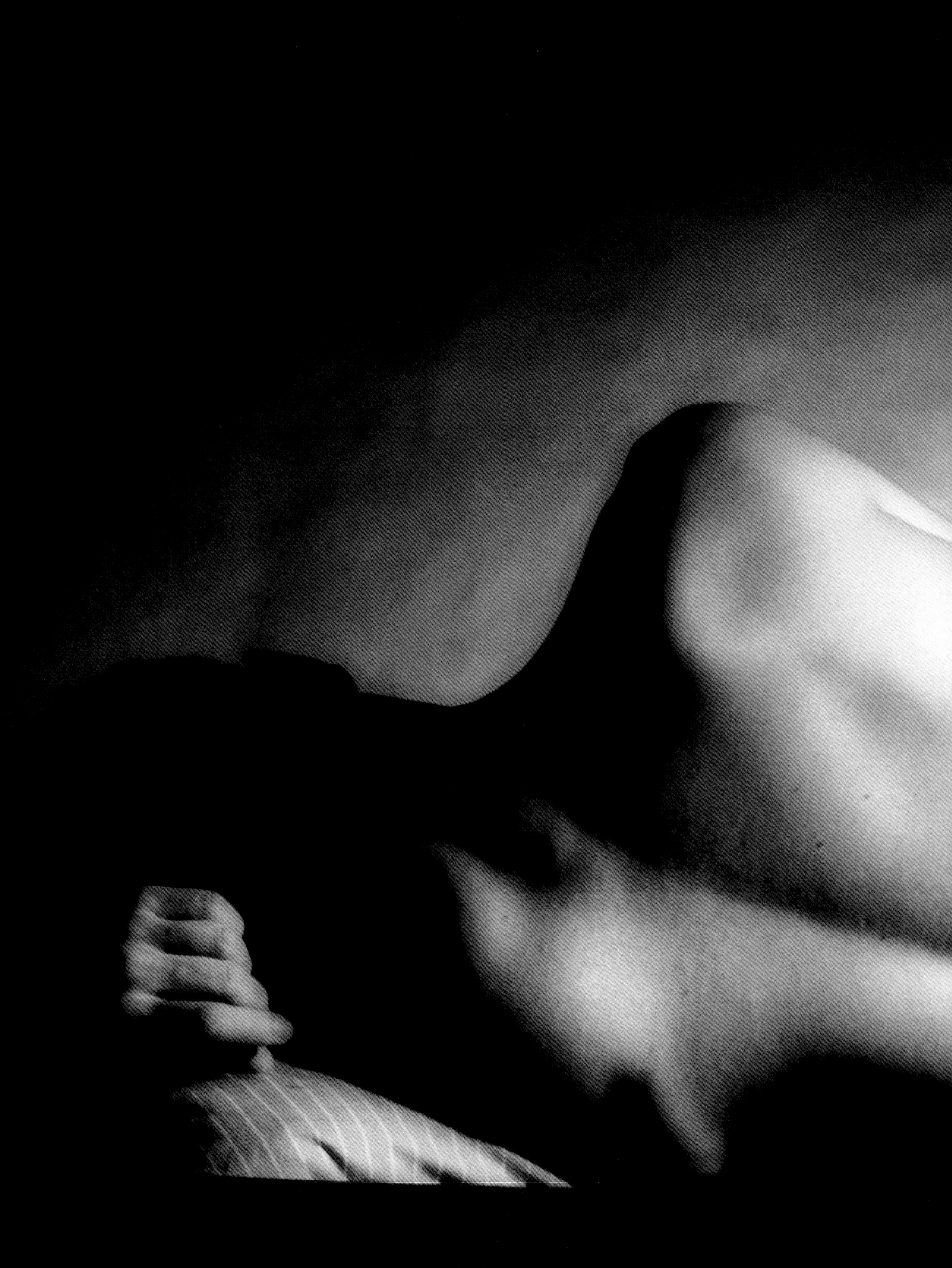

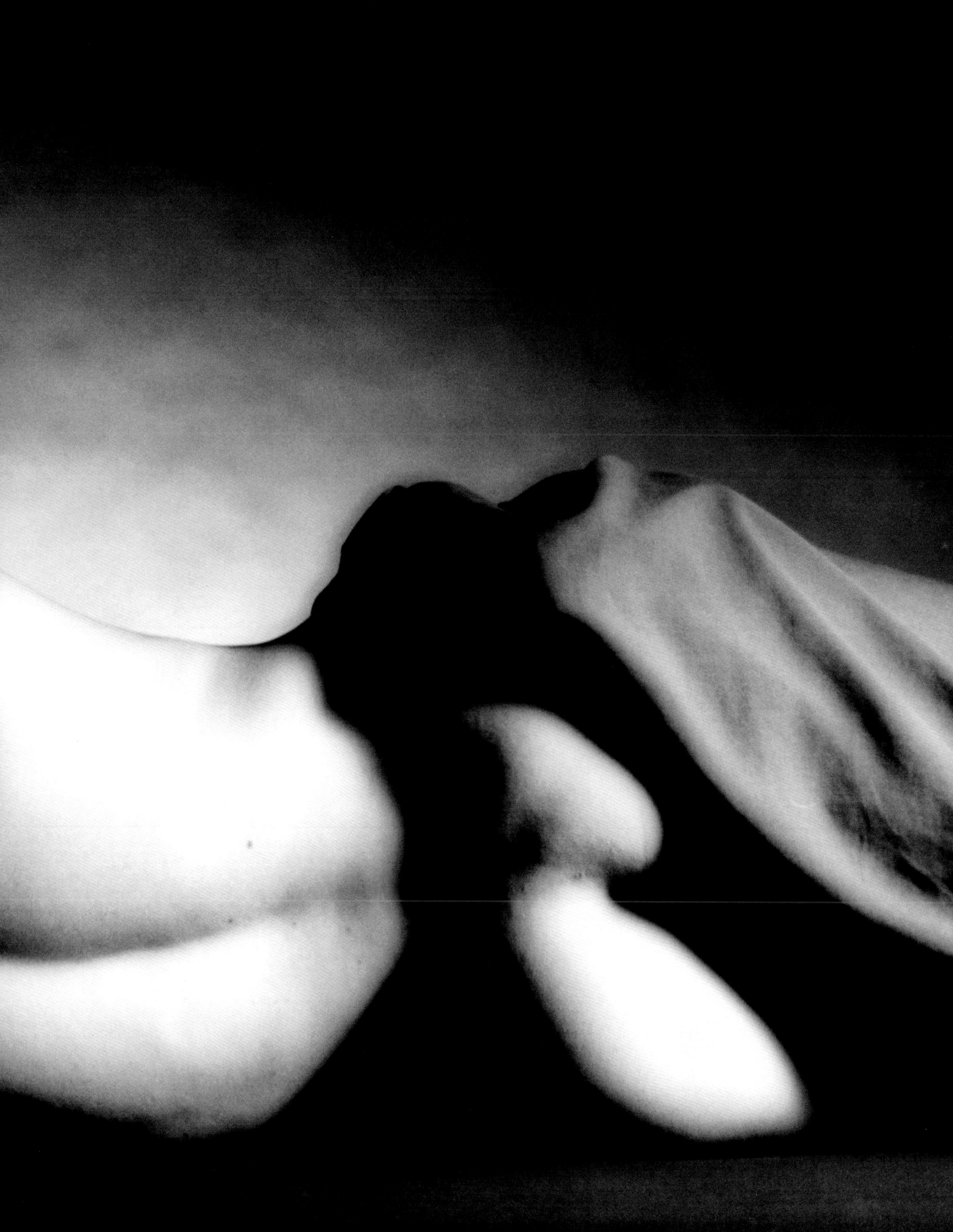

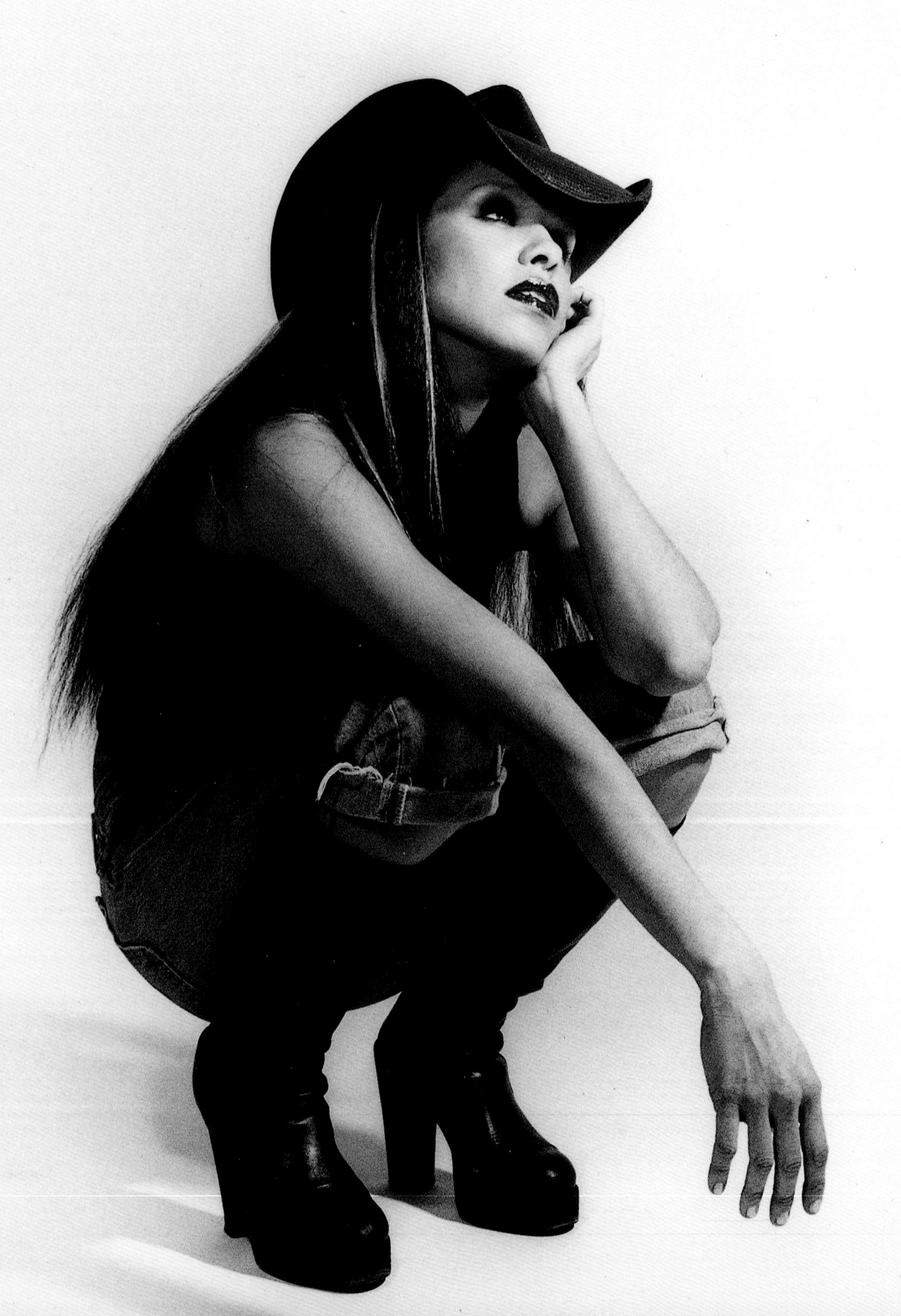

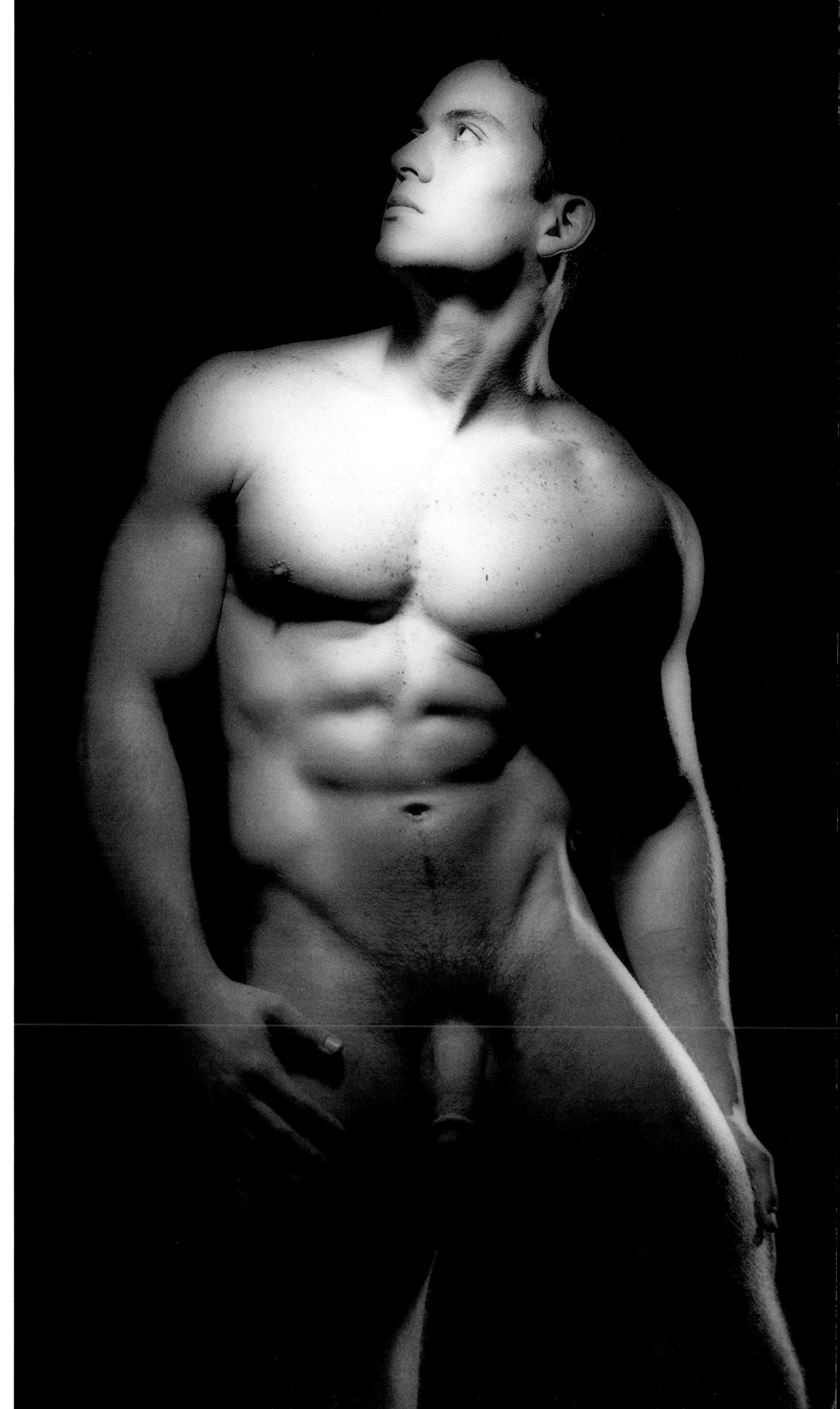

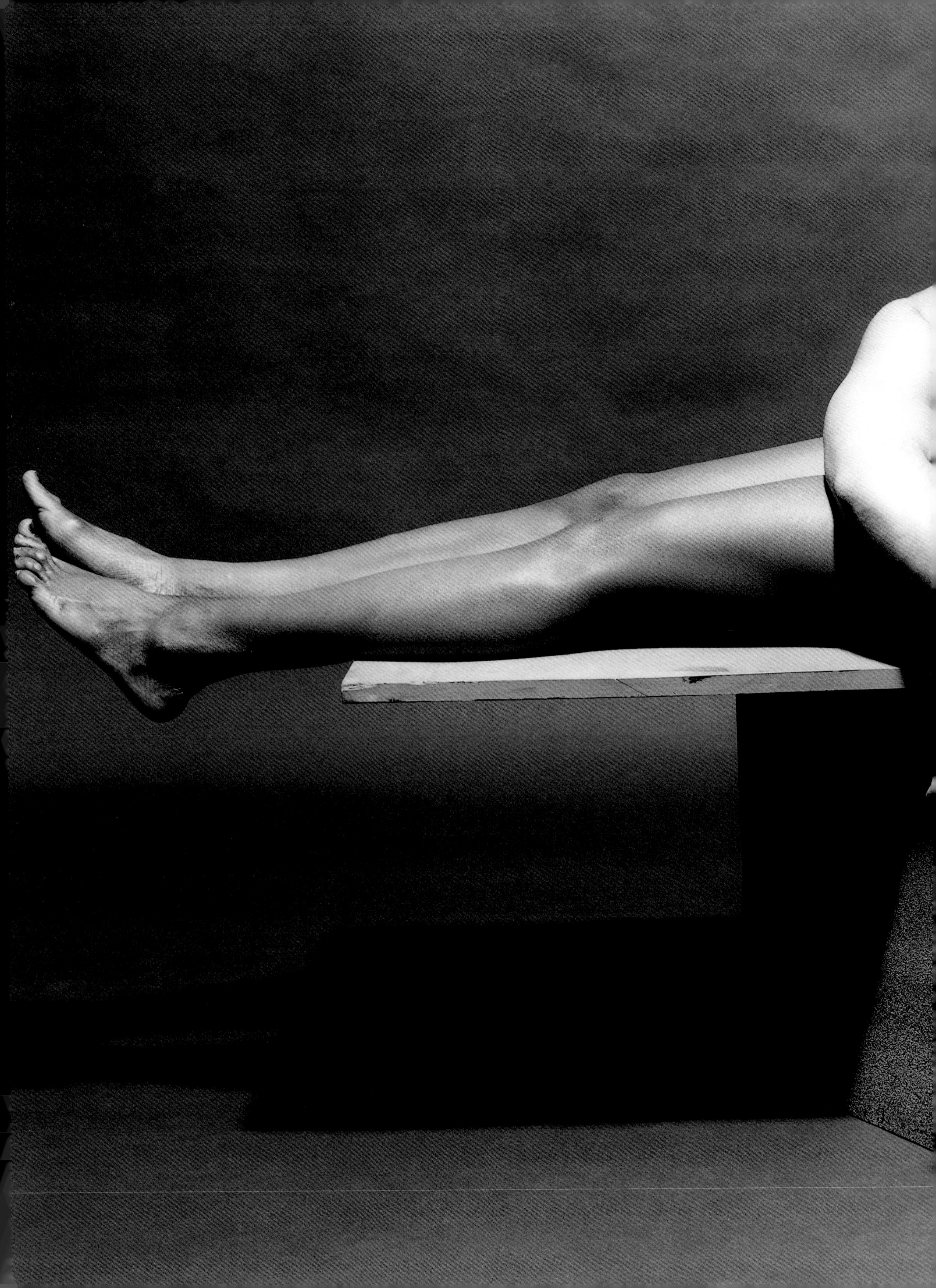

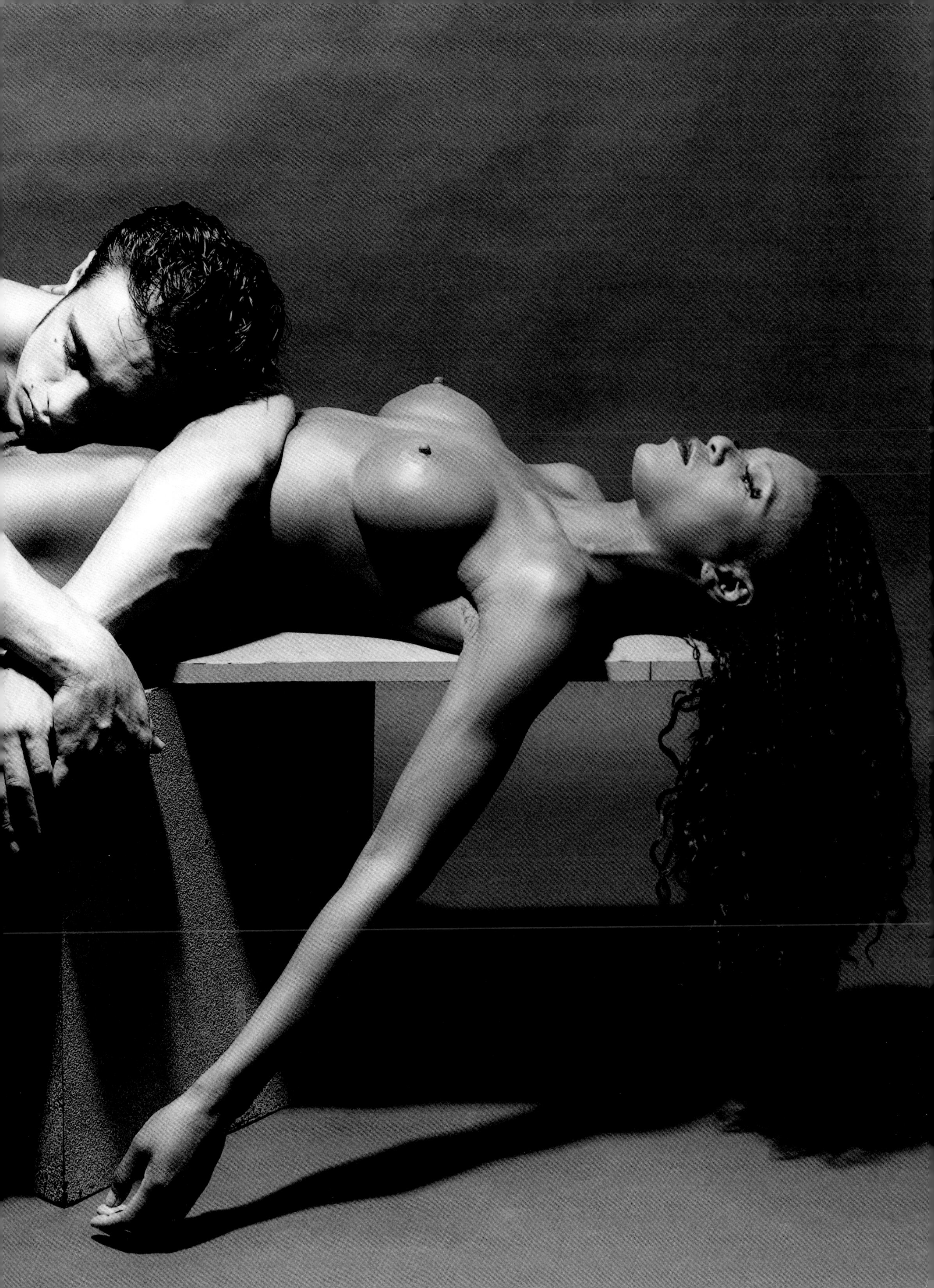

# acknowledgments

Very special thanks to Robert Anglund, Gordon Boelzner, Ken Roberts Detelich, Arthur Lambert, and David McAninch for their invaluable help in creating this book. Thanks also to the models and agencies whose participation made this book possible.